THE GARDEN STATE PARKWAY MURDERS

A Cold Case Mystery

CHRISTIAN BARTH

WildBluePress.com

THE GARDEN STATE PARKWAY MURDERS published by:
WILDBLUE PRESS
P.O. Box 102440
Denver, Colorado 80250

WILDBLUE PRESS is registered at the U.S. Patent and Trademark Offices.

ISBN 978-1-948239-76-9 Trade Paperback

ISBN 978-1-948239-77-6 eBook

Interior Formatting by Elijah Toten
www.totencreative.com

THE
GARDEN STATE
PARKWAY
MURDERS

TABLE OF CONTENTS

AUTHOR'S NOTE

The Garden State Parkway Murders is a work of nonfiction. Nevertheless, in certain instances throughout the book, names have been changed to protect the privacy of certain individuals.

INTRODUCTION

This is the true story of the unsolved murders of Elizabeth Perry and Susan Davis, college friends who were brutally knifed to death during the early morning hours of May 30, 1969, in the woods between mileposts 31.8 and 31.9 of the Garden State Parkway near Ocean City, New Jersey.

A culmination of more than nine years of research, this book is compiled from multiple sources, including interviews with retired New Jersey State Police detectives, law enforcement officials from other jurisdictions, federal agents, possible witnesses, victim family members, as well as information gathered from FBI case files, letters, journals, libraries, newspaper articles, and university archives.

Throughout this time period I interviewed, or at least attempted to interview, every person whom I thought might lend valuable insight toward solving this cold case. Although my first public records request to view the Perry-Davis investigative file was submitted to the New Jersey State Police in 2000, I didn't begin researching the case in earnest until immediately following the completion of my first book, *The Origins of Infamy*, a fictionalization of the 1969 Garden State Parkway murders published in 2009.

My interest in this story was borne from a distant childhood memory. One dusk, when I was about twelve or thirteen years old and we were driving along the northbound lanes of the parkway somewhere near Ocean City, en route home from a vacation at the Jersey Shore, I overheard my mother say to my father, "They never found out who killed those girls, did they?" My memory of that passing conversation remained dormant until 1993, when I'd read a fascinating *Philadelphia Inquirer* article by columnist Larry Lewis. Ted Bundy was attending Temple University, the story read. He'd confessed to a prison psychologist that he'd slain Davis and Perry, claiming they were his first two killings. The memory resurfaced once more, seven years later, when I had decided to write a short story about the parkway murders before embarking upon *Origins*. Yet even with that book's completion the case still gnawed at me. I needed to know more.

Over the years my investigation took some ominous turns as the project meandered toward completion. After the weeks following the publication of *Origins*, a victim's younger sibling sent along a Facebook friend request, followed by a heartfelt accusation that I'd disrupted what closure she'd attained upon concluding that Ted Bundy had murdered her sister. About a year later, in a lengthy, typewritten response to a letter I'd sent to him at the New Jersey State Prison in Trenton, convicted serial killer Richard Cottingham, better known as the "Torso Killer" because of his affinity for dismembering Times Square prostitutes, offered to create a psychological profile of Susan and Elizabeth's killer, but only in exchange for my delivery of a $250 food package to him. The steep price, he insisted, was necessary to ensure that I wasn't a police officer posing as an attorney. "A cop," he surmised, "would be too cheap" to spend $250. He further insisted that I accept one dollar from him to seal the bargain, so that our conversation would remain bound by attorney-client privilege. On another occasion a Minnesota minister's wife sternly reprimanded me when she learned I had attempted to speak with her husband, who'd delivered the eulogy at Elizabeth Perry's funeral service. I withstood her blistering torrent, for in the midst of her scornful lecture she repeatedly pledged to have her husband return my call.

He never did. On another occasion a Vietnam War veteran, whose late brother was friends with a potential suspect when they both were teenagers, called me to utter some threatening remarks less than an hour after our phone interview, suggesting he knew where I lived, and having forgotten that we'd just spoken. His sister profusely apologized for his behavior, saying he continued to suffer from PTSD.

Yet with each setback, every call not returned, formal records request denied or scathing rebuke, my resolve to solve this case only strengthened. Amidst the many obstacles thwarting my pursuit of learning what killer had slain these two girls on the cusp of womanhood, I met a number of courageous men and women who offered spiritual guidance and moral support along my journey, encouraging me to continue forward with my seemingly futile and time-consuming quest.

Obsess over an unsolved case long enough and you begin to notice it affects you in a surreal manner. Strange, though nevertheless true, on each occasion when self-doubt would cloud my inspiration, when futility interfered with my fervent hope that my work would one day yield results despite such daunting odds, upon the advent of each Memorial Day weekend I would invariably cross paths with at least one light-blue, 1966 Chevrolet convertible, reminding me that all my efforts hadn't been for naught. I'd see this make and model in various permutations, some slowing past me with rusted panels and missing hubcaps, others gleamingly restored to their original showroom luster or slunk low to the ground, parked for sale at a gas station parking lot. I interpreted these signs as totems prodding me forward, suggesting deeper spiritual forces were at play. After all, except for family members, who really speaks for the victims? And were these victims speaking to me?

"Everybody counts," former Atlantic County Prosecutor James McClain told *Fox News* reporter Cristina Corbin, who in 2013 reported on the unsolved murders of four prostitutes found decapitated in a drainage ditch outside Atlantic City in 2006. "Every person is a child of God...we view every person, every victim of every crime, particularly crimes of violence like this, as worthy of our best efforts."

As I write these words another Memorial Day weekend looms, yet the murders of Susan Davis and Elizabeth Perry remain unsolved. Despite the passage of fifty years, I'm encouraged that some facet of this story will inspire the New Jersey State Police and Atlantic County Prosecutor's Office to reactivate the investigation and have a closer look at the several suspects discussed within these pages, hopefully leading to formal charges, thereby bringing much needed closure to this sad and troubling Jersey Shore mystery.

CHAPTER ONE

Be Careful

As Susan Davis and Elizabeth Perry shuffled about the porch in the early morning darkness, hefting their suitcases as they prepared to leave, the screen door creaked open behind them.

Close friends from Monticello Junior College in Illinois, the girls had just checked out of their eight-dollar-a-night room on the second floor of the Syben House, a three-story Dutch Colonial at 712 Ninth Street in Ocean City, New Jersey, where they'd enjoyed several fun-filled days tanning on the beach, strolling the boardwalk, and dining out each night in celebration of the end of their school year and the beginning of summer vacation. More importantly to both, the trip was a commemoration of their enduring friendship. They'd soon be going their separate ways, for Susan had just graduated and was moving on to pursue her bachelor's degree from Ithaca College in New York. Although they were a month apart in age, Elizabeth had enrolled a year later than Susan and would be returning to campus that autumn without her companion by her side.

The boardinghouse where they'd been staying, situated amidst a clustered row of similarly framed inns and pastel vacation cottages spanning the south side of the block between Atlantic and Ocean Avenues, fronted a busily traveled sidewalk a hundred yards from the entrance ramp to the boardwalk. Upon their arrival early Tuesday afternoon, three days earlier, they'd scrawled their names in the guest registry near the fireplace in the downstairs den: *May 27. Liz Perry, Minnesota; Sue Davis, Hbg, Penna.*

The girls were joined on the porch by their landlords, a retired man of German descent named Walter Syben and his American-born wife, Frances. A tanned, fit sixty-four-year-old with a thatch of wavy silver hair and narrow blue eyes fixed into a worrisome expression, Walter was protective of his young female guests. The father of two sons and a daughter who were about the same age as Susan and Elizabeth, he made certain no suitors snuck through the back door or climbed through the first-floor windows after he locked up at night. A hand-painted sign hanging above his front door cautioned *Gentlemen Wait Outside.* While Walter spent his days tightening leaky faucets, caulking holes, and running errands, Frances bustled about the three stories, laundering sheets and tidying rooms, sweeping the front porch free of sand tracked in by her guests.

Cars were few at this hour, the sidewalks empty, the surf a distant murmur. Farther down Ninth Street, the darkened restaurant lights and Victorian rooftops framed a faintly visible contour against the gathering daylight, offering the illusion of dusk. Susan and Elizabeth had told Walter they'd be leaving at 7 a.m. The idea of driving home this early troubled him, and he had reason for concern. It was dark yet, the girls had been up all night, and they would be traveling unescorted out on the desolate highways between the shore and Philadelphia. The Sybens reiterated their pleas, hoping their guests would reconsider their decision to leave now or at least hold off till daylight. Anxious to get a jump on the Memorial Day shore traffic, the girls weren't persuaded by their kindhearted urging to delay their sudden departure. "There are two of us and we'll be all right," they reassured the doting couple, promising to pull over somewhere and sleep if they became too tired to drive.

Susan and Elizabeth showed Frances the gifts and souvenirs they'd bought for their families. Five-feet, seven inches tall, with light-blue eyes and dark blonde hair that reached past her shoulders, Susan wore a denim jacket over a navy, patterned summer dress, and her eyeglasses. She smiled excitedly, revealing a slight overbite, saying how much she was looking forward to attending her older brother's college graduation in a few days. She was nineteen-years old.

Susan's slenderer, less talkative companion would be accompanying her this morning on the trip to the Davis home in Camp Hill, Pennsylvania. From there, the girls planned to join Susan's parents for the drive down to Duke University in North Carolina to see their son receive his diploma. Elizabeth bore a slightly darker complexion than her fair-skinned friend and stood two inches taller alongside her. Her chestnut-brown hair, also styled long and parted evenly down the middle, fell atop the scoop of her green dress. A black leather purse hung from her shoulder. When Frances asked of her plans for the summer, she eagerly told of the lifeguarding job she'd lined up at her family's country club near her Minnesota lakefront home. A native Midwesterner, this was Elizabeth's first visit to the seashore. She promised to write the Sybens, for they'd made her feel at home during her brief stay in Ocean City and gave off good vibrations.

The girls seemed excited to get going. "We're going to be late; we were supposed to meet them at 4:30," Frances overheard Elizabeth whisper to Susan. They kissed their hosts goodbye and bid them good tidings, saying they hoped to stay with them again when they returned to Ocean City next year. With their luggage and shopping bags in tow, they proceeded down the short driveway alongside the house.

Frances noticed a pair of dawdling young men, whom she later described as "hippie-types," seated next to one another on the curb in front of the Coral Sands Motel across the street, beckoning Susan with calls of "Sue! Sue!" Their pleas were either ignored or not heard by the young women as they continued through an alley out back and into the vast parking lot outside Watson's Restaurant, where Susan had left her car. Walter stood at the edge of his property as they loaded their belongings into the trunk of her Marina-blue, 1966 Chevrolet Impala SS convertible, then watched as they drove out of the parking lot. It was nearing 5 a.m.

The horizon glowed faintly behind the wooded swamplands to the east as Susan and Elizabeth crossed the moonlit causeway over the Great Egg Harbor Bay. The giant electric arrow of Tony Mart's nightclub and the street sign for Bay Shores Café, both dimmed at 2 a.m., stood darkly silhouetted against the indigo sky. Dock lights glimmered atop the low tide mark along the seawall as fishing boats passed under the drawbridge towers on their way out to sea. At the Somers Point roundabout, looming ahead as the women descended the Ship Channel Bridge, the perception of night hadn't yet faded, as if captured in time within the grayness of dawn shading its edges. Carloads of youthful revelers who'd returned from seeing Gary Puckett & The Union Gap perform at the Steel Pier in Atlantic City, and then made last call at the late-night bars in Longport and Mays Landing, looped toward the Point Diner. Their headlight carouseled through the dusky tidal mist, tinted orange at the turn beneath the Gulf station sign. Lonesome stragglers and tightly knit groupings of college kids who'd been up all night partying along Bay Avenue quickened toward the diner from opposite directions. They paused along the curb until the cars passed by, then trod through the grass in the middle of the circle, aiming toward the only place to eat that was still open, or, as they knew it, never closed.

After finding a spot in the bustling diner parking lot, Susan and Elizabeth went inside. Following a short wait they were seated at a booth near a window facing the bay just as the sun brimmed the eastern sky. The diner was filling quickly, and a waitress hurried to take their orders. At the counter stools near the pastry display patrons browsed the front pages of the *Atlantic City Press*, griping about the record-breaking heat. The temperature had reached ninety-nine degrees yesterday, and the forecast called for more of the same this afternoon. The aisles behind them clamored with overlapping conversations and young patrons shouting out names, jangling silverware, and Top 40 hits crackling from the table jukeboxes. Outside, the line to get in grew longer.

After being seated for a time, Susan and Elizabeth agreed to share their booth with three clean-cut college men who'd been standing by the hostess stand, waiting for a table to open. By all accounts, the girls were in good spirits as they got up to leave their table after finishing breakfast, walking unaccompanied through the front entrance of the diner at approximately 6:15 a.m. Locals seated at the counter didn't notice any drifters who in retrospect seemed out of sorts among the regulars who ate there every morning. No suspicious-looking hippies were seen following the girls outside. No employees saw them go down the front steps, walk across the parking lot, or open their car doors and drive away.

The Ocean City Memorial Day parade began along the boardwalk at 9:30 that morning while soldiers from the local VFW Color Guard gathered for ceremonies at Veterans Memorial Park. Reverently poised, they raised their rifles to their shoulders, firing a three-volley salute in solemn gratitude of patriots slain on faraway battlefields. As the smiling Girl Scouts of Troop 37 strutted proudly along the Asbury Avenue parade route, waving the American flag toward a deepening blue sky, a brigade of station wagons tied down with bicycles and beach rafts lurched forward along the glutted inbound lanes of the Route 52 causeway.

Ninety miles distant from the pageantry and excitement marking the start of summer, far removed from the holiday crowds plunging merrily into the frigid Atlantic Ocean, a similarly buoyant mood had tensed into an unsettling quiet inside the Camp Hill, Pennsylvania, ranch house belonging to Wesley Davis Sr. and his wife Marjorie. Their daughter and her guest were two hours late, expected home long before now. They had heard nothing from either of them and were beginning to worry.

CHAPTER TWO

Worst Fears

Something isn't right, Wesley Davis knew. He fought to remain positive, but the willpower sustaining his optimism seemed outmatched against the premonitions burdening his spirit. He enjoyed a close relationship with his oldest daughter and trusted her judgment completely. She never abused the many privileges he extended to her, and in return she acted responsibly. In matters ranging from her allowance to the use of her car, she was encouraged to speak freely with her parents if something was upsetting her. If her car had broken down, or there had been some sort of emergency, she would have called him from a booth along the side of the road, he thought. To just take off on a jaunt like this without telling them was not like her. "She wasn't the type to jump into something and let the chips fall where they may," Davis said.

Although Susan's parents grew more concerned with each passing moment, they rationalized that any number of plausible reasons might explain the delay. After all, it was another steamy day in the Lehigh Valley, with the mercury expected to top ninety for the second day in a row. Perhaps the girls had merely stayed at the beach to go swimming and forgot to call home, or there'd been some miscommunication as to when they were due to arrive.

Noontime came and went with still no word. Sustained by a stalwart devotion to their faith, the Davises kept their plans to go out for the evening despite their mounting fear. When they returned home at midnight, the girls still hadn't been heard from. "By about 2 a.m. we got panicky," Davis, the president of a Bethlehem, Pennsylvania soft drink distributorship, admitted to a reporter several days later. A genteel, plainspoken patrician with North Carolina roots, he telephoned the Sybens in Ocean City and learned that his daughter and her friend had checked out of their boardinghouse at about 4:30 a.m. the day before. It was at this point, Davis said, that he feared the worst, as if their disappearance was a logical prelude to a self-fulfilling prophecy.

Davis contacted the Perrys at their home in Minnesota. The anguishing parents of both women began calling their daughters' friends and acquaintances, asking if Susan and Elizabeth had arrived unannounced or stopped for a visit on their way home. Nobody they spoke with had heard from either of the women or knew whether they'd been sidetracked.

By early Saturday morning Davis notified the Camp Hill Police Department, relaying the license number of his daughter's car. According to a report in the *Ocean City Sentinel Ledger*, at 3:15 p.m. he called the Ocean City Police Department, asking them to check again at the Ninth Street rooming house where the girls had stayed. Detectives Joseph Nesgoda, John Divel, and James Nickles of the Ocean City Police Department began an informal investigation, searching among streets, driveways, and parking lots for signs of a light-blue Chevrolet convertible. Just as police dispatchers in urban areas assign low priority to reports of prowlers, whom an overwhelming majority of the time turn out to be nothing more serious than a peeping voyeur or a jilted ex-lover out snooping, the Ocean City Police Department initially gave lower precedence to what was first characterized as an "attempt to locate," thereby lacking the urgency of an official missing persons alert. That same day their police department received a second call and a telegram, this time from Elizabeth's father, distraught when he learned that the police hadn't yet found the car.

The fathers arrived in Ocean City on Sunday at 10 a.m. They met with Detective Nickles, whom at 10:35 a.m. requested the New Jersey State Police substation at Cape May Courthouse to send out a bulletin over the police radio network to all stations in Cape, Atlantic, and Cumberland Counties. The *Atlantic City Press*, however, reported that the bulletin didn't air until 2:25 p.m. on Sunday. At 6:50 p.m. Detective Nesgoda rechecked to make certain that the message, which by this time had developed into a 13-state alarm, had been transmitted. One state trooper concurred with the decision to wait at least a day before sending out an official alarm, saying that missing persons reports on teenagers at the Jersey Shore were "rather common and usually unfounded."

Exasperated not so much by the uncooperativeness of authorities as by their initial reluctance to assist in what they deemed a low priority search, the fathers notified Congressmen John E. Hunt (R., N.J.) and Clark McGregor (R., Minn.), who solicited the intervention of federal authorities. Joseph D. Jamieson, special agent in charge of the FBI's Philadelphia office, said their offices hadn't joined the search because they lacked jurisdiction, as there was no indication of forcible kidnapping across state lines. Though in a few months they would quadruple the amount, the fathers initially offered a $5,000 reward for information concerning their daughters' whereabouts. They promptly withdrew this offer, however, when the FBI warned them it would only attract crank calls.

Davis sought the help of his Camp Hill neighbor, Pennsylvania Attorney General William C. Sennett, who was only thirty-six-years old when appointed as the youngest attorney general in Pennsylvania history by Governor Ray Shafer. Today, ironically, he bears the distinction of being Pennsylvania's oldest living attorney general. "Boy, I sure do remember that father calling me," says Sennett, reached at his hometown of Erie, Pennsylvania, where he returned to private practice once his term ended. "I remember it well. It was a tragic situation. I had a bunch of young kids at the time, and I told him 'we'll do whatever we can.'" He recalled the frantic urgency in Davis' voice. "At that point they didn't know what had happened; their daughters had disappeared, and the police weren't treating it effectively because kids ran away all the time."

After hanging up the phone, Sennett immediately called Frank McKetta, Superintendent of the Pennsylvania State Police, asking him to further the investigation to the extent that he could. Because nobody knew Susan and Elizabeth's whereabouts, or whether they'd crossed over into his jurisdiction, McKetta was reluctant to engage his police force in any significant capacity until more information became available.

Elizabeth's father, Raymond Perry, flew from Minneapolis to Harrisburg in a private plane to join the Davis family in the hunt for their missing children. A vice-president of the Bemis Company, a Minneapolis-based bag manufacturer, the dignified Harvard blueblood was also recognized as a highly successful inventor who owned several patents.

Fraught with concern, and certain they'd need to take the initiative in tracking down their daughters, the fathers chartered a helicopter that weekend. Their pilot swept low above the marsh creeks while his passengers peered down among the clearings underneath the forest canopy. They canvassed the vast watershed spanning Wildwood north to Atlantic City, fearing that Susan's car had careened into a ditch and out of sight of passing motorists. They found no signs of wreckage in their aerial sweep of the surrounding woods, however. Several of the teens they spoke with at the

Ninth Street boardinghouse had met Susan and Elizabeth during their stay. None could offer any leads or suggestions where they'd driven once they'd left the house, or where the fathers might search next.

The shore section of the Garden State Parkway, beginning south of the Raritan River and paralleling the Atlantic Ocean, commands a markedly brighter scenery than its denser northern counterpart. Much of the road wending down to the Delaware Bay is bordered by a wilderness of low coastal savannas and scenic wetlands, with a large portion of the flatland woods in Ocean County protected as part of the historic New Jersey Pine Barrens. Wind fires ignite easily during dry spells here, rutting thousand-acre swaths of pygmy pine and blackjack oak, charring a vast undulating plateau of skeletal ruins as far as the eye can see. Crossing over into Atlantic County, the countryside abruptly changes as the road twists toward the southern shores. Shoulder-high cattails rim the sharp bends of estuarine creeks, threading between poor backcountry hollows and pastures native to the Lenni-Lenape Indians. Amateur explorers often excavate arrowheads and other artifacts submerged along the same mud banks where tribesmen once foraged oysters, trapped waterfowl, and netted fish. Closer toward sea, the sun-bleached duck boats and half-sunken trawlers moored to the rickety pilings can cause a traveler awakening dazed from a heavy slumber to ponder whether he has woken somewhere deep within the South Carolina low country.

Two New Jersey state troopers had been assigned early morning patrol of this sleepy southern corner of the parkway on Memorial Day 1969. Trooper James E. "Hawk" Dunbar, twenty-four-years old and a four-year veteran of the force, was stationed at the Avalon barracks off exit 13 in Cape May County. He went on the road at approximately 6 a.m., cruising a forty-mile loop that included a thickly wooded stretch of maritime forest in Egg Harbor Township, a few miles north of the Atlantic County line. He returned to the barracks at approximately 7:30 a.m. The report he logged shortly after his shift ended read that he hadn't noted anything out of the ordinary, no hitchhikers avoiding his glance or disabled cars on the side of the road that might otherwise prompt him to pull over and explore further.

Dunbar was relieved by parkway trooper John Louis Sterr, a seventeen-year veteran also stationed in Avalon, a wealthy barrier island community twenty minutes south of Ocean City. That morning Sterr was covering the same area as his predecessor. He sighted no disabled cars upon first crossing Patcong Creek and the Steelmanville Road overpass. However, at about 8:15 a.m., during his second tour north of the creek, the trooper spotted an unoccupied light-blue convertible with its top down, parked on the northbound shoulder near mile marker 31.9. He slowed his cruiser, turning onto the shoulder to investigate.

Upon approaching the convertible, Sterr observed that the keys were missing. He didn't notice any skid marks or obvious signs of a mechanical breakdown, as a raised hood might indicate. A transistor radio and a straw purse lay in the front seat. Because its contents were seemingly undisturbed and he recognized no immediate signs of foul play, Sterr presumed the vehicle was abandoned.

Within ten minutes of arriving at the scene, Sterr completed a "hot sheet" check with the FBI's National Criminal Information Center database in Washington, D.C., and learned that neither the car nor its tags had been reported stolen. He called in a routine teletype query for a code 15 "lookup" on Pennsylvania license plate number 828595 to the parkway troop E headquarters, who relayed the message to the Pennsylvania Motor Vehicle Department for the identity of the car's owner. Although it has been rendered nearly obsolete with the advent of computer e-mail and text messaging, in 1969 the teletype machine was the primary nationwide interstate communications system utilized by police precincts to exchange urgent bulletins to one another across telephone wires. When the teletype was received in Harrisburg, a clerk at the Commonwealth Department of Records transmitted a faulty return teletype which read that the tag had been issued for a Pontiac owned by William J. Quinn of Camp Hill.

Based upon this information, Sterr officially classified the blue Chevrolet as abandoned and a safety hazard, ordering it towed to Blazer's Auto Service lot in Northfield, New Jersey. He logged this information at the Avalon barracks before his shift ended that morning and then left town for a weekend fishing vacation. After impounding the convertible in his fenced-in junkyard on Tilton Road later that same morning, the tow-truck driver, Howard T. Blazer Sr., stowed the straw handbag in a metal cabinet in his garage office, where it remained for the next three days. He also left town for a fishing trip, driving to Cobb Island, Virginia, with parkway trooper Eddie DeHaven.

Throughout the weekend, the Davises and Perrys remained unaware that Susan's car had been found. When he reported for duty on Monday, June 2, at 8:15 a.m., Sterr read the description of the blue convertible from the missing persons bulletin and immediately alerted his superior, New Jersey State Police Sergeant Lewis Cavileer, who notified Det. Captain Norman D. Young of the Ocean City Police Department that they had the missing vehicle in their possession.

Young phoned Perry. Elizabeth's father spoke with grim foreboding upon hearing news of its recovery, a story first reported by the *New York Times*: "There's no other explanation but foul play," he told a reporter. "I'd stake my life on the proposition that the girls simply would not leave for another destination without notifying members of their family. The girls are not temperamentally suited to just driving off without telling us."

Davis was equally doomful, adding, "We feel there is foul play along the line, but we don't know where. We've contacted her friends along the Eastern Seaboard, but nobody's seen her."

At 11:15 a.m. Monday authorities ordered a massive search of the vicinity where the automobile had been discovered. With traffic whooshing behind them, uniformed troopers joined state highway maintenance workers clad in jumpsuits. They went to their knees and formed a human chain, peering down storm drains and searching for evidence along each square inch of the grassy shoulder and treed parkway median between Somers Point and Ocean City.

Elwood Faunce was a parkway employee stationed out of the highway's Maintenance Division 6, which consisted of a cluster of aluminum sheds housing tractor trailers, pickup trucks, and grass-mowing equipment. Twenty-years-old, until this moment he thought the search "was a huge joke," believing there was little likelihood of finding the missing coeds, especially when he considered the dense vastness of the surrounding wilds that he and his crew were assigned to cover this balmy afternoon.

Workers and volunteers hacked a wide swath through the swampy terrain. They hoisted tree stumps and lifted tangled vines, delicately opened pricker bushes, sifted under pine needles and fallen oak branches as the afternoon mosquitoes swarmed their necks. At 1:30 p.m., just ten minutes after beginning his search, Faunce and co-worker Richard Silvius caught sight of something buried underneath a swept pile of fallen leaves, arranged as if to conceal what lay beneath them. Faunce would lose his voice for two weeks after realizing what held his focus. "I became so nervous, I just stood there," he said. "After a couple of seconds, I came to my senses. It was a blonde girl. She was covered with leaves, but I saw her nude body. I started to whistle to call the other guys over.... My heart dropped to my stomach."

Susan and Elizabeth were discovered approximately three hundred-fifty feet south of milepost 31.9, about two-hundred feet from the edge of the parkway shoulder, within a thickly jungled stretch of woods separated from the shoulder by a grassy embankment. The secluded area, situated within a vast pig farm owned by James Flanagan of Egg Harbor Township and twenty feet from a firebreak path scattered with broken beer bottles, was familiar to locals as a "trysting place for young lovers," according to the *Sentinel Ledger*. Mainland Regional High School students were known to sneak off here to guzzle cheap gin on weekend nights or smoke a joint with friends between classes.

Susan lay facedown in the nude, her long mussed hair crusted with blood and speckled with broken leaves. Her partly decomposed body, savaged by multiple stab wounds to the chest and throat, was bruised throughout her torso. The blue dress and navy jacket she'd worn the morning of her departure were folded neatly beside her, along with her undergarments. Her shoes were still on her feet.

Elizabeth, fully clothed in her green dress, was found sprawled on her back approximately twelve to twenty feet from Davis, her clothes "torn and frayed," according to the *Lebanon (PA) Daily News*. Her body had also been heaped with leaves and twigs, and she'd been gashed repeatedly in the chest and front of her neck with a sharp instrument. Her leather handbag, containing three dollars and a smattering of coins, was strewn near her body. Two newspapers reported that her panties were missing. A three-karat diamond ring, passed down by her grandmother, remained untouched on Elizabeth's right pinkie. She was also found wearing a fourteen-karat charm bracelet, another family heirloom. A state police source recently confirmed that one of the girls, likely Susan, had her neck tied to a tree with her bra. According to two other sources with knowledge of the investigation, the bra had been tied into her hair. As with the diamond ring and charm bracelet, this was a fact never publicly disclosed. There was no drag path through the underbrush, indicating that the murder had taken place at, or very near, the exact location where the victims were found. Both victims had superficial cuts on the right side of their necks, leading state police to conclude they were held at knifepoint. With the exception of a small amount of blood spattered on the trees, and of course the severity of the wounds, there were no broken tree limbs, scuff marks on the ground, or other signs that a violent struggle had taken place as the girls wrestled to free themselves in the course of their abduction.

A reporter called Wesley Davis, notifying him that two bodies had been found that matched the description of Susan and Elizabeth. As word of Faunce's discovery leaked to the press, a bevy of newsmen lit upon the Davis home in Camp Hill. The despondent fathers were seen exiting the front door of the house. Davis maintained his composure, as if reconciled with this grim eventuality long before now. Perry, stunned silent and in a daze, walked unsteadily toward a station wagon waiting to rush them to Harrisburg Airport for the thirty-minute flight to Atlantic City. Crippled by grief, Susan's mother Marjorie had to be sedated and remained inside her home. Several tearful neighborhood women squeezed Perry's hand and kissed him in the driveway before the fathers left town. They offered prayers to both men, wishing them well as they prepared to face their darkest fear imaginable. Their grave expressions, bearing the full weight of hopelessness, reflected the bleak certainty of the fate awaiting them at their next destination.

CHAPTER THREE

Accidental Misfortune

New Jersey State Police officials were rushed by helicopter to the murder scene immediately after the bodies were discovered. Scores of official state vehicles and patrol cars swooped onto the parkway shoulder, so that from a distance they appeared to have slid into one another down an icy hillside. A storm of news trucks from local stations sped in soon thereafter. With their arms akimbo, uniformed state troopers Kenneth Crawford, Thomas "Moonbeam" McCreight, and Thomas Innocente alternately stood guard on either side of the weeded pathway leading into the woods, securing the entrance from press photographers eager to snap crime scene photos.

Clad in narrow dark ties and white shirtsleeves, New Jersey State Police detectives Robert Saunders, William Hunter, Raymond McIlhenny, Martin Brenner, Jr., James J. Hart, and Jack Kreps were among the first to arrive at the scene. Troopers maneuvered around them with metal detectors, sifting for clues as the detectives entered the forest. State police spokesman Joseph G. Kobus, hemmed in by news cameras, tape recorders, and microphones, stood by the parked cruisers on the shoulder of the road with his notebook in hand, patiently fielding questions under the glare of a blazing sun. His answers were brief, yielding what scant details he was permitted to reveal. Crime scene investigators in surgical gloves photographed and sketched the scene hidden in the woods behind him, taking detailed measurements and cordoning off the area with crime tape.

Approximately four hours later, five men emerged grim-faced from the forest hauling a pair of stretchers bound with bulging white sheets. Detectives Crawford and Brenner hoisted the victims, zipped in dark plastic body bags, aboard a waiting hearse parked on the embankment between the woods and the gravel parkway shoulder. Local funeral director Wallace Stroble immediately transported the bodies to the morgue at Shore Memorial Hospital in Somers Point.

"The Drysback, Anglemeyer, and Adamucci murders, I've worked on all of them," Detective Saunders commented. "So many I guess I want to forget. I wish you could forget. But you can't. None of us will ever be able to forget this one. I've seen worse in the way of injuries and violence. But to see two nice young kids who just a few days ago were alive and happy with nothing facing them but a full future…to look at them in those woods…no matter how hardened you get, you'll never forget that sight. This was a bad one."

Recognizing the names of the victims broadcast on local television and radio stations that afternoon, two of the three young men who said they'd eaten breakfast with Susan and Elizabeth at the Point Diner on Friday morning arrived at the Absecon barracks and voluntarily provided statements.

They told police that they joined the women in their booth at approximately 5:15 a.m. Elizabeth, who'd recognized the fraternity regalia woven on their jackets, invited the young men to sit beside them because no other booths were open. They knew the women were in a hurry to get home to Camp Hill, and initially told detectives that they watched them leave the restaurant while the men were still eating. They claimed to have no knowledge of their whereabouts after they exited through the front door, and nothing that Susan and Elizabeth told them during their brief time together led them to conclude that the girls were waiting for somebody, planning to meet with another person immediately after they left the diner, or had been approached by any suspicious characters during their brief stay in town.

A hostess at the diner told a reporter that the two parties had a disagreement over settling the check when the men insisted on paying the entire bill, and that a security guard was called over to settle the dispute. Thomas McReight, one of the state troopers who helped carry the bodies out of the woods, interviewed the three young men. Long since retired from the force, the Medford, New Jersey, resident recalls a different version of events that helps explain the discrepancy between the story reported in the papers and what actually transpired. "They told the girls they'd pay for their breakfast," he says. "What they did was, they took the girls' check and skipped out on their own. They didn't do anything at all. They were all shook up, these kids, and wanted to come forward. They weren't interviewed extensively." Despite the differing accounts, McReight and his supervisors deemed the young men credible, and they were free to leave.

One of the three young men who shared breakfast with Susan and Elizabeth that morning was William J. McMonagle, who'd spent a distinguished career as head of the Philadelphia Family Court bench warrant unit, where the former marine would regularly pursue and arrest "deadbeat dads" delinquent in their child support payments. He remembers nothing unordinary from that Memorial Day morning. After a night of partying, he and his two friends were on their way back to Ocean City, where they were staying for the weekend, when they drove into the diner parking lot in McMonagle's green Corvette to use the bathroom. He says that "the diner was packed" as he and his two friends walked inside. When McMonagle, a graduate of Cardinal Dougherty High School in Philadelphia, returned from the bathroom, his two friends, each of whom attended local Philadelphia colleges, were sharing a booth with Susan and Elizabeth. As McMonagle recalls, his friends were teasing the girls, asking to see their ID's. "We didn't believe they were in college," says McMonagle. "They looked like a couple of high school kids." He recalls a discrepancy with the check, rather than a full-blown dispute as the newspapers reported. "What happened was, I'd left money on the table and went to pay the check for myself and the girls. My friend took the check with him." McMonagle voluntarily returned to the New Jersey State Police barracks in Absecon to give a statement when he learned of the murders while playing a pick up basketball game at LaSalle University in Philadelphia. He says that several years after he'd passed multiple lie detector tests, he learned from the New Jersey State Police that either Mr. Perry or Mr. Davis wished to speak with him personally, but neither father made any attempt to contact him.

Around the time these three men were questioned, state troopers met the victims' fathers upon their arrival at Bader Field Airport in Atlantic City. Before heading to the hospital morgue, the troopers drove them to the substation garage in the rear of the Absecon barracks, where the convertible was stored after being towed from Howard Blazer's garage. Davis was shown the light-blue, Super Sport Impala, which he confirmed had belonged to his daughter. What slim hopes he'd clung to were swiftly dashed as he positively identified the car he'd bought for her. Two soft drink cups and a rubber overshoe were scattered on the front floor of the convertible. A child's red mitten lay in the front seat, and two umbrellas covered the back floorboard. Nothing indicated that the vehicle had been forced off the road. The gas tank was three-quarters full and the battery charged, confirming Trooper Sterr's conclusion that the girls hadn't pulled over due to a mechanical problem. Owing to unforeseen delays, it would be several days before the Chevy was transported to the police lab in West Trenton for fingerprint analysis.

The fathers were escorted to Shore Memorial Hospital after leaving the barracks. They emerged from the side doors leading out of the basement morgue an hour later, whisked by the police toward a waiting patrol car. The toll of crushing despair carved deeply into the downcast gaze of Mr. Davis. With the sleeves of his white shirt rolled to the elbows, a pen clipped to his shirt pocket, the tall, bespectacled forty-seven-year old appeared twenty years older than his true age when he politely muttered to reporters, "Thank you for your interest, gentleman," before leaving the hospital at around 5 p.m.

Atlantic County Prosecutor Robert N. McAllister, Jr., was also at the morgue that day. A mild-mannered, country lawyer with his own practice in the town of Northfield, McAllister was tall with sparse blond hair that blew crooked in the wind. With his plaid sport jacket, fair complexion, and boxy, tortoise-shell glass frames, the keenly insightful forty-two-year-old had an air of a college professor lecturing a roomful of sleepy students on the vicissitudes of market equilibrium. Yet his impactful daily press briefings, a responsibility he shared with state police officials, captivated the hordes of anxious newsmen bunched into the Absecon barracks each evening in the week following the murders. The intervening decades haven't silenced his demons. "My clearest memory of this case that comes into my mind, when I'm really down and tired and upset about something, is walking in and looking at those dead bodies with the parents," says McAllister, who served on the Ethics Committees of the Atlantic County and New Jersey State Bar Associations upon returning to private practice in 1972. "It was possibly the saddest moment of my life. I'll never forget it."

***

Albert Hickey Jr., a part-time security officer affiliated with the Somers Point Police Department, provided state police with a substantial lead just as the fathers left town.

Hickey is in his early seventies, a robust, energetic man with a callused grip and thickly boned forearms sprinkled with sawdust. He owns a small discount furniture store that he runs with his wife Joanna in Egg Harbor City, New Jersey, a short drive from the old Absecon barracks. New and used pieces clutter his modest showroom floor. A credenza in need of sanding stands against a stairwell leading to a second floor, beside a marked-down sofa. An unfinished dining set near the front entrance doubles as a work space, a nook where he can greet customers as they enter his store, sit with them to review a sales agreement, or savor a coastal breeze before he tackles his paperwork at the end of a long day.

In addition to his duties as a security officer, Hickey worked as a freelance photographer and was often dispatched by newspapers to cover local crime scenes. Coincidentally, on Monday evening he was at Shore Memorial Hospital on behalf of the Associated Press, preparing to photograph the arrival of the victims' fathers, when he casually asked a reporter standing next to him what make of car the women had been driving. When he learned that a convertible had been found, he suddenly became a potential witness and was hurried by squad car to the Absecon barracks to give a statement. The image of what he saw that morning hasn't changed in over forty years. He stands resolutely by the account he gave to police and reporters that night.

He remembers that he'd worked at the diner Friday morning until approximately 4:15 a.m., remaining on the premises for a cup of coffee once his shift ended. At around 4:30 a.m. he was standing outside the diner, chatting with fellow security guard John Bates on the landing at the top of the stairs leading to the glass doors. Facing the Somers Point traffic circle, Hickey glimpsed two pretty, young women in a convertible entering the circle from the direction of Ocean City. Their car top was up.

"I'm trained to observe anything around my area," Hickey told a reporter at the time. "That's one reason I looked that way." When the car was directly opposite him across the circle, in front of the Jolly Roger Cocktail Lounge about fifty yards away, the women stopped and picked up what appeared to be a clean-cut hitchhiker wearing a yellow shirt and dark slacks. Hickey remembers that the hitchhiker, about five-feet, seven to five-feet, nine inches tall, was carrying a satchel similar to the complimentary flight bags that used to be given out by major airlines. "He looked fairly clean-cut, not like a beatnik or hippie…neat, but shaggy," he told a reporter. "The girls stopped, and the hitchhiker ran up to the side of the car. The girl passenger said something to him and then opened the door and let him in the back." Hickey said that the car, which had Pennsylvania tags, was either blue or black and sped off down MacArthur Boulevard in the direction of the parkway. But when asked by state police to positively identify the convertible now stored at the barracks garage, he said that although it looked similar to the car he had seen at the circle, he couldn't be certain. He candidly admitted he never saw the women eating at the diner or entering and leaving the premises.

The autopsies were performed at Shore Memorial Hospital two hours after the fathers identified the bodies. Dr. Edward Albano, chief medical examiner for the state of New Jersey, Dr. William A. Joy, Atlantic County medical examiner, and Dr. Henry E. Seidel, a pathologist at Shore Memorial Hospital, concluded that Susan's death was caused by a stab wound to the right side of the neck inflicted by a short blade that perforated her larynx. As opposed to a penetrating wound with one entry point, in a perforated injury the weapon punctures both points of surface and leaves an exit wound. That the murder weapon, thought to be a penknife or paring knife, pierced the tough outer layer of cartilage and muscle composing the larynx elucidates how forcefully the killer thrust his jabs. The report also revealed three stab wounds on the left side of Susan's abdomen. Her torso was marred with contusions. As the report did not indicate that her beating was caused by a blunt instrument such as tree branch, a baseball bat, or a lead pipe, it was likely delivered by a flurry of hard blows.

Elizabeth, also the victim of a rage-fueled killing, was similarly bruised above her waist. Her assailant focused his attack on her upper torso, hammering the knifepoint five times into her chest. She died from a gaping wound that pierced her right lung. Scrapings from under their fingernails were submitted to the state police lab for evidence of defense wounds, with hopes they might yield skin samples.

Earlier that day, Elizabeth's older sister Suzanne received a letter addressed to their parents' lake home in Minnesota. It had been postmarked in Ocean City. "I'm having a marvelous time, but am eager to get home and see you all again," Elizabeth wrote.

Ray Perry flew home to be with his family after returning to Harrisburg that evening. A day later he told reporters that the discovery of the bodies confirmed his worst fears. "There simply was no other explanation for their disappearance," he said gloomily. "The girls simply were not temperamentally capable of driving off some other place without letting us know."

At 6:40 p.m. Monday, Walter Cronkite reported the story of the murders on the *CBS Evening News* while troopers continued scouring the parkway woods and nearby marshes for evidence. Among the items the search teams uncovered were Susan's eyeglasses and a skin diver wristwatch. The police had initially hoped to treat the latter find as a "holdback," or a "control," terms used by detectives when they withhold a crucial piece of evidence from the public, so that during interrogation and lie detector tests wily suspects can't attribute their knowledge of it to what they read in the paper or saw on television. This practice is also useful in discouraging mentally unbalanced, publicity-seeking individuals who habitually offer false confessions to satisfy a compelling need for notoriety. News of the watch's discovery, however, was leaked to the *Philadelphia Inquirer* and reported in the following morning's edition. Although police confirmed it had been found, the make and model—a Belforte Sea Diver retailing for $39.95 at local surf shops—wouldn't be disclosed to the press for several weeks.

"I was so shocked that I couldn't watch the television reports last night," said Mary Bryson from Milwaukee, one of Susan's best friends from college. "I couldn't sleep. It's like I can still hear their voices. What a ghastly, horrible thing this is. One minute you're saying 'Goodbye' and 'Don't forget to write'-and then they're dead. What kind of person could've done this?"

New Jersey State Police Colonel and Superintendent David B. Kelly appointed Lieutenant James F. Brennan to preside over a task force of thirty homicide detectives assigned to work the double murders. A twenty-two-year state police veteran, with fifteen of those years spent as a detective with the Criminal Investigation Division out of Troop A headquarters in Hammonton, Brennan's command was overseen by Captain Mario Paterra and Major Victor E. Galassi, sent from division headquarters to supervise the investigation.

Stocky and balding, with a crooked nose busted in a childhood mishap, Brennan bore an uncanny resemblance to 1950s television actor Broderick Crawford. He'd served in the Navy during World War II and was a devout Irish Catholic who lived with his wife and three children in nearby Stone Harbor, where he ushered at St. Paul's Roman Catholic Church.

Kelly's selection was ideally suited to shoulder the heft of a high-profile murder case. The top-ranking detective out of the Hammonton barracks, Brennan was familiar with the handling of high-publicity crimes, having extensively worked on the Harry Anglemyer murder case scheduled for trial in September of that year. He was known by his peers as a methodically patient man whose easygoing demeanor belied his reputation as a tenacious cop with fifteen years experience solving violent crimes throughout southern New Jersey.

Late Monday evening at the Absecon barracks, Brennan stood solemnly before a gaggle of expectant reporters squeezed into the small lobby outside an office door. To his left was Robert McAllister, whose prosecutor's office was under directive from the New Jersey Attorney General's Office to assist Brennan and the state police in any way possible. McAllister's staff humbly complied in the coming weeks, joining their fellow lawyers and the investigators beneath them in tasks as mundane as fetching coffee or driving daily investigative reports between the Absecon barracks and division headquarters in Trenton.

Brennan paused for a moment to listen as Assistant Prosecutor Solomon Forman, standing to his right, slung an arm over his shoulder and pulled him closer, whispering in his ear. The police had no suspects or leads, Brennan bluntly announced to the newsmen, who barraged him with questions at the first press conference in what was to become one of the most highly publicized murder cases in New Jersey since the Lindbergh baby kidnapping. The boarders who'd stayed at the Sybens' boardinghouse hadn't been interviewed yet, Brennan said, but none were under suspicion. Detectives were awaiting lab results to determine if either, or both, of the women had been raped, the lieutenant calmly stated before turning and retreating to his office. The

Chicago Tribune, however, reported that "there had been some evidence of sexual assault."

The state police had little reason for optimism at this juncture, an attitude reflected in Brennan's terse statement. They hadn't yet located the murder weapon. The culprit had long since vanished from the scene, and a strapless diver watch was all he'd left behind. Robbery, a likely motive, was ruled out as Susan's purse was untouched, and Elizabeth's money had been left behind at the scene. Worse, their bodies lay outside in the humid climate for three days, exposed to insects and scavenging animals, accelerating decomposition and making it more difficult for pathologists to harvest useful forensic evidence.

Top state police officials assembled at Trenton headquarters to strategize their next phase of action. Detectives and troopers were enlisted from neighboring barracks, including Bass River and Port Norris. They worked throughout Monday night, fervent in their hunt for a witness they were certain had seen something vital between the Somers Point traffic circle and mile marker 31.9 of the parkway but hadn't come forward yet. A newspaper headline suggested that the police had already targeted a suspect: *Youth Reported Seen With Coeds Before Slaying. Hitchhiker Sought in Killings.* What information were they withholding from the press? Was the murderer still in town, pacing the boardwalk in search of his next victim, or had he already fled? Had Susan and Elizabeth run into him at the nightclubs in Somers Point, or have the accidental misfortune of picking up a random psychopath hitchhiking at the traffic circle?

John Divel, a retired lieutenant with the Ocean City Police Department Detective Bureau, visited the crime scene extensively in the days following the murders. Although his department lacked jurisdiction, he nevertheless tracked the investigation's progress, compelled by a duty to lend whatever help he could to the beleaguered state police force. "It was one of the warmest summers we'd had in a long while," he says. "I know that the way the bodies were left, the person who killed those girls had an excellent knowledge of chemistry, knowing that the three things you need are heat, moisture, darkness, and the proper point of acidity to eliminate evidence. All of that was accomplished. It was remarkable."

CHAPTER FOUR

An Incomplete Portrait

Due to its proximity to the murder locus, and because it was under the prosecutorial jurisdiction of the Atlantic County Prosecutor's Office, in 1969 the Absecon barracks at 244 East White Horse Pike in Absecon was designated as temporary headquarters for the Perry-Davis murder investigation. Formerly a sleepy road station outfitted with bunk beds where troopers could nap between shifts, the ground floor of the modest, shingled brick building was suddenly transformed into a war room command post. Living quarters were hurriedly dismantled and spare rooms partitioned into new offices equipped with filing cabinets, wall charts, and new phone lines to be utilized solely for the expanding investigation. The hotline number—609-646-2088—was distributed to local newspapers, along with a message from Lt. Brennan imploring the public to call and provide state police with "any scrap of information that might help us solve these crimes."

Teams of detectives fanned out through the region early Tuesday. They spoke with jewelry store and surf shop owners to learn who carried Benrus brand watches, sifting through piles of receipts to see whether they'd sold any of the Belforte Sea Diver model recently. Closer to home, investigators sought out people who'd been with Susan and Elizabeth or had seen anyone in their company in the hours before they were murdered. They were primarily interested in speaking with the young men Frances Syben had overheard Elizabeth alluding to on the porch Friday morning.

Walter Syben told reporters that the girls had been out for the evening, returning when he was on the porch locking up his house. "The girls had planned to leave sometime Friday morning," he said. "But my wife and I were on the porch at about 2 a.m. Friday and the girls came back from the boardwalk. They said they changed their plans and would leave at 4 a.m." They walked back in the direction of the boardwalk, he said, returning at 4 a.m. to pack. "One of my guests told me that they were beaten to death," Syben told a reporter for the *New York Daily News*. "I couldn't believe it. My wife became so upset she wants me to get rid of the place. I cried too."

The father of one of the young men who Susan and Elizabeth met with before they left town, and who may have been the persons Frances Syben overheard Elizabeth referring to on the boardinghouse porch, spoke anonymously to a reporter for the *Philadelphia Daily News*. He said that his son and a friend first met the two girls on the beach earlier in the week and spent much of the next two days with them. The girls had a camera and, according to what the son told his father, snapped photos of people they'd met at the beach, including the two hippies who'd been pestering them to take their picture. During their time in Ocean City, Susan and Elizabeth had been to the father's house to visit with his son and the friend, and while there Susan had called home to Camp Hill. The father, however, didn't say whether the pair had been with the girls between 2 and 4 a.m. Friday. He confirmed that they said goodbye to Susan and Elizabeth just before the girls left town the morning they were slain but couldn't confirm the exact time their parting took place or at what specific location in Ocean City. When asked how he knew this, the father replied that he was at his house when his son left with his friend to go meet the girls that morning and was there when they returned home. He was adamant that his son couldn't have eaten breakfast with Susan and Elizabeth at the Point Diner, however, for he and his companion returned home before the girls were seen at the diner. The two young men met with detectives on two occasions, told them what they knew, and were cleared of any wrongdoing.

Police also located and spoke with the two "hippie-types" Frances Syben saw loitering on the Ninth Street curb across from the boardinghouse early Friday morning, allegedly shouting toward Susan. Coincidentally, these turned out to be the same men that had been pestering Susan and Elizabeth to take their photo. Identified from the camera film developed by police, they voluntarily submitted to questioning, provided an alibi for the time of the murders, and were released.

Investigators logically returned to the Point Diner, the first place the girls were spotted after leaving Ocean City. In addition to Albert Hickey, eight waitresses, three busboys, and several cooks were working at the diner early Memorial Day. Mrs. Eleanor Ryan, who was hostessing before dawn Friday morning, recalled seeing only "a mass of long-haired boys and girls," not anybody matching the specific description of Susan or Elizabeth. Cashier Gloria Cressey didn't recall seeing them either.

William Magill, manager of the Point Diner, said that some two hundred customers had eaten in his restaurant early Friday morning, but nobody saw Susan or Elizabeth. "Logic would put the two girls in our place before starting on their trip," Magill told a reporter. "I have not heard from any of our people that they believe they served them."

Magill's family had owned the diner since 1950, back when it was a sixty-five-seat dining car. In 1982 he sold the establishment to the present owners before embarking on a second career as an insurance salesman with MetLife. Like trooper Thomas McReight, Magill offers an explanation for the inconsistent accounts detectives were provided. "At that particular time of the day, the diner was extremely busy," he says. With the bars letting out in the early morning hours, "It was practically a situation where we had a standing line to get in twenty-four hours a day. It was gangbusters."

Detectives theorized that after leaving the crowded diner, Susan made a right turn out of the parking lot and entered the flow of traffic. To reach mile marker 31.9 of the parkway from this point, they would have driven three quarters of the way around the circle and taken the MacArthur Boulevard exit, consistent with Hickey's account. At the end of MacArthur Boulevard there is a light where the road intersects with Route 9. From here it turns into Laurel Lane, a leafy, two-lane suburban road that ends at a toll booth before the entranceway to the northbound lane of the parkway.

Doug Bartlett of Sea Isle City was the lone collector on shift early Friday morning at the Ocean City-Somers Point toll plaza, which sits in the middle of the three-mile stretch between the diner and the murder scene. Bartlett said he didn't notice the convertible go past his booth. A toll collector, he explained, rarely takes note of any but the most unusual vehicles. He said he "certainly could not have missed the two" young women driving by in their light-blue convertible at that hour if the top was down. After all, he said, it was a damp, chilly sunrise at the time the girls supposedly drove through the booth, which meant that he simply didn't see them after they dropped their coins in the bucket, they didn't take this route, or, as his statement implies, the top to their convertible was up. Bartlett himself discounted the possibility that the girls' car didn't pass through the Somers Point interchange, for the alternate routes they might have chosen—due west on Mays Landing Road, north on Route 9, or northeast on Shore Road—would have been impractical, leading them in an opposite direction from where they were headed.

Given such sparse feedback by the authorities, the press turned to local proprietors to find out where and with whom the women had spent their time during their three days in Ocean City. Davis summarized his daughter's activities in the days preceding her murder: "They called Tuesday night and again Wednesday," he said. "They had gotten a bit too much sun; they'd been shopping; they said they met a few boys on the beach, but nothing exciting." He added, "They were not boy-crazy types."

Interviewed in the den of his home, Walter Syben told reporters that Susan and Elizabeth had spent most of their time at the Ninth Street beach, unofficially coined "College Beach" because of the throngs of undergrads that congregated there each summer between Shriver's Pavilion and the Music Pier, a grand Spanish hacienda-style building still used for weekly summer concerts given by the Ocean City Pops Orchestra. The girls paid between forty-eight and sixty dollars cash for a three-night stay in a room with two single beds, two windows covered by Venetian blinds, one dresser, and a chair. When they checked in on Tuesday, May 27, three boys were staying there, Syben said. On the morning Susan and Elizabeth left, the house was filled with forty vacationers. "Most of the day they were at the beach, and at night they would go out with friends, I think from some college," he told reporters. "They were in at two every morning, just as I asked because I like to lock up soon after that." He added, "They were very sophisticated girls. They were well-bred and sort of plain. None of that heavy makeup and stuff. You could just hear them say anything and know they had a good education."

There were indications that the girls had applied for summer jobs while in Ocean City. Fred Celebre, a pizza restaurant owner on Asbury Avenue, refused to hire them. "They were not the type that would associate with riff-raff," he said. "They were too high class." He distinctly remembered Susan because she had visited his shop in summers past. While she and Elizabeth were at his shop, Susan was vivacious and talked a lot about college, but her friend sat silent, he said.

"Both wanted jobs," he said. "But they were not the type to be picked up. They would have to know the guy first." He added, "I need the type that makes it with the guys."

R. Lee Swigart, a nineteen-year-old student from McVeytown, Pennsylvania, was one of the three young men staying on the second floor of the boardinghouse when the girls checked into a room across the hall from them on Tuesday afternoon. A psychology major at Elizabethtown College in Pennsylvania, that summer he was working at a boardwalk luncheonette. He was listening to the radio at his parents' home in Pennsylvania, two-hundred-thirty miles away, when he first heard that the girls were missing. Upon his return to Ocean City on Monday, June 2, he drove to the Absecon barracks and volunteered all he knew, spending most of the night answering questions.

Swigart was interviewed at length by the *Philadelphia Bulletin*. He told a reporter that he and Susan, whom he described as outgoing and friendly, quickly struck up a conversation upon her arrival at the boardinghouse. All five of the boarders went out as a group Tuesday evening, had something to eat, then strolled the boardwalk. They joined one another for breakfast together the following morning, with Susan and Elizabeth insisting on paying their own checks. The same group spent Wednesday afternoon on the beach. Susan went swimming in the ocean a number of times, Swigart recalled, listening to her radio and singing to herself while Elizabeth tanned. At some point in the afternoon the girls made acquaintances with a couple of young men from the University of Pennsylvania. Susan eventually went off to be alone with one of them, as did Elizabeth with the other. It is unclear whether these were the same young men who'd allegedly met with them in the early morning hours before they started for home.

On Wednesday evening, May 28, Swigart, Elizabeth, Susan and some other boys drove across the causeway to Somers Point for a beer party. Because everyone in their group was under age (In 1969 the legal drinking age in New Jersey was twenty-one.), another youth bought two six packs of beer in Somers Point, where they sat together in a car alongside the roadside and drank, smoked cigarettes, and talked. "We didn't get drunk," Swigart insisted. He said they returned to the rooming house at a reasonably early hour that night. Swigart checked out Thursday afternoon, May 29, the last time he saw Susan and Elizabeth alive.

According to Swigart, Susan was the chattier of the two girls, maintaining control of the conversation. Elizabeth, he said, "held back a little and didn't talk too much about herself. She was just Sue's sidekick," whereas Susan "didn't want to be too serious about anything. If the talk got too serious, Sue would holler, 'Whoa!' and would change the subject. She wouldn't let us talk about marriage, children, schoolwork, or anything else serious."

Although Swigart volunteered to take a lie detector test, he was never given one, or at any point considered a suspect. He believed that one man killed the girls. "This guy might be right here. He may be one of the guys we know, one of the guys that was with us." As to the possibility of Susan pulling over to offer a stranger a lift, he said, "Sue wouldn't have picked up a hitchhiker unless she knew him."

At least publicly, Lt. Brennan agreed with Swigart's assumption. He told *Atlantic City Press* reporter Jon Katz, "From what I know about them, it doesn't appear they would pick up someone they didn't know."

But on Wednesday, June 4, three young men from Susan's hometown told reporters she had picked them up hitchhiking in Camp Hill eighteen months earlier. The seventeen and eighteen-year-old boys, who asked not to be identified, made the disclosure to a reporter on the beach in Ocean City, where they were on a class trip with sixty other seniors from Trinity High School in Camp Hill. They were trying to hitch a ride to a hamburger drive-in about a half a mile away, they recalled, when Susan stopped and offered them a ride without knowing them. She was apparently driving her father's car, accompanied by a friend unknown to the boys.

"We were hitchhiking, and Sue stopped and said, 'Where are you going?'" one of the boys recalled. "We told her McDonalds." They quickly got in the car. "She was real easy to carry on a conversation with," he said, later recognizing Susan from her picture in the local newspaper.

The scant feedback provided by local storekeepers and fellow boarders, all of whom had limited interaction with Susan and Elizabeth, formed an incomplete portrait of the girls. The statements made by the numerous young men who'd courted them during their brief stay in Ocean City were of little use to detectives either, providing no new direction for their investigation. Lt. Brennan himself had misjudged Susan, suggesting that she wouldn't offer a lift to a stranger. A closer study of Susan and Elizabeth, revealed through recent interviews with their former hometown neighbors, schoolmates, and acquaintances, offers a more thorough portrayal of the victims. This insight provides a deeper understanding of their vulnerabilities, a narrower profile of their murderer, and a clearer explanation how they likely encountered him.

CHAPTER FIVE

Fertile Hunting Grounds

Susan Margarite Davis was born on March 14, 1950. She was raised in the affluent Beverly Park neighborhood of Camp Hill, Pennsylvania, a borough in eastern Cumberland County located two miles outside the state capitol of Harrisburg. Founded in 1735 as a settlement along the historic turns of the Susquehanna River, Camp Hill was the site of The Skirmish of Sporting Hill, a pivotal battle between Robert E. Lee's Army of Northern Virginia against the Union forces during the Gettysburg campaign of the Civil War.

Laurel Lane, the leafy cul-de-sac where Susan grew up, is located near the fairways of the West Shores Country Club, where the Davises were longtime members.

The family was originally from North Carolina, led north by Susan's grandfather, Francis W. Davis, a prominent attorney in Durham, North Carolina. Upon relocating to Harrisburg, Pennsylvania, the family patriarch founded the Bethlehem, Pennsylvania-based Davis Beverage Company in 1943. Susan's father, Wesley Sr., ran the business for several decades before turning over leadership to his firstborn child, Wesley Jr., who eventually sold the distributorship to Dr. Pepper.

Susan was educated at Harrisburg Academy, the K-12 private school that she'd attended since grade school. Caitlyn LeGrande, a former classmate from nearby Mechanicsburg,

Pennsylvania, carpooled with her to school each day during Susan's senior year at the academy, a day school comprised mostly of children of the Harrisburg elite. "For forty years a lot of us have wondered what happened," LeGrande says. "I haven't talked to anybody about the murders in thirty years," for her classmates refuse to discuss the issue whenever the topic is broached at school reunions. Susan, she recalls, was a talkative, cheerful girl known for her effusive kindness. "She didn't have a malicious bone in her body. I can't stress how nice she was," says LeGrande. She remembers when the Davises chaperoned parties for Susan and her classmates and hosted sleepovers in their downstairs den. LeGrande seems reluctant to qualify her poignant assessment of her former schoolmate. "Susan was a very different girl….She was a very nice girl, but socially awkward. She was the kind of girl who, if you were standing around in the hallway, in front of boys, she might tell you, 'Your slip's hanging out.'" Legrande added, "She didn't have a lot of friends, only because she was socially awkward. But you didn't dislike her."

Joan Romig, Susan's art instructor at the academy, recalled that her former pupil showed potential as an artist. "There was a delicate, spiritual feeling that came with her work," she told a local newspaper, noting that Madonnas were a favorite subject of the young painter. She said that Susan planned to continue her artwork. "This was deeply instilled in her. I would say this was one of her great loves."

Susan worked for her father's bottling company during summer vacations and was a member of her church's Methodist Youth Fellowship chapter. In the quote under her photograph in *The Spectator*, the school yearbook, she attested to her outgoing disposition, playfully amending English poet Thomas Carlyle's proverb, "Silence is golden," to include "But she prefers silver." At the suggestion of her brother's fiancée, in the fall of 1967 she enrolled at Monticello Junior College in Godfrey, Illinois. The all-girls school near St. Louis closed its doors in 1971. The buildings remain, however, encompassing the scenic two-hundred-fifteen- acre campus of Lewis & Clark Community College.

Monticello catered to debutantes from old midwestern families, much like the all-female finishing schools of the rolling Virginia countryside that to this day continue to enroll descendants of the southern aristocracy. Susan was often bored during her first year away from home, miffed by the college's strict enforcement of its 11 p.m. weekend curfew. In a letter to a friend from New York, she referred to the school as a "nunnery," once quoting the oft-played refrain from the Animals song, "We Gotta Get Outta This Place," to describe the desolate winter months and arctic prairie winds of southwestern Illinois.

Despite her grumblings, Susan fit in well at "Monti," as she referred her school, immersing herself in extracurricular activities and embracing its traditions and rituals, like being tossed into the showers if you were lavaliered by your hometown boyfriend, or submitting to a playful spanking on your birthday. She joined the field hockey team and also served on the senior staff committee. An adviser to the student resident counselors, she led the school's Spanish Club while living at Caldwell Hall, graduating with her Associate of Arts degree a week before driving to Ocean City. She befriended Elizabeth after they met one another through a "Big Sister" program toward the end of Susan's second year.

The memory of Susan's death lurks with Caitlyn LeGrande as a traumatic episode from her adolescence, evading closure. "Finding her killer might at least give her family a little peace at this point. I know it would give me some."

***

Elizabeth Potter Perry was born on January 10, 1950. She was the younger of two daughters born to Margaret Eggers Perry and Raymond Potter Perry. The family hailed from St. Louis originally, relocating to the Minneapolis suburbs when Elizabeth was eight-years old.

Elizabeth was known to her friends and family as "Ibby," a nickname derived from the mispronunciation of her name when she and her sister Suzanne were children. Like Susan, she was a child of means, a former Girl Scout raised in a grand Victorian home on Lakeview Avenue in the wealthy Cottagewood section of Deephaven, Minnesota, a Minneapolis suburb situated on the forested shores of Lake Minnetonka.

Elizabeth enjoyed a sheltered upbringing in this cloistered neighborhood of winding driveways and yacht clubs, playing tennis in backyard courts and swimming in pools sheltered by tall, manicured hedgerows. A childhood friend, today a prominent attorney, remembers how the Perrys would throw birthday parties for Elizabeth at their home on the lake, inviting over her classmates and friends for winter skating parties. Her parents were members of the Wayzata Country Club, where her father served on the board of directors.

Janet Kordonowy, Elizabeth's classmate from the 1968 graduating class of Minnetonka High School, recalls Deephaven as an idyllic town whose privileged youth were impervious to the revolutionary zeitgeist that had consumed other teens during the late sixties. In this wealthy Minneapolis suburb it was still a time when girls remained fearful of sullying their reputations, where at football games they continued to wear Bermuda shorts with matching knee-high socks and wool crew-neck sweaters rather than bellbottom jeans and fringed leather jackets. Instead of marching in anti-war protests or experimenting with drugs, "We went to drive-ins, tried Colt-45 or cherry vodka, puked and went home and hoped our parents didn't find out," Kordowny says.

Elizabeth had been enrolled in the Minnetonka public schools since the fourth grade. Former classmates recall her as a shy, withdrawn girl. Throughout her teens she attended church every week and was a Sunday school teacher at her parish, where she was also active in the Young People's Fellowship. "She had an abundance of compassion for those in need," said the Rev. Edwin J. Eilertsen of St. Martin's-by-the-Lake Episcopal Church in Minnetonka Beach.

"I basically was her friend through high school," says former classmate Connie Carbonell, who also remembers the Rockwellian scenes of their Minnesota youth, a time of autumn hayrides and kids dashing between neighborhood homes to play Yahtzee and Monopoly. "I don't think I was in touch with her after high school. We shared a lot of talks in Mr. Bauman's tenth grade English class, especially about boys. She seemed boy crazy, although I don't remember her ever having a boyfriend. She was excited about going off to college. She was relatively shy and a bit gullible, maybe a bit too trusting. Perhaps that was why she was vulnerable."

Annette Ahern and her husband John lived next door to Elizabeth on Lakeview Avenue for several years, before the Perrys moved to Mercer Island, Washington, in the year following their younger daughter's murder. Avid tennis players, they and the Perrys would often play mixed doubles on the Ahearn's private court.

"Ibby was a different kind of girl," Mrs. Ahearn recalls. "She was a sweet, sweet girl. She wasn't extremely popular. My mother-in-law's house was next to us here, my nieces and their parents lived in the next house, and the Perrys lived on the other side of us. I never knew Ibby that well because she wasn't, well, I guess she was socially immature, and she didn't draw people that much." Elizabeth often visited Mrs. Ahearn's mother-in-law because she was very approachable, offering guidance and wisdom to the awkward teenager.

According to Ahern, Margaret Perry was more outgoing than her husband. A proud alumna of Sweetbriar College in

Virginia, the same finishing school that her daughter Suzanne attended, Margaret headed the women's group at her church, helping to sew quilts later auctioned to fund community outreach programs. She shared Elizabeth's love of animals, allowing the stray cats and dogs she rescued the run of her Lakeview Avenue home, which she used as a temporary shelter. Raymond was quieter and spent much of his free time in the basement, busily sawing or fixing something. He grew more withdrawn once his daughter died. "It was so hard," Ahearn says, vividly recalling the Memorial Day afternoon when Marge Perry approached her, worried that Susan and Elizabeth hadn't returned from Ocean City. "I was gardening, and she said, 'we haven't heard from them, we're sort of concerned.'"

Although she was an average student, Elizabeth attained an excellent attendance record in high school, where she actively participated in the fine arts and theatre programs. Her Monticello classmates remember her having a more difficult time adjusting socially than Susan, but she nevertheless immersed herself in activities, joining the chorus and play committees and managing the swim team. Like Susan, she was an art major, and the following autumn was scheduled to serve as assistant to the resident director of her dormitory. Elizabeth was "very alert...a very responsible kind of girl," said Monticello College Dean of Women Marguerite Shewman. "She was easy with adults, didn't have the traditional kind of hang-ups."

"Sue was a more feminine, makeup, boy-oriented, partying kind of girl," says Karen Greiser, who lived across from Elizabeth in Baldwin Hall. She remembers Elizabeth as a soft-spoken, reserved young woman who chose her words carefully, speaking in measured cadences. Pamela Hartwick, Elizabeth's best friend, says Ibby was painfully homesick her first year away at school, and had lost weight, which might explain the person described by her Monticello classmates as shy and oftentimes withdrawn.

Ken Lippert, from Wood River, Illinois, had dated Elizabeth for a short time before she died. "We broke up about three weeks ago," he said to a reporter two days after the bodies were discovered. "She was a real nice girl; she was a decent little girl. She wasn't wild or loud or anything like that. She was pretty quiet."

Ocean City's residents were shocked as to how two conscientious, intelligent young women like Susan and Elizabeth, both tall and fit, could have been so swiftly subdued by a diabolical killer, in of all places their Christian seaside oasis at the Jersey Shore. It wasn't that an act of cold-blooded murder in the area was unprecedented (Five years earlier, flamboyant civic leader Harry "Fudgy" Anglemyer, owner of the Copper Kettle Fudge Shop chain, was found bludgeoned to death in front of the Dunes nightclub on Longport Boulevard, a case that was never solved.), the randomness of the crimes, or lack of any apparent motive that made the murders of Susan and Elizabeth seem so incomprehensible. More perplexing was how a person capable of these atrocities wasn't recognized during his time here. Bewildered residents openly wondered how he could have gone undetected, anonymously immersing himself within the throngs of teenagers loitering outside the Chatterbox Restaurant, the mix of frat boys and sorority queens sunning themselves on the Ninth Street beach, and the older crowd drinking and dancing the night away at the Somers Point bars. After all, this was a vacation community marketed toward God-fearing families, a resort where parents could rest assured knowing that their college-aged children, if left alone with friends to rent a beach bungalow for the weekend, were likely to be safe. Though storeowners, innkeepers, and local authorities were accustomed to a certain amount of mischievous spiritedness from their younger visitors, the gruesome slaying of two innocent college girls was an entirely unexpected tragedy for which they were completely unprepared.

The affluent island where Susan Davis and Elizabeth Perry spent their last days began with the idealistic visions of four Methodist ministers. The three brothers among them, the Revs. S. Wesley, James E., and Ezra B. Lake, together with the Rev. William Burrell, set out to establish a Methodist seaside retreat "where the sanctity of the Sabbath should be preserved and the sale of alcoholic beverages is prohibited." First known as Peck's Beach, a sparsely inhabited seven-mile barrier island of sand dunes, cedar swamps, and mud flats named for English whaler John Peck, the island initially served as a fishing destination for local Indians, a grazing land for wild cattle herds, and a scenic picnic spot for mainland residents.

Strictly enforced, the island's blue laws originally prohibited "non-essential shopping" as well as "dancing, singing, fiddling or other music for the sake of merriment" on Sundays. Although these restrictions were loosened in 1986 to allow shopping on Sundays, the sale and consumption of alcohol anywhere on the island is still against the law, contained as a restrictive covenant with every deed of land sold, public or private.

Aside from the untarnished beauty of its gilded sands, Victorian gingerbread architecture, and lush tidal wetlands, the residing image of a family-oriented vacation destination has always been the island's true appeal. Touting itself as "America's Greatest Family Resort" on its weekly tourist pamphlets and in city newspapers since 1920, the island has always enticed visitors with the promise of wholesome fun. Residents take pride in their reputation as a safe Christian beach community where upper middle-class parents, primarily from the Philadelphia and southern New Jersey suburbs, can bring their young children on vacation for a week in the summertime to sun, swim, and enjoy the boardwalk amusements.

Like-minded persons run Ocean City's businesses. "I happen to love the fact that it's a dry island," says Clara Plowfield, former owner of Serendipity Bed & Breakfast at 712 Ninth Street, the same house where Susan and Elizabeth stayed, before selling it in 2017. "You're not going to walk by a bunch of drunk guys at night," says Plowfield. "It's a very safe place and the fact that there's no alcohol is a big part of that."

Despite its relatively small population (In 1969, the island had an estimated population of 7,550), Ocean City has produced a disproportionate number of celebrities since its founding. Among the more notable inhabitants included Grace Kelly, whose family owned a Spanish-style mansion at Twenty-sixth Street and Wesley Avenue. According to local historian Fred Miller, Prince Ranier, Caroline, and Stephanie visited the Kelly vacation home on numerous occasions over the years, before the Princess' untimely death in 1982. Acclaimed writer Gay Talese, the author of the controversial best-selling novel *Thy Neighbor's Wife* and the husband of famed publisher Nan Talese, grew up along these shores.

Former MTV host Kurt Loder was also born here, graduating from Ocean City High School in 1963. Actress Anne Heche was a member of the class of 1987. MSNBC political commentator Chris Matthews, a native Philadelphian, spent a summer as a singing waiter at Your Father's Mustache, a bar in Somers Point. He also worked at Watson's Restaurant on Ninth Street, where Susan and Elizabeth had parked their car the morning they disappeared.

Today, a stroll down the Ocean City boardwalk on a late July evening reveals a scenery largely unchanged since 1969. With its twirling Ferris wheel lights aglow within a humid twilit haze infused with the scent of caramel corn, the promenade seems preserved within a kindred timelessness revered by natives and returning guests alike. Gulls scavenge trash bins. Shriver's Candy Store, located at Ninth Street and the boardwalk, a short walk from the boardinghouse where Susan and Elizabeth spent their last night alive, continues to churn vats of salt-water taffy behind a glass viewing partition. Vacationers stand in line for soft ice cream at Kohr Brothers and fresh slices at Mack and Manco Pizza. Though Simms' Seafood Restaurant was swept up in a towering blaze, and a pounding nor'easter tide reclaimed the Shriver's Pavilion, the Wonderland Pier on the north end of the boardwalk still bustles nightly with scurrying children stopping to plunge tokens down slots for a game of skee-ball, or waiting their turn for the go-carts and Tilt-a-Whirl.

Separated by two and a half miles from Ocean City is the mainland port of Somers Point. Located just over the line dividing Atlantic County from Cape May County, the former clamming port is named after John Somers, an Englishman who settled on Great Egg Harbor in 1693. He deeded his land, then known as Somers Plantation, to his oldest surviving son, Richard, on November 5, 1720. Richard built a brick home upon the foundations of his father's cabin, laying the groundwork for Somers Mansion, which today sits atop a fractured cement rampart overlooking the Crab Trap Restaurant and the Ocean City skyline, across from the Somers Point Diner.

Unlike its abstemious neighbors across the bay, for a time the inland settlers were actually required to maintain a tavern and inn for the benefit of their outlaw patrons, many of whom were rum runners and smugglers. Known as "ordinaries," these establishments were constructed pursuant to the 1688 Ordinary Law, according to Ocean City and Somers Point historian William E. Kelly in his book *300 Years at the Point*. Maintaining its piratical origins, upon the repeal of prohibition over two hundred years later a slew of barkeeps opened shop along Bay Avenue, catering to the sinful indulgences of Ocean City beachgoers.

Throughout the fifties and early sixties, Ocean City and Somers Point enjoyed a profitable symbiosis. As the postwar economy boomed, men found work building hotels along the boardwalk, profiting from a tourism industry that thrived on a summer crowd comprised largely of young families and college kids whose exuberances and indiscretions were constrained by their conservative social mores. These educated young professionals, who'd board overnight at summer guesthouses or rent houses for the season, routinely headed across the bay for decadent nighttime excursions. The famous Bay Avenue nightclubs such as Tony Mart's, Bay Shores Café, and the old Anchorage Hotel prospered during this era, luring thousands over the bridge with continuous live music and nightly seven-for-the-price-of-one beer specials.

Tony Mart's was the best known of these saloons. The joint jammed nightly from Memorial Day through Labor Day, offering midweek limbo contests, popular house bands, and gyrating go-go dancers hired to bat their doll lashes and strut in micro-mini skirts on the platforms between the three stages. Bill Haley and the Comets performed their timeless anthem "Rock Around The Clock" here. The renowned group The Band, which started as Levon and the Hawks, got their start at Tony Mart's. Bob Dylan, it is said, placed a call to lead singer Levon Helm, who was seated at a pay phone in the rear of the noisy bar in the summer of 1965, persuading Helm and his band mates to cut short their weekly gig on Bay Avenue, so they could join the famous singer's tour.

"The setup was great," Robbie Robertson, songwriter and former lead guitarist for The Band, recalls of Tony Mart's. "There were three bands on three stages, so there was always music and dancing. Plus, there were a lot of pretty girls in Somers Point. We would go to the beach during the day sometimes in Ocean City, meet girls and invite them to the club at night."

The movie *Eddie & the Cruisers*, a cult hit starring Ellen Barkin and Tom Berenger, was filmed in part at Tony Mart's in 1982. But by this time the bar scene along the bay had lost its following. Faced with a diminishing crowd and competition from Atlantic City once gambling was legalized, in 1984 the locally famous bar, like Bayshores Café three years before it, was bulldozed. A succession of businesses opened at these locations in the years that followed, but none were able to replicate the success of their predecessors.

Ocean City business owners, who'd always tolerated the rowdy antics of its youthful crowd, perceived a noticeable shift in their behavior by the mid-sixties. The erstwhile polite, well-groomed set, whose nightly pilgrimages to Bay Avenue comprised the limits of their rebelliousness, slowly gave way to a new generation united in their defiance of the establishment. Town officials found themselves in a precarious position; on the one hand they needed to appease the local innkeepers who depended upon the business of the younger generation. Yet on the other, they recognized their responsibility toward property owners and vacationing families suddenly contending with inebriated packs of renters smoking marijuana, urinating in bushes, vomiting on porch stoops, some even stumbling into the wrong house upon their return from Somers Point.

The Ocean City Police Department fought to enforce local laws drafted to curtail the opprobrious conduct among the raucous summer guests. Their ordinances were an ineffective deterrent to the sun-seeking hedonists once word got out of the debauchery offered here. Soon Ocean City acquired the nickname "The Fort Lauderdale of the North." In July that year, *Time* magazine published an article about the hottest summer vacation spots for the college crowd, offering unwanted publicity for a beach town intent on remaining understated and keeping true to its morally upstanding origins. "The place with the wildest reputation is Ocean City," the article noted. "After sunning all day at Ocean City and partying all night at Somers Point, the conclusion is frequently sexual."

"I like it down here," said eighteen-year-old Gregg Fawthrop. "There aren't any parents, no one to tell me what to do. You can blow your mind, drink, do anything you like."

Florida native James F. Penland, former Director of the Ocean City Fine Arts League and founder of the Ocean City Arts Center, owned an art studio on Asbury Avenue before moving to Millville, New Jersey, where he died in 2006. A mystical, ponytailed bohemian of Cherokee Indian ancestry, he moved to Ocean City in 1949 after graduating from art school in Philadelphia. He proudly referred to himself as "Ocean City's first hippie," speaking in a gravelly baritone timbre, which purred wistfully as he recalled the city's gradual transition from a teetotaling seaside resort in the 1950s, reliant on a summer tourist trade composed of day-trippers, seasonal renters, and college kids, to a decadent playground for old and young alike in the decade that followed.

"I was avant garde when I moved here in 1949," Penland said, seated on a stool in back of his studio one clear September morning as sidewalk browsers paused to view the works perched on easels outside his front door. "I was the first person in this town to wear Bermuda shorts. They looked at me like I was crazy." He once owned the Connoisseur Shops along the boardwalk, a cluster of stores that included a café where teens mingled and a fine arts gallery where he and other local artists displayed their paintings. Of the local scene in the 1960s, he says, "From an artist's point of view, it was nice to see a change from staid, little-old-suited ladies with white button earrings, to something more in tune with my gypsy likings." He vividly recalled Ocean City's transition from a family beach town to a nationally known summer mecca for local college students. "The boardinghouses were loaded with kids. They started as early as February and March, applying for summer positions. You could have a hundred at your door in April."

Before long the Hare Krishnas appeared, beating their drums outside the city yoga center and gathering under the shaded alcoves of the music pier. Under the boardwalk, hippies formed circles, passing flowers among one another. "Everybody grew long hair; the guys wore beads," Penland said. The self-indulgent lifestyle he recalls wasn't limited to teenagers looking for a good time in the new era of free love. Middle-aged husbands and housewives discreetly partook in the bacchanalia on summer weekends as well. "There was more booze delivered across that bridge that you can ever imagine," he said. The parties that I knew went on were outrageous. Wife swapping was a big deal."

Tens of thousands of college kids were streaming into town each summer weekend by the summer of '69. A line of cars would back up onto the Garden State Parkway each weekend, snaking through Somers Point and gridlocking the bridges leading onto Ninth Street. As reported in the *Sentinel Ledger*, Memorial Day that year "was the biggest early season holiday within memory, and possibly of all time."

Contending not only with massive crowds, the island suddenly found itself helpless to withstand the onslaught of a counterculture movement whose recreational activities involved the rampant usage of illegal substances. A *Philadelphia Inquirer* article, published shortly after the Davis-Perry murders, reported that for the first time in its history Ocean City was admittedly contending with a drug problem among its young vacationers. Amphetamine use was prevalent, with a young man from Baltimore dying in town the previous winter from an overdose of barbiturates.

There was no better example of the generational rift dividing the town than seen in the *Sentinel Ledger*. The editorial section overflowed with scolding letters to the editor composed by local residents concerned with the precipitate rise in the amoral conduct of the teenagers. In response to the arrest of two seventeen-year-olds from Plymouth Meeting, Pennsylvania, on charges of narcotics possession, one resident wrote that Ocean City "is a new haven for real and pseudo hippies....It behooves the city government, backed by concerned citizens, to rid the town of this youthful element. It does no good to preach that the great majority of Ocean City young people don't take dope and don't subscribe to the anti-social creed of the hippies."

Another resident, chastising the lenient treatment of ordinance violators at a recent municipal court session, said, "The fact is that the fines were so modest that they will hardly be deterrents. The members of the Bedlam Set are part of the affluent society and a $25 fine doesn't impress them much...Unfortunately, a large number of those in Court Monday left sneering at the judge, the 'fuzz' and the entire establishment...Ocean City prides itself on its 'traditional tone' and believes that the town's Sunday and liquor restrictions attract nicer people. Then, why do these undesirables show up in increasing numbers?"

Hippie communes were suddenly prevalent throughout town. The Warlocks motorcycle gang rented a house for the summer on Roosevelt Boulevard. *Sentinel Ledger* columnists unabashedly sided with the homeowners in their clash with the "undesirable element" crashing their beaches. Practicing McCarthy-era enforcement strong-arming, city officials attempted to stop the circulation of what they termed an "underground" newspaper, the *Philadelphia Free Press*, which ran from 1968-1972. The publication, which Ocean City officials said contained "hard core obscenity" in the form of a cartoon with four-letter words, was described by the *Sentinel Ledger* as a paper favored by "hippies and beatniks," and "slanted toward the extreme left wing." Ocean City Police Chief Benjamin Dugan ordered their confiscation, and Public Safety Commissioner Chester Wimberg personally snatched several copies he saw being handed out on the boardwalk. In an alarmist editorial in response to the incident, the *Sentinel Ledger* publisher wrote:

The hippies and fellow travelers and others of their ilk must not be allowed to take over here and do as they please. They are a menace to what this community stands for and the sooner we get rid of them the better....we do not intend to let Ocean City be turned into an East coast version of the Haight-Ashbury section of San Francisco. There, what hippies touched they ruined.

Despite the increase in illicit substances, the straight-laced, affluent, middle-aged family crowd still represented the substantial majority of seasonal visitors. The Ocean City Police Department, understanding the needs of their business owners to keep the summer dollars rolling in, fought to uphold the city's pristine image, doing their best to maintain a balance between free-spirited teens and reserved families. They loosely enforced an 11 p.m. to 6 a.m. curfew for those under eighteen. Citations, rather than arrests, were handed out for sleeping under the boardwalk. Hitchhiking, common in town and on the causeway leading out of it, was an infraction for which tickets were seldom issued, though the practice was banned by statute, and recent articles had highlighted its perils, especially for young women.

The deaths of Susan and Elizabeth occurred a little more than two months before the Tate-LaBianca murders in Los Angeles riveted the nation, exposing America to the more sinister facets of the beatnik lifestyle. In Ocean City, concerns once written off as the scolding rants of older folks were now legitimate fears possessed by everyone.

Nightly telecasts of the "Mephistophelean guru," as Charles Manson was labeled by *Helter Skelter* author Vincent Bugliosi, reinforced a stark warning that glib psychopaths lurked at the fringes of peace-espousing communes, marches, and protests. The clean-cut image of several of his disciples exemplified the ease with which they could infiltrate this new culture of permissiveness, while revealing the dark side of recreational drug use. "The mantra of the era was 'peace, love and sharing,'" said Bugliosi, interviewed by *Time* magazine on the fortieth anniversary of the slayings. "Before the murders, no one associated hippies with violence and murder, just drugs, peace, free love, etc. Then the Manson family comes along, looking like hippies, but what they were all about was murder. That was their religion, their credo. That shocked a lot of people and definitely hurt the counterculture movement."

Before they fell under his sway, several of Manson's cohorts appeared no different than any other young college students. Leslie Van Houten was once her high school's homecoming queen. Manson's lieutenant, Charles "Tex" Watson, wore his hair relatively short and was a star high school athlete and straight-A student from a small town in Texas. Neighbors from his hometown were stunned to learn of his involvement in the Tate-LaBianca murders. "Charles was the boy next door," said one resident from McKinney, Texas. "It was the drugs that did it," his uncle told reporters, adding, "He started taking them in college and that was where the real trouble started."

Four months before the Somers Point murders, among a desolate stretch of dune grass and pine woods eight miles from Provincetown, Massachusetts, police discovered the decapitated remains of Mary Ann Wysocki and Patricia Walsh buried in a shallow grave not far from the road. Both had been repeatedly shot and stabbed. In a case with facts eerily similar to the Perry-Davis investigation, the pair had been staying at a guesthouse, checked out one morning, and went missing. Their car was found a month later, near their shallowly buried corpses. Twenty-four-year-old Cape Cod carpenter Antone Costa, a divorced father of three who'd been staying at the guest house, was found guilty of their murders, along with the killings or two other women whose bodies were discovered near the first two. He, too, had spent time immersed in the Haight-Ashbury district of San Francisco. Costa's defense attorneys blamed their client's behavior on his frequent use of barbiturates, LSD, and marijuana, arguing that these illicit substances reacted negatively with his schizoid personality disorder. In a chilling confessional penned by Costa before he hung himself in his jail cell, he claimed to be under the influence of LSD when he committed the murders.

Whereas a person in the 1950s was more readily classified and distinguishable based upon his physical appearance, Watson and Costa exemplified how two reasonably well-groomed sociopaths in the late sixties could easily veer from one social group to another without drawing attention to themselves, despite their sinister intentions. Who could really tell, at first glance, who was good and who had it in him to murder somebody? Persons whose suspicious demeanor might have spooked their peers during an earlier time were now camouflaged by an embracing sea of youth wearing tire-treaded sandals, hemp garb, and sporting long unkempt hair and muttonchop whiskers, united in their love of rock music and defiance of conventional norms.

With its weekly influx of attractive young women from fine homes, a copious supply of mind-altering psychedelics to color the sunsets, a crowded beach, and the prevalence of singles bars a five-minute drive over the causeway, vibrant summer resort towns like Ocean City were fertile hunting grounds for attractive, unbalanced men in the summer of 1969. Its ample supply of guesthouses, motels, even the shelter of a safe boardwalk to crash under if their rooms were filled, offered the perfect cover. Buses, arriving and departing hourly from the Ninth Street stop, ferried passengers to Philadelphia and all points north, providing a quick means of escape. Owners of cozy inns, boardinghouses, and rustic seaside hotels, who for years had stocked their rooms with fun loving, if somewhat rambunctious young guests, were now unwitting hosts to the fringe elements of an entirely different clientele. When one considers the ingratiating nature of young people during the Vietnam era and the slackly-enforced local laws prohibiting hitchhiking, it isn't difficult to envision how a psychopathic charmer could sweep into Ocean City or Somers Point virtually unnoticed, hold his thumb out while leaning against a telephone pole, or beneath the Gulf station sign at the traffic circle. Neither is it hard to fathom how an engaging, handsome predator, delirious with sleeplessness at 6 a.m. and perhaps strung out on narcotics, might unhinge if provoked.

That Susan and Elizabeth made no enemies in town, weren't seen in the company of any unsavory men, or offering a lift to anybody as they left Ocean City, cemented the detectives' initial conclusion that the girls had picked up a stranger in the moments after they left the diner.

"When we found out the theory was she picked up a hitchhiker, it made sense to all of us because she was, I hesitate to say 'boy crazy,' but that's what she was," said Susan's high school friend, Caitlyn Legrande. "But she never would have acted on it. There would have been no sexual reason behind her picking up a hitchhiker, but she's exactly the kind of girl that would have done that."

Several weeks would pass before the state police engaged the services of a renowned criminologist to assist in preparing a psychological sketch of the murderer. Judging by the savagery of the victims' wounds and the ease with which the assailant convinced two random girls to offer him a ride, from the start of the murder probe detectives likely reckoned that the person they sought wasn't the twitchy vagabond with bloodshot eyes furtively avoiding glances at the end of a Bay Avenue bar, or the pervert opening his raincoat and exposing himself to old ladies walking home from sunrise service. Rather, he was a cunning, self-possessed young man who could readily assume the role of hippie, armed forces veteran, or fun-loving frat boy, whatever the situation demanded.

Would Susan have been even more susceptible to the charms of a good-looking young man thumbing for a ride, rather than a bedraggled hippie propping up a cardboard sign bearing a destination city?

"Absolutely," Legrande said. "Without a doubt. That was the social awkwardness and naiveté she had. If he was cute, I can just see her saying, 'let's pick him up; let's give him a ride.' The Susan I knew in high school would have done that in a heartbeat."

Mary Bryson, a classmate from Monticello and one of Susan's closest friends, disagreed with the hitchhiker theory, as did several other students who'd known the pair. "There is no doubt in my mind that whoever did this had to either force their way into the car or somehow threaten Liz and Sue," she told a reporter for the *Alton (Ill.) Evening Telegraph*. "They would not have gone along willingly."

The state police had scant information at this juncture, even less they were willing to share with newspapers: a five-foot, nine inch hitchhiker who had shaggy hair, wore a yellow top, and may have been wearing a diver wristwatch, was the only information made public. Behind the scenes they knew that a bra had been used to bind one of the victims and that a watch had been found nearby. Their lone witness, security guard Albert Hickey, was admittedly uncertain about the color of the convertible he'd seen at the traffic circle. Furthermore, the time he remembered seeing two girls stopping to pick up the hitchhiker was nearly an hour before the three boys said they'd eaten breakfast with Susan and Elizabeth. Worse than these inconsistent accounts was the head start the murderer had on detectives. Time, a crucial ally in any murder investigation, had been irretrievably lost due to the three-day delay between when the girls disappeared and were found. Those vital seventy-two hours, beginning early Friday morning when Louis Sterr called in the Chevrolet's plate numbers, and ending early Monday afternoon when Woody Faunce stumbled upon the bodies, was proving to be a major impediment to accurately reconstructing the hour leading up to the murders. Compounding their frustration, detectives surmised that the assailant might have actually been in the woods when Trooper Sterr slowed down his cruiser to investigate.

"Those three days were so critical," said a former high-ranking state police official who was one of the detectives initially assigned to the murder investigation. "I think every living teenager within a hundred-fifty-mile area was in Somers Point that weekend. But after they left, they weren't there. You had to find the witnesses, and you didn't even have an idea who they were. Everybody was gone, even the toll collectors."

The odds were stacked against Lt. Brennan's men. With every hour, every minute they spent on the investigation without locating another witness or narrowing in on a possible suspect, their chances of apprehending the assailant grew worse as he returned to his old life, conjuring up viable alibis. The possibility that he might claim two more innocent victims was fast becoming a harrowing realization for state police. Faced with the diminishing probability of capture, the pressure to make an arrest intensified.

CHAPTER SIX

A Tan Mustang

The New Jersey State Police continued to focus their investigation on the vicinity of the crime scene and neighboring towns. On Tuesday, June 3, at approximately the same time of morning when the coroner estimated that Davis and Perry were killed, troopers set up a roadblock near where Susan's convertible was found, hoping to speak with commuters who frequently traveled the parkway and might have seen something on their drive into work four days earlier. They halted each motorist on the southbound and northbound lanes, asking if they'd traveled that same route early Friday morning and noticed anything unusual between the Somers Point interchange and mile marker 31.9.

They stopped eight people who claimed to have seen a light-blue convertible near the murder scene at 6:30 a.m. Friday morning. All agreed they'd seen another car parked behind it. While each witness recalled that both cars were unoccupied, only one of them, a local maintenance worker with the Ocean City Water Company, identified the second vehicle as a tan Mustang. He spotted it at 7:30 a.m., located a short distance behind the convertible. He told investigators he saw a youth seated in the sports car and another "sprawled lazily on a grassy plot" at the roadside.

Detectives cross-checked New Jersey and Pennsylvania motor vehicle records, tracking down anybody who owned a tan car. Any young man who'd registered such a vehicle or was in possession of a similar make and model, was pulled out of class or yanked from his ROTC line and questioned. Troopers appeared unannounced at workplaces, recalled Marta McCoy. She was employed at the payroll department of the W.T. Grant department store in Moorestown, New Jersey, when a pair of detectives arrived at the Camden Avenue location and began inquiring about her boyfriend, who also worked there. They intensively questioned the Marlton, New Jersey, man, even though the tan car he owned wasn't a Mustang. "It was a shock to see these state troopers coming into my store," she said. Though her boyfriend was never charged, it was an experience she's never completely shaken and exemplified the thoroughness and expanding scope of the investigation.

Detectives hit the streets as soon as tips poured into the Absecon barracks. Sergeant-in-Charge Edward Blackburn's full-time job was to answer the multitude of incoming calls flooding the hotline number. As the assistant station commander he fielded collect calls from lands as distant as Honolulu and Midway Island, compiling the leads from each conversation into the station record notebook before passing them along to investigators.

State police continued their search for a murder weapon Tuesday morning. Again using metal detectors, they covered a six-hundred square-foot area surrounding the crime scene. As authorities ran down every lead, they learned that another waitress at the diner, Mrs. Ann Kloehs, recognized Susan and Elizabeth based upon pictures distributed by police to local newspapers that afternoon.

She remembered the girls, she said, because they stopped her from closing the drapes next to the booth where they were eating Friday. "The sun was just coming up, you know," she explained to a reporter, "and it was glaring on them. So I started to close the drapes, but they said, 'No, we like the sunshine.'" Kloehs set the time of their breakfast between 5 a.m. to 5:30 a.m. Friday. Because sunrise was at 5:34 a.m., Kloehs' timeline seems the most accurate of the diner employees. The autopsy report lent further credence to her story, as did the fact that the Point Diner was the only restaurant in the area open for business that time of the morning. Kloehs stated that the girls came into the diner by themselves and were joined in the booth by "two clean-cut boys" after she'd tried the close the drapes, likely among the same young men already questioned and released by police. She didn't notice whether the boys left with the girls, she said.

Reporters awaiting the Tuesday night news briefing in Absecon observed a trooper carrying a clear plastic bag into the barracks. They watched as he removed a wrinkled, heavily soiled yellow turtleneck and held it up for inspection to a roomful of detectives. Shortly thereafter, a short, middle-aged woman entered the front doors with a curly-haired teenager thought to be her son. He pointed to a map on a rear office wall, presumably pinpointing the location on the parkway where he'd found the shirt, leading reporters to speculate that it had turned up near the murder scene. The woman and young man refused to speak with reporters as they left the investigation headquarters. Had these Samaritans delivered the same shirt worn by the man Hickey claimed to have seen at the circle, or was this nothing more than an article of clothing discarded by a lusty couple in the throes of a passionate embrace? Detectives were non-committal again, leaving reporters to draw their own conclusions.

By Tuesday's end the police had interviewed nearly one hundred people, administering lie detector tests to five of them. Though the FBI hadn't yet intervened, they were closely monitoring the case.

On Wednesday morning, June 4, Lt. Brennan held a ninety-minute meeting with his detectives in Absecon. When it ended, he called a press conference. "We went over all the information we have received," he announced. "We are now concentrating our investigation on the people who have seen the car or the girls. We have some information we received that someone saw the girls walking back into the woods. We are now in the process of checking that out."

Over forty police trainees were transported by bus to Egg Harbor Township from the State Police Academy in West Trenton. They spent that afternoon scavenging the forests for clues before commencing a hands-and-knees search of the forty-yard wide grass center strip between either side of the parkway. They discovered a pair of stockings and a soiled girdle, both of which were sent to the state police lab. Tests determined, however, that neither article of clothing belonged to the girls.

At a late afternoon press briefing, state police announced that they'd confiscated a yellow turtleneck sweater from a young man arrested early Tuesday evening in Somers Point and charged with public intoxication. As with the soiled shirt brought into the barracks, interest in the man arose due to Albert Hickey's earlier statement that he'd witnessed two women offer a lift to a hitchhiker wearing similar clothing. The man was reportedly in custody following his arraignment after "failing to give a good account of himself," according to a state police spokesman, who said the man had been found drunkenly sprawled on Longport-Somers Point Boulevard. Brennan emphasized that the young man, whom he described as in his twenties and "neat in appearance," had been questioned by a detective but wasn't a suspect at this point. However, the lieutenant acknowledged that the yellow shirt, which he described as having "red and brown" stains, had been submitted for analysis to the state police laboratory.

Built in 1888 to resemble a New England seaside chapel, St. Martin's-by-the-Lake Episcopal Church in Minnetonka Beach, Minnesota, is located steps from the water on the southern shoreline of a narrow woodsy isthmus jutting out into Lake Minnetonka. From the steepled belfry tower atop its gabled roof, St. Martin's offers a panoramic view of Lafayette Bay, with the north-facing rectory window looking out over the greens of the exclusive Lafayette Club golf course.

Some three hundred classmates, neighbors, and townspeople attended memorial services for Elizabeth Perry, held beneath a cloudless Wednesday afternoon sky on June 4, 1969. The harrowing eulogy was delivered by the Rev. Edwin J. Eilertsen, who'd known Elizabeth since she was eight-years-old. Evoking the unflagging spirit that church founder George Camp hoped to inspire in generations of future congregants who question their faith whenever God claims the young, Rev. Eilertsen quoted from the 23rd Psalm of the Episcopalian Book of Common Prayer. From the 46th Psalm he read, "God is our refuge and strength, a very present help in trouble..." The affable rector shared anecdotes, recalling that Elizabeth and her family joined his parish eleven years earlier, just after they'd moved from St. Louis. Elizabeth, who'd been very active in church affairs, had "an abundance and compassion for those in need," Rev. Eilertsen said, and would offer to help anyone in every way she could. Services concluded with a stirring rendition of Elizabeth's favorite hymn "All Things Bright and Beautiful." A piece of stained glass was fitted into the chapel window as an eternal memory of her short time on Earth.

That same evening in Absecon, the first rays of light forked the swirling gloom clouding the police barracks, buoying a collectively diminishing morale. Reporters, by now accustomed to hearing the crackling strain afflicting Lt. Brennan's voice as he addressed them, sensed a palpable buzz circuiting through his staff. Troopers and investigators appeared relaxed and smiling, hinting to reporters that there had been a significant development in the case and that an announcement would be made the following morning, or by afternoon at the latest.

The rumored breakthrough involved three hours of questioning late Wednesday afternoon between detectives and a twenty-one-year-old man from Delaware County, Pennsylvania. He admitted that he and his two teen companions had slept alongside milepost 31.9 of the parkway in a tan Mustang around the time when the slayings occurred.

The three young men, all from Delaware County, had already met with investigators a day earlier, though police managed to keep this information out of the newspapers. They told police that they were driving home to Pennsylvania from Wildwood at approximately 4 a.m. Friday when their car ran out of gas. They'd decided to wait until daybreak before continuing their trip and pulled over to the side of the parkway to sleep. At approximately 7 a.m., they awoke to the sight of an abandoned blue convertible parked approximately one hundred yards in front of their car. Two of the young men, who went in search of gas upon rousing from their slumber, were curious about the car and started toward it while the third stayed behind in the car. One of them held out his thumb, and they were given a ride before they reached the convertible. They were let off on the Black Horse Pike via exit 36, the next turnoff on the parkway, where they purchased several gallons of fuel from Phil Weis, the owner of a local Esso station across from the Searstown Mall in Northfield. Weis told the *New York Daily News* that he'd opened his station at 6 a.m. that morning but wasn't certain the exact time when the boys arrived. Afterward they hitched a ride back to the Mustang, filled the tank, awoke their sleeping friend and drove away.

On crutches, the twenty-one-year-old man hobbled into the Absecon barracks with his father for a second round of questioning beginning at 3 p.m. Wednesday. Lt. Brennan said that he'd injured his leg in an accident after returning from his Memorial Day weekend at the shore. When asked why the young man had returned to the station, Brennan responded that he'd done so voluntarily. "He came down here and offered more information." A part-time gas station attendant at a Sunoco station at the corner of MacDade Boulevard and Castor Avenue in Folsom, Pennsylvania, he spent three hours with investigators, reiterating what he and two of his friends had already disclosed to investigators Tuesday night.

Because it was called at such an unusual hour, a post-midnight press briefing held early Thursday morning led reporters to believe that Brennan was prepared to disclose that an arrest had been made. He offered no bombshells, however, squelching rumors that somebody had seen the killer enter the woods with the victim. Instead, he utilized the conference as a forum to transmit his plea for that elusive, reluctant witness. "Someone must have seen them go into the forest," he said. "We have absolutely no leads at this point. We are virtually back where we started."

Funeral services for Susan were held on Thursday afternoon at the Grace United Methodist Church in downtown Harrisburg. Several hundred mourners, among them Susan's Harrisburg Academy classmates and her father's business associates, filed somberly past a closed bronze casket shrouded with yellow roses. The Rev. Dr. Sheridan Watson Bell, Jr., who baptized Susan nineteen years earlier in the same church, officiated the brief eulogy. Behind his pulpit the cathedral streamed prisms of violet through a stained-glass rendition of Christ's Ascension. "She loved life as a normal young American girl," Rev. Bell offered, adding, "Despite what happened, this is still a loving world, a caring world." Drawing from the words of famed orator Robert Ingersoll, philosopher William James, poet William Blake, and the

Greek historian Plutarch, Rev. Bell said, "The mystery of life and death we cannot comprehend. Man alone destroys the symmetry of God's world; man alone violates its laws." Following the brief service, Marjorie Davis removed the roses from the casket, handing one to each of her daughter's pallbearers.

Caitlyn LeGrande, Susan's classmate and carpool partner, attended the services. "It is the most horrible memory of my life," she said. "I will never forget Susan's mother screaming at the front of the church. None of us had been through anything like that before. I was nineteen-years old. It was horribly emotional and gut-wrenching."

Susan was buried at Rolling Green Memorial Gardens in Camp Hill. "The worst thing I had to do, aside from identifying my daughter's body, was to call Mr. Perry and tell him his daughter was dead," Wesley Davis said, an obligation he undertook because their daughter had been Susan's guest. "He's stoic," Davis said, when asked how Perry had been coping with the shock of his own daughter's death. "Is that the proper word? He's quite a fine man."

"You've got to pick up the pieces, keep going," Davis said, left to his thoughts in the den of his home, speaking with reporters for the *Inquirer* and *Bulletin*. "My biggest concern is my wife, Marjorie," he said, "because I have my work to keep me busy and she's basically a housewife." He added, "But she is not hysterical."

When asked about the person who murdered his daughter, Davis answered a reporter, "At this point I am too numb to have any specific feeling about the person who committed the crimes. I really haven't thought about him. I am undecided about the value of capital punishment. In any event, we have got to get the criminal off the street to prevent this from happening to other girls." He further stated, "Basically, rather than say I believe in capital punishment, I say I don't object to capital punishment."

Reverend Bell attended to the Davis family in the days immediately after the murders. A selfless community icon in his own right, Dr. Bell once offered his church for use by members of Temple Ohev Sholom when their synagogue was ravaged by the floodwaters of Hurricane Agnes in 1972. At his passing in 1982, "Sherry" Bell was eulogized by his son as "a loving man of conviction, warmth, generosity, passion, impulse, flamboyance, gusto, humor, spontaneity, balance, dedication, support, vocal gifts, drama, wise counsel, compassion, and faith."

"This is a very religious family," Rev. Bell said of the Davises. "There is a well-worn Bible in every bedroom." He seemed far less forgiving toward the murderer than Mr. Davis. Perhaps drawing justification from the Book of Exodus, he hinted that Susan and Elizabeth's murderer should be condemned to death. "I think there are times there should be justifiable retaliation for depravity," the minister said. "I just question when we give the man who commits the crime the benefit of our laws and forget about the victim."

"If it hadn't been for religion, I don't think I could have lived with myself," Davis reflected. "You have to live day by day. You certainly have to have faith. You learn to live with these things. Life has to continue. I know that in the world there have to be many different types of people, some good and some bad. That's the way the world's always been." He recognized the agonizing readjustment period that lay ahead for him and his family, coping with the void left by their child's death. "The next week and the week after are going to be very difficult weeks at home."

New Jersey State Police detectives weren't altogether convinced that Susan Davis and Elizabeth Perry were the occupants of the convertible identified by security guard Albert Hickey. After all, the statements offered by the diner waitress, and from the three boys who'd eaten there the morning of the murders, each placed the girls at the Somers Point circle after Hickey claimed to have spotted them stopping to give a ride to the young man in the yellow shirt. Nevertheless, investigators continued to rely upon the security guard's recollection of the man's clothing as their investigation moved forward. Maybe he *had* seen something, or someone, and simply mixed up the time. That they arrested a drunken youth wearing the same color shirt and were seen in the barracks examining a yellow turtleneck found in the woods, shows that the state police were seriously considering each witness's account, despite the inconsistencies.

This painstaking, time-consuming strategy finally paid off, as the yellow shirt Hickey allegedly saw the hitchhiker wearing would indirectly implicate a young man from Norristown, Pennsylvania. Today he remains under suspicion, even though his actions years later made him a public figure for different reasons, overshadowing this harrowing incident from his youth.

CHAPTER SEVEN

A Hair's Breadth Away

Sixty miles from Absecon, on the same Wednesday afternoon that New Jersey State Police detectives again questioned one of the three boys who'd fallen asleep along the parkway shoulder, the Philadelphia Police Department received a tip from a store clerk at North Thirteenth Street in the Market East section of the city. Before the near thorough demolition of this block south of City Hall in the 1990s, the area was a red-light district replete with seedy taverns, pornographic bookstores, and second-run movies playing at the Mark III Cinema. The *Philadelphia Bulletin* reported that the call to the police station came from a clothing store.

The store clerk called to say that a tall youth wearing a yellow turtleneck had been in his store earlier that afternoon at around 3 p.m. He overheard the young man bragging that he'd known the two slain girls at the shore, meeting them on the boardwalk in Ocean City. His interest was piqued, he told police, because in a local newspaper he had read security guard Albert Hickey's account of seeing a shaggy-haired man in a yellow shirt climbing into a convertible at the Somers Point circle. The clerk notified the Philadelphia Police Department immediately after the man left his store. They approached him a half-hour later at another location near Thirteenth and Arch Streets, close to the Quaker City bus terminal garage. Carrying a small overnight bag, he was taken by squad car to police headquarters several blocks away, where he agreed to be questioned.

Known as the "Roundhouse," the Philadelphia Police Department headquarters at Eighth and Race Streets is comprised of three massive circular concrete buildings. Within the Homicide Division on the first floor of the Police Administration Building, Mark Thomas, described by police as a six-foot, five-inch "hippie-type" from nearby Norristown, Pennsylvania, was placed in an interrogation room. At around the time he was questioned about the Somers Point slayings, Thomas had already been involved in two minor skirmishes with the law. Court records reflect that on February 20, 1969, he was arrested in Philadelphia and charged with loitering and prowling at night. On April 15, 1969, just a month and a half before the murders of Davis and Perry, he was convicted of providing alcohol to a minor and was sentenced to thirty days in a Montgomery County, Pennsylvania, prison.

Thomas initially told police that he'd gone into the clothing store to buy a shirt for his father and that he had no information or knowledge about the slain women. But as his interrogators grew more persistent, he finally acknowledged that he had referred to Susan and Elizabeth while in the store but was merely "shooting off his mouth" and didn't actually know them. The *Daily News* reported that Thomas told police he'd been staying at the 3200 block of Powelton Avenue in the University City section of Philadelphia, comprised of a block of row homes adjacent to a Southeastern Pennsylvania Transit Authority train yard. His parents, he said, were separated and living at different residences in Norristown.

Powelton Village, the neighborhood where Thomas reportedly resided, was a hub of radical activity for anti-war protesters in the 1960s. Hippie enclaves were prevalent among its shabby Victorian rowhouses. "Powelton Village was like a commune with traffic lights," said one prosecutor. In later years this section of the city drew national attention for two separate incidents. One was a police standoff with the radical black-liberation group MOVE in 1985, resulting in the catastrophic deaths of several children when Mayor Wilson Goode gave the order for police to firebomb their Osage Avenue compound. The other event was the 1979 arrest of infamous counterculture guru Ira Einhorn. Known nationally as "The Unicorn Killer" and the co-founder of Earth Day, his estranged girlfriend Holly Maddux was found dismembered and stuffed in a steamer trunk at Einhorn's 3411 Race Street apartment.

Detective George W. Dix, lauded by one attorney as "perhaps the leading expert on the subject in New Jersey," headed the New Jersey State Police polygraph unit from 1975 to 1979. After his retirement from the state police he served a twelve-year term as mayor of Pleasantville, the next town over from Atlantic City. In his early nineties, today he lives in Absecon, New Jersey, not far from the Perry-Davis investigation headquarters in 1969. Next to Lt. James Toth, the senior polygraph examiner who also headed the New Jersey State Police Field Services Bureau, Dix was the most experienced of a group of four detectives authorized to administer lie detector tests. Both Dix and Toth received their training at the world-renowned Keeler Polygraph Institute in Chicago.

The polygraph, more commonly known as the "lie detector," measures physiological responses such as breathing rate, pulse, blood pressure, and perspiration in response to questions designed to assess the subject's truthfulness. The underlying theory of the polygraph is that people get measurably nervous when they lie, with the test results reflected on a graph as a series of peaks and valleys recorded by the machine's needle.

Dix, who resided in Atlantic County at the time of the murders but was stationed out of state police division headquarters in West Trenton, was enjoying dinner at home with his family on Wednesday evening, June 3, when he received a call from one of the five examiners for the Philadelphia Police Department Polygraph Unit, headed in 1969 by Joseph M. Brophy. The examiner updated Dix on the results of a test given to the suspicious young man they'd picked up for questioning that afternoon.

After first reporting to the state police barracks in Turnersville, New Jersey, to meet with and polygraph the three Delaware County youths who had fallen asleep in their Mustang, Dix was picked up at the barracks by fellow detectives Harvey T. Burns and Harry Patterson in Captain Mario "Red" Paterra's cruiser. Together they drove to Philadelphia to join the questioning of the intriguing eighteen-year-old drifter.

The three New Jersey detectives arrived at the Roundhouse at a few moments past midnight. By this time Thomas had already been interrogated for approximately eight hours by Philadelphia Police Department detectives, who said he had given "fuzzy answers to crucial questions" on three lie detector tests. According to an internal unpublished newspaper memo written by *Philadelphia Inquirer* reporter Robert Shoemaker, "the young drifter flunked badly when he answered 'no' to questions as to whether he stabbed the two girls, did he cause their death, and was he withholding information. He 'half-flunked and half-passed' when answering 'no' as to whether he was lying on the grass on the parkway and whether he went into the woods on the parkway." However, according to Shoemaker's memo, "Police said there was a history of mental illness in Thomas's family, and that if he was a victim of it too, this could throw off the whole test."

Thomas admitted to New Jersey detectives that he'd been in Ocean City on Thursday, May 29, arriving by bus sometime that afternoon. He said he'd slept under the boardwalk Thursday night and was awoken at approximately 5:30 a.m. Friday by a group of fishermen. After waking, he dallied in the area of Ninth Street and the boardwalk until about 9:30 a.m., at which time he started hitchhiking back to Philadelphia. He claimed that he met a friend from Blue Bell, Pennsylvania, at a Ninth Street diner in Ocean City for breakfast on Friday morning before he began hitchhiking home. But when police contacted the friend, he said that it was Saturday, not Friday, when he and Thomas had met. Thomas further alleged that his first ride home took him from Ocean City to Blackwood, New Jersey, in Camden County, via the Garden State Parkway and Atlantic City Expressway. He said he'd received four other rides before arriving in Philadelphia on the afternoon of May 30.

After reviewing the peaks and valleys of Thomas's charts, presented to him shortly after he and the other detectives arrived in Philadelphia, "I was pretty convinced we had our man," Dix said. He and Harry Patterson took turns interrogating Thomas into the deepening night. According to Dix, during these early morning hours of Thursday, June 5, they had their suspect "a hair's breadth away" from a confession to the parkway murders. They admittedly pressured him, with one unidentified police official threatening, "We're going to shoot you up with 50,000 volts and leave you in a pile of ashes." There were several turning points when the detectives thought a confession was imminent. Yet whenever they'd leave the room for a few moments to grab a cigarette or a cup of coffee, oddly enough, Thomas would pound on the door, summoning Dix and Patterson to return to what they expected would be an admission of guilt. Instead, according to Dix, the eccentric hippie kept aimlessly ranting, "I can't leave the world without a child, I need to have a child to leave to the world." Tweaked by his bizarre behavior, detectives continued. No matter how hard they pressed Thomas, he wouldn't admit to any involvement in the murders.

At approximately 8 a.m., Lt. Donald L. Patterson of the Philadelphia Police Department advised detectives Dix and Patterson that they'd have to release Thomas. By now he'd been interrogated upwards of seventeen hours, and there was simply not enough evidence to hold him any longer without charging him. A decorated Army veteran associated with the Special Forces, Lt. Patterson, who died in 2016, spent twenty-five illustrious years with the department, attaining the rank of Inspector of the Detective Bureau. Patterson didn't recall the interrogation taking place on his watch, but conceded that he was the lieutenant of the Major Crimes Squad in May 1969, and that in such a scenario he would've consulted with Richard Sprague of the Philadelphia District Attorney's office, which in 1969 was led by future United States Senator Arlen Specter. Similarly, Dix doesn't recall Lt. Patterson being present either. Instead, he recalls that Homicide Sgt. H. Robert Snyder was the supervising official on duty that night.

Lt. Patterson's ultimatum—either charge Thomas or release him—placed Dix and Harry Patterson in a quandary; Dix felt certain they had their man, but the New Jersey authorities didn't have jurisdiction to place him under arrest and extradite him to New Jersey, question him further, and hopefully extract a confession. The two detectives had a heated argument with one another. Dix wanted to bring Thomas back to New Jersey. Patterson, however, knew that without an extradition order the pair risked a charge of kidnapping.

Strangely, though free to leave, Thomas volunteered to accompany the three detectives to New Jersey and submit to another round of questioning.

Before leaving Philadelphia, Dix called state police headquarters in Trenton for further instructions. He was directed to bring Thomas to the barracks in Berlin, New Jersey, on Route 73 South, adjacent to the Berlin traffic circle. Like the Absecon barracks in Atlantic County, today the small colonial style building, occasionally used for police business, seems abandoned in comparison with the onslaught of recent commercial development along this major artery. In 1969 it was nothing more than a rural route comprised of peach orchards and garden centers, offering a shortcut to the Atlantic City Expressway. The need for secrecy in the transport of Thomas was undoubtedly due to the ubiquitous swarm of newspapermen camped at all entrances of the Absecon barracks, awaiting news of a break in the case.

As Thomas was escorted out of the city, another odd incident befuddled detectives. Dix was in the back seat next to him, with Patterson and Burns in front, when the men realized they didn't have enough change for the Ben Franklin Bridge toll to cross over the Delaware River and into New Jersey. According to Dix, Thomas volunteered to pay, reaching into his pocket and handing Harry Patterson fifty cents. The teen's actions beg the obvious: why would a young man who has just endured over eighteen hours of intensive police interrogation agree to accompany his accusers for another round of questioning, especially when he was free to leave?

The three detectives and their suspect were met by a bevy of police personnel upon reaching the Berlin barracks. Among them was Lt. Toth, the senior lie detection examiner, who was prepared to hook up Thomas to the polygraph machine and conduct his own exam. Also present were Robert McCallister and Assistant Prosecutor Solomon Forman, who both remained in a separate room as the suspect was further questioned.

Neither the New Jersey State Police nor the Philadelphia Police Department disclosed to the press Thomas's entire account of his whereabouts on the morning of the murders. According to Dix, he told investigators that after one of his rides dropped him off on the Black Horse Pike near or around Hammonton, New Jersey, he stopped to eat at a diner, ordering a peculiar flavored milkshake that required him to give special instructions to his waitress how to properly mix the ingredients. Detectives, as Dix recalls, interviewed the waitress, who confirmed that she had served him. Dix is unsure of the name of the diner, but certain it was located in the Collings Lake neighborhood of Hammonton, at the corner of Cains Mill Road and The Black Horse Pike. This spot, which today stands as an empty lot across the pike from a Wawa food store, was once the site of the Collings Lake Diner. In 1969 the diner was a regular stop for buses traveling to all points along the south Jersey coastline from Atlantic City to Cape May. The owner had a contract with the bus company, mandating that they stop for at least fifteen minutes at his diner, with the passengers disembarking to enjoy a milkshake or a slice of pie. Might Thomas have stopped in and ordered a milkshake in an attempt to establish an alibi when he had actually ridden the bus home?

At some point following his release from the Roundhouse, Thomas voluntarily accompanied New Jersey State Police detectives to the Royal Diner on 312 East Ninth Street in Ocean City. They brought along with him the friend with whom Thomas said he'd eaten breakfast the morning of the murders. The pair were also shown to the employees at the Seaway Diner on Ninth Street and Haven Avenue in Ocean City. None of the staff recalled seeing them on Memorial Day. The police also brought both men to the Point Diner, but officials refused to comment publicly whether anybody there could place them in that diner at the time Perry and Davis were slain, suggesting that whatever information they'd acquired there was being maintained as a holdback.

Both men were returned to the Berlin barracks for more questioning on Thursday afternoon. At the same time Robert McAllister addressed reporters at the Absecon barracks, saying that the murder investigation had run out of any substantial leads. The prosecutor seemed in a hurry, unwilling to elaborate, perhaps because he was eager to get to Berlin and oversee the interrogation of Thomas. Among the questions McAllister refused to answer was whether police had lifted any fingerprints from the blue convertible. Asked if the diver watch had been linked to anyone, McAllister responded, "No comment." As to whether the murder weapon had been found, he replied, "Not yet." McAllister deflected the focus from Thomas when queried about the Norristown suspect during this 3 p.m. press briefing, saying that he didn't think the questioning was going to produce a major break in the investigation. Detectives were in Philadelphia routinely questioning the suspect and several other Pennsylvania youths, he told reporters, though Thomas was presently being interrogated in Berlin.

Because Thomas hadn't slept the night before, Toth and Dix agreed they wouldn't get an accurate polygraph reading, known in police parlance as "a bad chart" or a "false read." Their suspect, whose acquiescence continued to befuddle detectives, agreed to be taken to a local hotel so he could sleep for a few hours before undergoing another polygraph test. Accompanied by troopers James Cuzzupe and Jeffrey Barnes, at some time in the late afternoon or early Thursday evening Thomas was led to an upstairs room at the Hotel White Way, a rustic two-story inn on the White Horse Pike in nearby Atco, New Jersey. According to police sources, while sleeping in the presence of the two troopers stationed to watch him, Thomas was overheard mumbling, "I had a vision that two girls were driving a convertible, and I was in the back, and their hair was blowing in the wind." As he exited the door to his hotel room, the lanky young man from Norristown allegedly asked, "Where are all the cameras? I thought the news reporters would be here."

The press was in Absecon instead, where Lt. Brennan announced that the man found wearing a yellow turtleneck when he was arrested for disorderly conduct in Somers Point had been officially eliminated as a suspect. He told newsmen his team had "positive leads" but wouldn't say whether he was referring to the interrogation of Thomas, whose identity was still being withheld from the press. Brennan also confirmed that a total of eight young men had been given lie detector tests in the case, and all had passed. These included the two young men who had dated the girls early Friday morning between the hours of 2 and 4 a.m., the three college boys who shared a booth with them at the Point Diner at 5:30 a.m., as well as the three Delaware County youths who had run out of gas and fallen asleep in their Mustang. Investigators, Brennan disclosed, were now leaning on the theory that more than one person killed the two women.

Susan's convertible had finally been towed from the Absecon barracks to West Trenton for laboratory examination, Brennan stated, but he didn't offer a reason for the inexplicable delay in its transport. He said that more recent pictures of the girls were distributed to teams of detectives who were fanning out in the Ocean City-Somers Point area in order to locate other persons who might've seen them. He confirmed that investigative teams had been stationed in Philadelphia police headquarters to run down any leads in that area.

Prominent criminal defense attorney Edward F. Kane of Norristown phoned McAllister at his Northfield, New Jersey, home at 1 a.m. on Friday. He said that he represented Thomas and demanded to know where his client was being detained. Kane, together with his partner and the young man's parents, who'd retained him, arrived at the White Way Hotel at 1:30 a.m. "The lawyer asked a state trooper if the youth was being held in custody, and he was advised that he was not," McAllister said. "The lawyer was permitted to see his client. They conferred briefly, and both left." When asked by a reporter if the youth was considered a suspect, McAllister responded, "Everybody is a suspect."

In the seconds following his extemporaneous utterance about seeing a woman's blonde hair blowing in the wind, blurted in the presence of two state policemen, did Thomas realize that his words might be construed as an admission of guilt? Or did his fear of facing another round of lie detector tests, this time to be administered by a New Jersey detective with a more acute knowledge of the crime scene than the Philadelphia detectives, cause him to suddenly clam up and invoke his right to counsel? Was he simply weary of being questioned, and decide that he'd had enough upon waking in the hotel room?

Just five hours after Thomas was released to his attorney, the New Jersey State Police released more candid photographs of Susan and Elizabeth, provided by their families. Detective Robert Saunders told reporters these were accurate likenesses of how the girls might have appeared the night they were last seen. One picture revealed a smiling Susan Davis in a graduation cap and gown, wearing thick-rimmed glasses. It was shot on May 25, 1969, the day she graduated from Monticello College. The other photo showed Elizabeth Perry in a frilled, two-piece bathing suit, a pendant dangling from her throat as she stood pensively next to the side of a house.

Detective Saunders reminded reporters that the Absecon barracks hotline number would remain open on a twenty-four-hour basis. "We are very optimistic with these pictures," he said. As if perceiving their cynical tone, he admonished the newsmen standing before him: "You people," he scolded, "would never make good police officers. You are too pessimistic. You've got to have stamina, a strong back, a receptive mind—and luck." Asked by a reporter if investigators were running out of leads, he added, "Well, there goes your pessimism again. We have every hope of finding the killer."

It was also reported that the young man acquainted with Thomas had been questioned and released along with him. Brennan told the press that although the two young men had been released, they weren't totally cleared of suspicion, and that either or both might be questioned again. Today, however, only two New Jersey State Police detectives remember there being a second suspect associated with

Thomas, and neither can recall his name. The other detectives who were interviewed insist that at this point the investigation was focused solely on Thomas.

As for his client, attorney Edward F. Kane told reporters later that night, "He was released to me but not in my custody. I have no obligation to produce him at any time."

The lack of a solid case against Thomas, who was questioned for a total of thirty-four hours before being released to his attorney, clearly frustrated Brennan, who had hoped to have an arrest by now. He announced that his detectives had no more immediate plans to question him again. When asked if "the Norristown youth," had been cleared of suspicion, Brennan replied, "He has been cleared, but not the way we'd like to clear him."

Lt. Brennan had slept a total of nine hours during the first four days of the investigation when he consented to be interviewed by an *Inquirer* reporter at his Absecon barracks office on Friday. For the tight-lipped police veteran to step down from his dais, loosen his tie, and allow a reporter access to his thoughts, seemed to mark a turning point for him. In an informal setting, might he speak candidly and elaborate more freely upon the investigation's progress?

"But for the .38 caliber Colt holstered to his belt, Jim Brennan could be taken for a businessman worn to the point of exhaustion by worry and frustration," the reporter described him. "His eyes at times peer glassily over the bags. His tie is pulled down, his white shirt open at the collar." Readers hoping to gather insight into the detective's psyche were sorely disappointed. The cranky lieutenant disclosed little to the reporter other than to clarify what he had said earlier in the week at the late Wednesday evening press conference, when an *Inquirer* reporter, gleaning from Brennan's buoyant mood that a break in the case was imminent, had allegedly misquoted him as saying that investigators had a "break" in the case that would "lead to the wrapping up of final details" later that same night. Brennan reiterated that he'd been misquoted and had never stated that he had two witnesses who saw the two girls entering the woods. What he meant to say, he explained to the reporter interviewing him now, was that a witness *could have* seen the girls entering the woods.

With no physical evidence connecting their suspect to the murders, the first official week of the investigation drew to a disappointing close. Brennan continued to withhold information from the public, a strategy seemingly designed to maintain the flow of leads and give the appearance that his department was desperately reliant on more information. "We have no primary suspects," he'd stated at the Friday press conference, refusing to answer whether detectives would question Thomas again. Behind the scenes, however, the lieutenant's actions betrayed his remarks.

CHAPTER EIGHT

A Set of Keys

Five days had now passed since Elwood Faunce's grisly find. Despite mounting public criticism aimed toward local and state police departments, Lt. Brennan soldiered forward, refusing to succumb to defeat as the weekend approached. With the resort area nearing capacity with its inundation of vacationers, he had his investigators retrace their steps, hoping they might have missed something earlier. He began Saturday evening's press conference by announcing that his men hadn't learned any vital new information to pass along. "Leads have not developed as we had hoped," he glumly confessed. He also stated that fingerprints lifted from the girls' car were still being processed, as they were "spotty" and needed closer examination. The state lab, meanwhile, was systematically eliminating prints of the girls and of the Blazer's Auto Service employees who'd removed their automobile from the parkway.

Having exhausted their sources, and with recent canvassing of the parkway, beach, boardwalk, town streets, and Somers Point bars turning up no new evidence or promising leads, Brennan implored once again for a crucial witness to come forth, pleading for any shred of information that would help account for the girls' whereabouts between 5:30 and 6:15 a.m. "We have them in the diner," he said. "We have people who saw them in the diner with three boys.

We have witnesses who saw them getting ready to leave but not actually going out the door. We have witnesses who saw the car at 6:15, but nobody who saw the car between 5:30 and 6:15. Why in the hell can't somebody who saw that car between 5:30 and 6:15 a.m. come forward? I am convinced that somebody saw the car during that period of time."

The Ocean City Police Department, meanwhile, was enduring a wave of criticism that the murderer hadn't been apprehended. "I've got a stack of letters from 'concerned residents' criticizing the department," Public Safety Commissioner Chester Wimberg told the *Philadelphia Inquirer*. "I thought I would because the victims vacationed there. What these residents don't realize is that the murders weren't committed here. But the town has received a lot of publicity, seemingly unfavorable. What can you do?"

Raymond Perry, adamant that the Ocean City Police Department was being unjustly criticized in the aftermath of his daughter's death, dashed off a scathing letter to the editor of the *Inquirer.* It was reprinted in the *Ocean City Sentinel-Ledger* for all its citizens to read:

Dear Editor:

I refer to the article headlined "Resort Being Criticized in Coed Deaths," which appeared in The Inquirer of Sunday morning, June 8. This only now comes to my attention in reviewing a stack of clippings which friends in your area were kind enough to send me.

It is truly a shame that the Ocean City residents-or anyone else-would have such narrow minds as to censure the Ocean City Police in this affair. I speak from the experience of having spent only two hours' time in Ocean City plus several telephone contacts with their police during the subsequent 24. Nonetheless, I am perfectly confident that I comprehend their quality quite more clearly than does any of these residents who presume to criticize them. This is not to suggest that every last man on the force is a Sherlock

Holmes, but it was apparent to me-and I'm sure I speak for Mr. Davis-that they are dedicated and competent people, trying to do a job against great odds.

What, we may ask ourselves, are those odds against which they fight? I would suggest a few:

1. Narcotics. And I'll bet that not all the pushers are from "somewhere else."

2. Stupidity-or to say the least, thoughtlessness. I had the occasion on Monday morning, June 2, to place a call to what I thought was the private line number of the Ocean City detective bureau. Wrong number-turned out to be and Ocean City residence. I apologized, explained to the woman who answered that I was the father of one of the two missing girls (at that point, they were only "missing") and that I would hang up and try my urgent call again. She retorted, "Don't you dare hang up! Tell me what is all this about two missing girls?" Her ear is still ringing, I should think.

3. Most of all, lack of concern-the press abounds daily with stories about someone needing help in an emergency, and no one willing to bestir himself to give it. Who is to say that such an episode did not occur momentarily before the murder of these two young ladies?

To those who would cast blame upon the Ocean City police, let me suggest that they ponder the above in connection with the observation of Benjamin Disraeli:

"This shows how much easier it is to be critical than to be correct."

Sincerely yours,
Raymond Perry

After a two-hour meeting among Lt. Brennan, Captain Paterra, and Detective Robert Saunders, on Saturday a consensus was reached to start an underwater search near the crime scene. Beginning at 4:30 p.m. Sunday, June 8, six

New Jersey State Police divers, members of their Underwater Rescue Unit, arrived near the murder locus in a specially equipped truck dispatched from division headquarters. Using underwater metal detectors termed "scuba looters," they scoured for the murder weapon and car keys in the vicinity of where the girls were found, beginning with the mucky bottom of Patcong Creek. The twenty-four-foot deep, thirty-foot wide brackish waterway, a tributary of the Great Egg Harbor River, flows southeast beneath the parkway at the village of Bargaintown, where it forms a loop around the crime scene a hundred yards or so from its banks. Bound in wetsuits, braving mosquitoes, horseflies, gnats, and other inquisitive water critters inhabiting the high marsh grasses and cattails, police divers George Hurden, Joseph Quinn, Martin Nesbitt, Steven Holmes, Robert Fuller, and Robert Nye reached blindly into the waist-deep water. Nye, long since retired from the state police, was among the divers who combed the narrow creek turns on either side of the parkway. He recalls the heat and the unbearable afternoon mugginess in which he had to work. To stave off sunstroke, he would periodically float on his back and dunk his head, allowing the cool estuarine waters to restore his clarity.

Lt. Brennan continued to beseech the public for help, emphasizing that the forty-five minutes after the girls were seen leaving the diner were "critical to our investigation." He urged anyone who saw anything, "no matter how insignificant" at the diner or on the parkway, to contact him immediately. "The killer or killers are still at large," he warned. "As long as they are loose, there is a danger to every girl, your sister, or our daughters."

Brennan issued a similar plea the following day, relaying his concerns to the newspapers: "We feel certain there is some helpful information that will remove a dangerous criminal or criminals from our society. We ask you please not to try to decide whether what you know might or might not be helpful to us. Call Area Code 609-646-2088, or stop at any police station, no matter how small or unrelated your information might seem. Your identity will remain confidential...Remember, there is still a killer or killers at large." Three teams of detectives, Brennan said, with a two-policemen team working in New Jersey, and two teams in eastern Pennsylvania, were working the case, he told reporters during a short ten-minute press conference.

Hampered by weeds and large lily pads, the next day police divers resumed their underwater search with an aluminum boat while troopers looked along the adjacent wooded banks. Although twelve knives were found and sent to the state police forensics lab, none were conclusively linked to the murders.

A ten-day sweep of everything within a mile and a half of the murder scene produced nothing of significance. An exhausting four-day search of the muddy creek bottom turned up nothing more than a screwdriver, hubcap, and a handful of rusty nails. State police had about given up hope of finding more pieces to the puzzle when on Wednesday, five days after the murders, a group of girls picking wildflowers near the parkway shoulder discovered a set of car keys. They'd stumbled upon their find near sundown in a grassy area by a section of the highway that runs parallel to and within forty feet of Fire Road in Bargaintown. Midway between the woods and the Black Horse Pike, the area is approximately two miles north of the murder scene. The children had played with the leather case containing the keys before turning it over to their parents, who immediately called police once they recognized the name of the owner printed on the inside fold: *SUSAN DAVIS.*

State police descended upon the area, sweeping with metal detectors a half-mile outside the grid of where they'd earlier looked. "That close to the parkway, they were most likely thrown from a car," said one police officer.

"The significance of the discovery of the keys is that we're now searching in a northerly direction," Robert McAllister told reporters.

The following day searchers discovered a small kitchen knife. The *Philadelphia Daily News* reported that the handle was made from bone, with a six-inch blade. The *Philadelphia Bulletin* described it as having a brown handle, located one-tenth of a mile from where the girls had found Susan's keys. As with the keys, it seemed probable that the weapon was tossed out a car window by the fleeing assailant. However, the knife bore no visible blood stains, according to McAllister. And because twelve others like it had already been unearthed by mine detectors, its discovery failed to excite the prosecutor, who indicated that it would be tested at the state police lab. Sadly, the results concluded that this was not the same knife used in the murders. A sense of despair swelled once again.

Up to this point, the witnesses who'd called the barracks hotline reported seeing the unoccupied light-blue convertible parked along the shoulder near mile marker 31.9. One man, a local maintenance worker, had noticed a tan Mustang parked behind it. But these witnesses were uncertain of the precise time they'd driven past either or both cars. On Sunday, June 14, state police announced that they'd finally located a crucial witness who'd heeded their persistent cries for help. State police confirmed that they had spoken with the witness earlier but had chosen not to reveal details of their conversation until they decided how much they would release to the public, and what parts they would withhold. Newspapers reports varied as to what exactly this person had seen.

According the *Atlantic City Press,* the witness saw Susan and Elizabeth in their convertible with an unidentified driver behind the wheel at about 6 a.m., just after they'd left the diner. The car was moving very slowly, with one girl seated in front and the other in back. McAllister confirmed that police had twice questioned the witness. When asked to confirm whether the person seen driving the convertible was a young male, McAllister replied, "I can only be quoted as saying no comment. We have our reasons." He added, "We've had several reports that the girls were seen in other areas. This pinpoints their location."

The *Bulletin*, however, reported that the witness saw the girls with a man in their car not far from where Susan's convertible was found abandoned on the parkway, suggesting that they'd been spotted with the man near mile marker 31.9. A source quoted the witness as saying, "The car was moving very slowly, and one girl was in the front seat and the other in the back."

The *Daily News* reported that while driving on the parkway, the witness noticed a young woman at the wheel of the blue convertible with the unidentified male seated in the passenger seat beside her. The other young woman, presumably Miss Perry, was in back. The witness could only give a vague partial description of the youth seated next to Elizabeth, describing him as a "non-hippie type."

Did this witness identify Susan and Elizabeth near the traffic circle, as suggested by McAllister, or near the murder scene beside the parkway? Who was driving the car?

Two days later, police decided to release more details of the witness's statement. According to a report in the *Press*, Detective Saunders said police were seeking the driver of an old, black Pontiac seen parked in front of the slain girls' car. He confirmed that the witness who saw this Pontiac was the same man who'd spied the stranger seated in Davis' convertible. The witness came to the barracks and told police he saw the two cars as he was traveling north on the parkway that morning between 5:30 and 6 a.m. As he passed the murder scene, he spotted a blue Chevrolet convertible "similar" to the one driven by Susan and Elizabeth. Police refused to comment on reports they'd narrowed their search for the killer to three suspects, one of them local. Saunders said the witness gave police "other information that we will not disclose because it might jeopardize the case." This account by the *Press* conflicts somewhat with what was earlier reported in the June 8 edition of the *Inquirer,* when Brennan stated, "we have witnesses who saw the car at 6:15 a.m...." Newsmen, who were now being told a different time than was originally provided, didn't seize upon another discrepancy between what Brennan was presently stating and what he'd announced a week earlier, when he clearly said "witness"....Did more than one person see a man in Susan's car in the moments before she and Elizabeth were murdered?

Brennan was pleased by this unexpected burst of useful information. Though he still didn't have an arrest, he was suddenly presented with a number of intriguing new questions to contemplate. Among them: when providing their statements to police, why didn't the three young men in the tan Mustang recall seeing the black Pontiac parked two cars ahead of them? Could he have pulled in front of Susan's convertible while the men were sleeping, yet after Susan had pulled over? Assuming that the murderer was driving the Pontiac, why would he pull over in plain view of a parked Mustang with three occupants, especially when he had a vast stretch of rural roadway and woods in which to slay the girls? A reporter immediately noted a coincidence that seasoned detectives likely knew within moments of the find: the keys were found on the same route that the three young men in the tan Mustang would've taken when they went in search of gas. Might one of them have tossed the keys from the passenger-side window, unbeknownst to the driver who'd picked them up hitchhiking? All three, however, had already passed lie detector tests.

The state police set up a mobile command post at the Somers Point traffic circle three days later, stationing an emergency operations trailer on a grass apron between the two entrances to the Circle Liquor Store parking lot, next to a bus stop shelter. It was manned round the clock with troopers and detectives, so that any witnesses who stopped by could offer information. A large white sign facing traffic was leaned on a cement pole near the back corner of the trailer for drivers heading east into Ocean City:

"WANTED"
CO-ED
MURDER INFORMATION
STOP HERE OR CALL
609-646-2088

On the same day, shore beat reporter Jon Katz, who covered the investigation for the *Press* and would go on to become a producer for the *CBS Morning News* and a *New York Times* bestselling author, interviewed Detective Robert Saunders at the Absecon barracks.

Second in command to Lt. Brennan, Saunders joined the state police in 1947 after serving with the U.S. Army Air Forces during WWII. A plainclothes detective since 1954, he and Brennan had worked together for more than seven years. In addition to being assigned to the Perry-Davis murders, over the years he investigated other famous cases, including the unsolved Anglemyer murder in Egg Harbor Township, as well as the 1965 shooting death of Frank Adamucci, co-owner of the Rickshaw Inn in Cherry Hill.

The movie-star handsome, forty-four-year-old with dark wavy hair echoed the urgent tone of his lieutenant. "There's a killer on the loose somewhere," he said, standing behind the walnut-paneled divider separating the barracks working area from a small foyer as he gazed contemplatively out at the traffic streaming down the White Horse Pike. "We don't know where he's going to be next. Somebody must have seen something relevant on the parkway that morning. We're positive somebody saw something, but for their own reasons aren't coming forth. Everybody we've talked to who saw something on the parkway the morning of the murders says that three or four cars passed them. We'll keep all sources confidential, but some people aren't coming to us.

"It isn't fair," he said, "for someone who knows something not to come to us. It isn't fair to the people who send their kids to recreational areas like these. What about the kid next door? What about the neighbors' children? Is it fair to keep information from the police for any reason? People talk about law and order. This is law and order. They don't owe anything to us, but they owe something to society. They have a moral obligation to call us and tell us if they know anything." The Northfield resident and father of three gestured toward the pike. "We'll meet them at the neighborhood drug store or on top of the Empire State Building if they want.

"Some people went to the murder scene on their own time," he continued, "using their money to make sure that they hadn't or couldn't see anything that could help us. But there's somebody who's sitting back with relevant information and not coming forth. Everyone we've talked to says they passed or were passed by cars on the parkway that morning. There simply has got to be somebody who saw something relevant."

Detectives questioned two Millville, New Jersey, men who were arrested in Atlantic City on Tuesday night, June 24. The suspects, Matthew Hignett, twenty-seven, and Herbert Kelley, thirty-six, lived in the farming town of Millville, about an hour's drive away. Kelley, a former U.S. Marine and Korean War veteran, was being held along with Hignett on charges of raping a twenty-two-year old woman and threatening to kill her with a shotgun. A state police spokesman said detectives were sent "to find out where [Hignett and Kelley] were at the time of the murders of Susan Davis and Elizabeth Perry." The results of the questioning were not disclosed, but the spokesman said their inquiry was "routine." Both men subsequently provided alibis, passed lie detector tests, and were eliminated as possible suspects.

Investigators were initially reluctant to divulge details about the watch found at the murders scene for the same reason they withheld disclosure of the bra possibly used to restrain one of the victims: in the future they might need the information to ferret out liars and deceitful suspects during interrogations and lie detector tests. Initially, they would only confirm that the watch was of the variety used by deep-sea divers and surfers. But with the month-old investigation bearing no fresh leads, state police were growing desperately reliant on the public's help, however weak or uncredible its source.

On the last Friday in June they distributed to the press a picture of the watch they'd found, asking readers to notify the state police if they had seen anyone who had such a watch and wasn't presently wearing it. "We emphasize the word HAD," said a spokesman. Waterproof and shock-absorbent, the watch face was attached to a "Time Elapse Band," a rotating outer bezel which gauges how long a diver has been submerged underwater. Newspaper coverage varied concerning the watch's condition when it was found. Most papers reported that only the face was recovered. The *Atlantic City Press,* however, indicated that a partial band was attached to it. The police close-ups, however, clearly reveal the face only, and every former detective who was interviewed concurs that the second report was erroneous.

The watch was found in generally good condition. A few nicks and scratches marred the stainless-steel casing, and the numbers embossed on the outside bezel appeared chipped in spots. No engraved serial number on the back plate meant that it couldn't be traced to any specific jeweler, and also signified that the watch was not military-issue. Although the manufacturer, Benrus Company, produced a military-issue dive watch in the late 1960s for use by soldiers, the retail model found at the crime scene was available at jewelry stores in the area. According to Rock Scarfo, a watch restorer from Suwanee, Georgia who served as a crew chief with the United States Air Force during his tour of duty in Vietnam, the Belforte 666 found at the crime scene would have been manufactured between 1965 and 1968. This model was popular with "river rats on the Mekong Delta," general infantrymen, and at PX bases in America and abroad because its waterproof casing resisted heat and humidity. But while such a watch might have been sold at a stateside exchange, detectives had already checked with local military bases, questioning and clearing all personnel on leave at the time of the murders. "This type of watch was really, *really* popular" with soldiers fighting in Vietnam, Scarfo said, so fashionable that many soldiers would remove the watch face from its rubber strap and have street vendors in Saigon customize their leather bands with colorful battalion insignia.

By the time that the New Jersey State Police released a photo of the watch, they already had a strong lead as to its owner. Although their statement in conjunction with the publication of the close-up implied they were seeking his identity, they may have been trying to locate him instead. A young woman had called state police officials one day in early June, in the days following the murders. She was adamant that she knew who owned the watch discovered at the murder scene, for she had seen him wearing it.

CHAPTER NINE

99 and 44/100 Certain

Francene Latkin was seated at her desk, processing claims at the local U.S. Social Security Office in Atlantic City, New Jersey, when the WFPG radio bulletin piped in through the office intercom: the slain bodies of Susan Davis and Elizabeth Perry had been found. The broadcast froze the space surrounding her. That she'd secretly foretold their tragic fate when she first heard the reports they'd gone missing a few days earlier did little to absorb the impact of this devastating news.

Twenty years old at the time, Latkin was living with her parents in Hammonton, New Jersey, a farming community not far from the Garden State Parkway. Like others her age, she was at a point in her life between high school and college, trying to chart a course for her future while commuting to her civil service job thirty miles away. The news that one of the murder victims was the same age as she and had long, dark blonde hair like hers—a seemingly incidental detail mentioned in passing during the broadcast—resonated with Latkin, tantalizing her with the mystery of its elusiveness. There was something beyond the scope of the senseless tragedy, another aspect of the story that the reporter hadn't announced, that circled in Perkionnen's mind, kindling her memory as she silently sat, unable to continue working. Her heart jumped as she suddenly drew the connection, recalling something her friend and co-worker Kathleen had told her earlier that same morning about a handsome young man the girls had met a short time ago while vacationing together in Florida.

In April of 1969, less than two months earlier, Latkin was joined by her sister Mimi and their friend Kathleen as they flew down to south Florida for spring break. At the time, Fort Lauderdale was the spring break capital of the world, "Dizzy" by Tommy Roe was the top Billboard song, and in the college bars the young throngs moved and grooved, flailing their hair while dancing "The Swim" and "The Monkey." Eager to join the craze, the three girls booked a room for the week at the Lauderdale Beach Hotel near the famed A1A strip between Los Olas and Sunrise Boulevards. They spent the next several days tanning poolside in their bikinis and partying the evenings away at the many bars along the beach.

One night at a local hotspot, the three girls were approached at the bar by a tall, strapping young man with sandy blonde hair, muttonchop whiskers, and light blue eyes. Athletically built, he spoke in a charming southern drawl, introducing himself as Ronnie Walden. At first he seemed harmless enough, an easygoing, glib twenty-two-year-old country boy who understood how to use his southern charm and rugged good looks to swoon young ladies. After introductions were made, Latkin, her sister, and Kathleen spent a better part of the evening dancing and drinking with Walden and his two friends. Numbers were exchanged, and a few days later Walden invited the three girls from New Jersey over to his place for dinner.

Walden's house, a local rental he shared with his two buddies and a fourth roommate, Robert Shelton, was a typical bachelor pad of the free-love era. Swirling drifts of marijuana and incense smoke curled beneath the ceiling lights. The refrigerator shelves held stacks of beer, with backup cartons piled alongside it. Bikini-clad girls and long-haired men traipsed through the kitchen and living room, pausing to chat with Walden and his houseguests while he cooked. The only peculiar thing about their host, Latkin observed, was his penchant for referring to himself by different names. In addition to being called Ronnie, he often referred to himself as Chad, and Chad Shelton. His favorite alias, however, was Bat Masterson, an Old West sheriff from Dodge City, Kansas, who was deputy marshal to Wyatt Earp. (An NBC series about his life aired in the late fifties.) Although Walden seemed like a sly maneuverer who was a tad too fast with a quip, Latkin kept her thoughts to herself. Perhaps he was immature, she told herself, a harmless eccentric eager to score with the ladies, trying all lines to see which worked. After all, her sister and Kathleen seemed to enjoy his company, and the last thing she wanted to do was dampen the fun.

Sitting next to Walden while they ate, Latkin was drawn to the attractively styled watch worn on his right wrist. He said it was a skin diver watch, and proudly held out his arm for her to view up close. She teased him when she noticed that the watch face, snapped onto a leather band, had been stamped with the word "jewels," even though it wasn't adorned with any diamonds or inlaid with gold. Strangely, as Latkin inspected the watch Walden kept complimenting her and reaching over to caress her hair. There was nothing untoward in his harmless flirtations toward her, however, for the wine was flowing and a general ease permeated the scene.

The stoned interlude was interrupted when Mimi spilled a small dash of red wine on the white shag carpet under the dining room table. The seemingly laid-back Georgia boy suddenly exploded, silencing the table. His sobering screams, summoned from some dark cavern within him, were hurled violently toward Latkin's sister. Even as the incident passed moments later, with Walden hurrying for a sponge to blot the stain, his unexpectedly volatile outburst frightened Latkin. Everyone but she seemed able to put the awkward episode behind them when the tension eased, even her sister. She couldn't easily shrug off what she'd just witnessed, as if the stranger seated next to her was possessed of a lingering evil only she could sense.

One day toward the middle of April, about a week or so after she'd returned home to New Jersey and settled into her old routine, Latkin learned that her friend Kathleen had been keeping in touch with Walden. He'd called her to say he'd be driving through New Jersey the following day en route to New York to visit a friend. He was going to be in the shore area for a while, maybe get a job locally, and had decided to look up her up. He told Kathleen he needed money, so she arranged to get him a job on the Atlantic City boardwalk with a friend of hers who owned a clothing shop named A Man and a Woman, as well as a room above the store where Walden could crash for a while.

The next day Walden appeared at their workplace, located on the busy street corner of Texas and Pacific avenues in Atlantic City. Latkin went outside to greet him, for Kathleen was temporarily preoccupied. Walden was driving a yellow Oldsmobile 442 with black racing stripes and wide tires. He opened the door for her. She slid into the passenger seat, so she could direct him to a place where he could park legally, as he was in a designated parking spot one block from the boardwalk and risked having his car towed.

The news that he'd have to move his Oldsmobile didn't sit well with Walden. He rocked back and forward in his seat, fuming as he sought to enter the stream of traffic. Struggling to suppress his rage, his face reddened with the simmering anger brewing within him, a physical reaction eerily similar to what presaged his violent outburst in Florida. As the car lurched forward, he inexplicably slammed his brakes. A short knife jumped out from under the passenger seat. "What's that?" a stunned Latkin asked as she noticed the blade, about six inches long with a small curve, slide out of its leather holder.

"It's nothing," Walden snapped, leaning over her lap to shove the weapon back under her seat.

Against her better judgment, Latkin let this incident pass without mention, much for the same reason she'd overlooked what she'd witnessed in Florida: though she was innately suspicious of Walden, and fearful of his behavior, her other friends weren't able to see this side of him.

In the wake of what she'd just heard over the intercom, Latkin immediately sought out Kathleen to relay her suspicions. She reminded her of the litany of events too coincidental to ignore: Walden had suddenly quit his job at the boardwalk clothing store and left town just as news of the murders broke. He was obsessed with her dark blonde hair, and one of the parkway murder victims had hair of a similar color and clear blue eyes like hers. There was the knife she'd seen, and the news bulletin had reported that both women were stabbed to death. But mostly Latkin recalled how easily Walden was angered, with this final connection cementing her intuitions.

Unbeknownst to Latkin, by this time a police report had already been filed against Walden. Atlantic City Police Chief Mario F. Foriani told the *Atlantic City Press* that Walden's employer at A Man and a Woman, proprietor Samuel Einstein, had signed an unlawful conversion complaint against him on June 6, 1969. Einstein told police that on June 5 Walden had agreed to sell him a motorcycle in exchange for seven hundred dollars worth of clothing and two hundred dollars cash. Walden allegedly accepted the cash and clothing but never delivered the motorcycle.

The newspapers indicated that Walden had been driving a 1969 Oldsmobile—comporting with Latkin's memory of the car he'd been driving when he arrived at her workplace in Atlantic City—but with an attached trailer that towed the stolen bike.

Acting upon her hunches, Latkin notified the New Jersey State Police after speaking with Kathleen. She is uncertain whether she drove to the investigation headquarters in Absecon or the Atlantic County Prosecutor's Office in Mays Landing. She also may have spoken with officials at the Hammonton Troop A barracks, headquarters of the Criminal Investigative Division.

Latkin arrived at one of these two locations a day or two after she learned of the murders. She was led into a sparse room with a two-way mirror and questioned by detectives as to why she believed Ronnie Walden was involved in the murders of Susan Davis and Elizabeth Perry. She told her interviewers that she'd had a hunch about Walden ever since he went crazy in Florida when her sister Mimi dropped the wine glass; she'd seen his knife and was the target of another of his unprovoked fits; he was infatuated by her blonde hair, and she had blues eyes too, just like Susan. But what struck Latkin as too patterned to be a randomly connected series of events was how quickly Walden fled the area after the murders.

During the interview, Latkin was repeatedly asked whether she recalled seeing Walden wear any jewelry. She thought it was strange that the police kept asking her this question and couldn't understand its relevancy. She'd always associated jewelry with rings, earrings, and bracelets. And of course, diamonds. Yet the detectives kept at her: Was Walden wearing jewelry? Finally understanding her confusion, they rephrased: Do you recall him wearing a watch?

Yes, she answered instantly.

They asked what type of watch. It was a skin diver watch, she said. She was certain of this because she'd sat next to Walden at the dinner table and had seen it up close. A detective then inquired, "If I showed you a picture of the watch, would you be able to identify it?"

They presented her with a blown-up photo of the watch found at the crime scene. Without hesitating, Latkin positively identified it as the same one Ronnie had been wearing in Fort Lauderdale. "We might have something here," they responded, assuring Latkin that they'd issue an all points bulletin (APB) on Walden that same night.

Before leaving the station that evening, Latkin was instructed to go home and take notes of everything she remembered about the time she'd spent with Walden. She did as requested, jotting down each tidbit of information she could recall, from the time they met in Fort Lauderdale to the moment he'd arrived in Atlantic City. Although over forty years have passed since the slayings of Davis and Perry, Latkin has kept her papers in safekeeping all this time, certain they might one day help solve the murders.

Her notes reflect that Walden had assumed aliases, most notably the last name Shelton. They also indicate he had a blonde girlfriend staying with him at the Fort Lauderdale house. A knife, she wrote, "possibly a dagger," shot out from under the front seat of his Oldsmobile, and in the Florida house she'd seen a skin diver's wetsuit that might've belonged to Walden.

The day following her visit with the New Jersey State Police, Latkin received a call from one of their detectives. Relaying to him the information she'd compiled, she was stunned to learn more about Walden's criminal background. Purportedly he was a schizophrenic who'd recently completed a stint at Central State Hospital in Milledgeville, Georgia, an overcrowded lunatic asylum whose attendants had a reputation for shackling patients to ward beds and physical abusing the mentally retarded. The detective told Latkin they'd obtained half a fingerprint from Susan's convertible. The partial sample drew a match with Walden but was unusable as evidence because it wasn't an entire print. The state police were "99 and 44/100 certain" they had the right suspect in Walden, the detective assured her. His use of that particular phrase, borrowed from a 1969 Ivory soap advertising jingle describing their product's purity, had always stuck with Latkin.

As the years passed, the information that Latkin possessed would continue to haunt her. She was reminded of the killings each year on their anniversary, and of the gritty hustler she was certain had committed them. She felt chilled by Walden's shadow, as if she'd wake to find him standing over her. Where was he now? Eager for a voyeur's peek into his future, and compelled by a need to validate her intuition, she sought to find out what became of him. She often wondered, why hadn't the New Jersey State Police arrested him after all this time?

In the early autumn of 2005, Latkin brought up the matter with an old friend who was still living in South Jersey. Her friend, who had a relative employed by the New Jersey State Police, placed Latkin in contact with Detective Fred Fife. During a telephone conversation, Fife, who would go on to receive the 2010 New Jersey State Police Trooper of the Year award, asked Latkin to fax him all her old notes, along with her collection of news clippings highlighting Ronnie's arrest. He also asked her to recall what she'd told detectives in 1969, and to explain why she was convinced Walden had murdered Davis and Perry. Latkin expressed concern for her own safety in disclosing all she knew. If Walden somehow learned she was a material witness, what lengths might he go to silence her?

Detective Fife allegedly told Latkin that the New Jersey State Police had no record of speaking to her in 1969, or any information concerning Walden's present whereabouts. She faxed Detective Fife all the documents in her possession. These included the notes she'd taken when speaking with the state police in June 1969, as well as a newspaper clipping summarizing Walden's detainment in Colorado. Latkin says Fife informed her that members of the New Jersey State Police Major Crime Unit were unable to locate Walden. At the time of their conversation, however, Walden was long since dead. This begs the question, why wasn't Detective Fife aware of this information when speaking with Latkin?

Yet another woman from Atlantic County had an encounter with Ronnie Walden around the same time he'd driven up from Florida and met with Latkin. In June 1969 Marjorie Garwood was twenty-years old, living with her parents in Egg Harbor City, New Jersey, approximately twelve miles from Somers Point. The Oakcrest High School graduate was taking a nap in her parents' living room one afternoon when she was woken by a call from a New Jersey State Police detective investigating the parkway slayings from a week earlier. He was interested in learning what Garwood knew about a young drifter from Florida named Thomas "Ronnie" Walden.

The name immediately resonated with Garwood, for a few days earlier she had gone on a blind date with Walden, set up by a girlfriend who told her "you have to go out with this guy." Walden came to pick her up at her parents' house driving a motorcycle. He seemed charming but fake to Garwood, trying too hard to impress her. She was immediately put off by his demeanor but allowed him to take her to dinner that night on the Atlantic City boardwalk, and to a movie afterward. Afterward, she recalls there was something very unsettling about him, a palpable bad vibe similar to what Francene Latkin had sensed. As Walden rode her home on the back of her motorcycle, he pulled over to the side of the road for no apparent reason, slowing the bike to a stop alongside a densely wooded area near the Atlantic Avenue entranceway to the FAA Hughes Technical Center, the same governmental aviation facility that had produced an aerial map of the Perry-Davis crime scene for state detectives in 1969. The bike seemed to be working fine, and there was no mechanical failure causing Walden to pull over, no landmarks to draw his attention. Immediately, Garwood immediately sensed something was wrong. "I was scared to death," she recalls, as Walden slowed to peer out into the darkened woods nearby. "I had very bad vibes, a sixth sense he was going to take me in the woods and kill me."

Much to Garwood's relief, after pausing for a moment to survey the woods before them, during which time she was certain Walden was searching for the precise location where he'd murder her, he rolled the throttle and peeled away, taking her home without further incident. Although she didn't know it at the time, Walden had likely given Garwood a ride on the same motorcycle he'd stolen from Atlantic City storeowner Samuel Einstein. As she was seated on the couch in her parents' living room, recounting her encounter for the detective, he told her Walden was a suspect in the parkway slayings, and police had made a match with the motorcycle tread to tracks found in the sand alongside the parkway. He also told Garwood that the parkway murder suspect was mentally ill.

The young man whom Francene Latkin and Marjorie Garwood are certain murdered Susan Davis and Elizabeth Perry was born Thomas Ronald Walden on February 5, 1947, in Cairo, Georgia. He was the younger of two sons born to Bernice Walden, who ran an infant day care center from their modest three-bedroom rancher on Sixth Street, in the northwest section of town. Walden's father Lindsey, a landscaper and retired career serviceman with the Air Force, was known around town as a mild-mannered, humorous man always quick with a riddle for the neighborhood children. He relocated his family to bases all over the world in locales as exotic as Panama before returning stateside. He settled in

Cairo after residing for a short period in Valdosta, following generations of Waldens before him.

Originally nicknamed "The Syrup City" because of its cane syrup factories, Cairo is located in the rolling lower coastal plain of southwest Georgia, thirty-five miles north of Tallahassee. Surrounded by fertile grazing pastures, livestock farms, and clapboard roadside churches, the small town is reminiscent of the Southern Gothic settings vividly explored in Flannery O' Connor's writings. Wisps of Spanish moss flutter from the live oaks and cypress branches overhanging abandoned carriage roads and haunted slave cabins. Alligators sun themselves along the white beach islands of the Ochlocknee River, the best spot in Georgia to land a Suwannee bass. Like many hidden towns in the Deep South, Cairo boasts wholesome homespun entertainment, like 4-H fairs, antique car shows, and festivals such as Mule Day. Neighboring Whigham hosts the annual Rattlesnake Roundup, a three-day hunt for prized diamondbacks. Yet despite its lack of stature or proximity to a metropolis, Cairo has produced its share of famous athletes. Baseball legend Jackie Robinson was from here, as well as Olympian basketball player Teresa Edwards and All-Pro NFL lineman William Stanfill, a former teammate of Walden's on their 1965 Georgia class AAA championship basketball team

Despite the passage of time, Cairo natives have no trouble recalling Ronnie Walden. In addition to being a top varsity athlete and three-sport starter at Cairo High School, he was nominated as a "Star" his senior year, an award bestowed annually upon students chosen by a faculty committee, then elected by the student body for exhibiting "good citizenship, intelligence, and ambition." In *The Raconteur*, the school yearbook, Walden is pictured on stage in a dinner jacket and bowtie, posing for the award next to cheerleader Mary Ann Hawthorne, the Miss Georgia Sweet Potato Queen. He was also social chairman of the Key Club, the nation's oldest and largest service organization. The quote above his 1965 yearbook portrait reads, "In theory there is nothing to hinder our following what we are taught," a phrase coined by the Greek philosopher Epictetus. Ironically, Walden left this phrase incomplete, for it next reads, "but in life there are many things to draw us aside."

Despite his notable scholastic achievements, Walden was a controversial figure who often drew attention to himself, and not always for the right reasons. Locals recall a much darker side to his personality, which revealed itself not long after he moved to Cairo from Valdosta when he was in his early teens.

Walden's older brother Roy characterized his little brother as "a superb athlete with a wild streak." He recalled an incident at the 1965 state basketball championship in Atlanta, when Ronnie and his teammates felt inferior to the opposing team, whose players had more money and donned slicker uniforms than the Syrupmakers. "He told his buddies to wait at the hotel," Roy Walden said. His younger brother returned two hours later with armfuls of shoplifted shirts and belts for his friends.

Cathy Moore graduated from Cairo High in 1969, four years after Ronnie Walden. She is the sister of former Pittsburgh Steelers punter Robert "The Toe from Cairo" Walden, a distant cousin of Ronnie's. Moore, a gracious southerner who speaks in a throaty drawl, has an awkward time speaking ill of a person, especially a neighborhood boy. However, she doesn't mince words when it comes to Ronnie Walden. "He was mean as a snake," she says, an expert at luring women into his fold. She recalls a young man who in his spare time used to break into houses, steal guns, and commit other unlawful offenses that went beyond his other mischievous pranks, such as shoplifting sporting equipment from the local sporting goods store, or stealing clothes for his teammates. Walden, she says, was "underhanded and sneaky."

Moore can remember discussing Walden with his mother, who once said of her younger son, "Ronnie could get a job wearing out couches, he is so lazy. Spoiled rotten."

Moore's depiction of Walden is similar to the sentiments shared by Saress Harrison Moye, who graduated in the same class with Moore and still lives in Cairo, where she owns and runs a successful organic farm.

Moye grew up on a large ranch bordering the Walden's more modest homestead. One of her childhood hobbies included riding her prized possession, a Tennessee walking horse named Dollie that she kept corralled in her front yard on the weekends when she wasn't parading him at shows and contests in Florida and Georgia.

One day when she was twelve years old and walking home from school, Moye noticed that Dollie was motionless in his riding ring, having collapsed to his side. She ran to the horse, resting his mane in her lap, when she noticed with horror that he had been shot dead center between the eyes. The police never told her who killed the five-gaited, bay mare. A local newspaper quoted them as figuring the bullet was a stray fired from a hunter's rifle. Years later, when Saress was old enough to handle the unreported version of the incident, her mother confessed to her that the Grady County Sheriff's Department had always suspected Walden was the culprit but weren't able to prove it.

After the incident, Moye never went near Walden again, remaining leery of him. "I always felt he was strange," she says. "I always had a funny feeling about him. Ronnie was jealous of anybody that had more than him. He was the type of person who, if he offered you a ride, you wouldn't get in the car with him. You just had that feeling about him, something that scares you. I can't explain it." The Waldens, Moye remembers, moved out of Cairo the same year their youngest son graduated from high school. "Everybody was glad when he was gone."

"Ronnie was sort of Mr. Everything in high school," says classmate and former girlfriend Lou Hurst Halstead. A year ahead of Walden in school, they went steady during her senior year of high school and part of her freshman year at Florida State University. When she moved to Tallahassee, leaving her lovelorn boyfriend behind for the remainder of his senior year, she began noticing changes in Walden's behavior during her visits home on the weekends. "Ronnie's high school principal called me in and said, 'Lou, you've got to do something,'" because Walden, a top student whom Halstead characterized as "very, very brilliant," had suddenly begun skipping classes and missing assignments, one of which was a senior year English thesis required for graduation. Often times he would inexplicably stand her up when they'd made plans. "He just quit caring how good he was. I saw a little mean streak in him. He just changed," she said.

Halstead broke up with her first love, for she'd grown weary of his erratic mood swings and had fallen for a Florida State classmate. While she freely admits this may have contributed toward Walden's downfall, unbeknownst to her at the time, he had secretly impregnated and married a girl in his senior class. The mother carried the birth to term, but the baby was stillborn. For Walden, who adored children and grew up in house filled with cribbed newborns and playful toddlers, the impact must have been devastating.

Walden derived his greatest joy from his gridiron feats, basking in the adulation of the cheering Saturday afternoon throngs. He was certain that his speed, toughness, and sure hands would attract the attention of one of the many talent-rich Division I programs in the region, like Florida State, or the University of Georgia in Athens. Instead, the scouts arrived in droves to witness teammate Bill Stanfill's heroic exploits, overlooking the Syrupmakers' scrappy wide receiver. Though Walden received partial grants-in-aid to attend both the University of Georgia and Florida

State University, these offers fell short of the full athletic scholarships he expected were forthcoming when his senior season ended.

For a year after their breakup, when she was home from school on vacation, a darkly brooding Walden would follow Halstead in his car. "I would come upon him just driving around town," she says. "I'd be at an intersection in a neighborhood and all of a sudden there he was. That frightened me. He didn't wave, he just stared at me."

If he couldn't have a full scholarship, Walden would have nothing. Despondent over his breakup with Halstead, grieving the death of his child, and deeply disappointed by his unfulfilled boyhood dreams of catching a touchdown pass at Doak Campbell Stadium in Tallahassee, Walden decided to distance himself from the source of his anguish. Following in his father's footsteps, he reasoned that a career in the service would earn him a steady if unspectacular living, allow him to see foreign ports of call, and revisit the distant lands where he'd lived a happy boyhood overseas. After graduating from Cairo High School in 1965, Walden left town for good, enlisting with the United States Air Force.

Perhaps it was the fear of being sent to fight in Vietnam, or the rigors of military structure, that derailed Walden. Soon after basic training, it became evident that a life in the wild blue yonder held little appeal for him. While stationed at Turner Air Force Base in Albany, Georgia, he went AWOL on or about December 30, 1966. In the months prior to leaving base he began writing and presenting bad checks and stole a money order from a fellow serviceman. He was arrested in Winter Haven, Florida, after fleeing when police tried to pull him over for driving with a bad taillight. Returned to base, he was court-martialed in February 1967 and sentenced to six months hard labor at Ft. Benning, Georgia, then issued a bad conduct discharge upon his release. It was soon after his discharge that he completed a stint at the Georgia State Mental Hospital. Whether he voluntarily committed himself, or his admission was a condition of his release from the Ft. Benning stockade, is unclear from his prison records.

When his undistinguished career in the armed forces ended, and after he was discharged from the asylum, Walden drifted around the country, his whereabouts uncertain until he landed in Fort Lauderdale in the spring of 1969.

On Monday, June 30, 1969—one month to the day after the parkway murders, and in the weeks after he'd fled Atlantic City—Walden surfaced at a Glenwood Springs, Colorado car dealer. A sparse frontier town located halfway between Aspen and Vail, Glenwood Springs is noted as the final resting place of Old West legend John Henry "Doc" Holliday. Ironically, the gunslinging outlaw was a nemesis of none other than Walden's alias, Bat Masterson. Might Walden have fancied himself as some sort of sharpshooter bent on fulfilling a vendetta? Walden wandered onto the lot under the pretense of shopping for a car. He took one for a short drive and returned to the dealer, and after testing a second, failed to return. At this point, the duped salesman looked over the car that Walden was trading and discovered that it had a Tennessee dealer's plate.

The Glenwood Springs Police Department issued an all points bulletin for a man fitting Walden's description, adding that he was considered armed and dangerous. On Tuesday morning the salesman told the story of the theft to a friend who was on his way to Aspen. The friend spotted the stolen 1969 Jeep almost as soon as he arrived at his destination. He notified the Aspen Police Department, who arrested Walden and transported him back to Garfield County Jail. A routine fingerprint check of Walden was forwarded to the FBI. They alerted the Glenwood Springs Police Department that Walden was wanted for crimes in other states including Georgia, Florida, Tennessee, and in New Jersey for questioning in the murders of Davis and Perry.

Bat Masterson and Chad Shelton were but two of his aliases, it was learned. He also went by the names Thomas Ronnie Chesnutt and Mark Reville Chesnutt.

Walden was detained in Glenwood Springs until Thursday, July 3, at about 4 p.m., at which point he was transported to federal district court, charged with auto theft, and had his bail set.

Back in New Jersey, newspapers got word there was a possible suspect in the parkway slayings. On Wednesday, July 2, a New Jersey State Police spokesman informed the *Daily News* that Walden was wanted in Atlantic City but only on bad check charges, and that no decision had been made on whether to extradite him to Atlantic County. The spokesman said that investigators were "interested only in routinely questioning" Walden on the murders because of his presence in the area on Memorial Day. "He is not considered a suspect in the murders at this time," the spokesman added. There was no mention of their interview with Latkin. "He is only one of many persons with criminal backgrounds that are being questioned."

Lt. Brennan told reporters, "We have reason to believe he was in the shore area when the murders occurred, but this thing is being blown out of proportion."

Armed with knowledge of Latkin's statement, and having confirmed Walden's location, New Jersey State Police detectives William Hunter and James Toth boarded a flight from New Jersey to Aspen on July 3 to question Walden and ask him to submit to a polygraph exam.

Les Eccher was undersheriff of the Garfield County Sheriff's Department in 1969. On the early evening of July 3, in the hours before the New Jersey State Police were scheduled to question Walden, and after he'd been returned to Glenwood Springs from federal court, Eccher received a frantic call from the sheriff's police dispatcher. She alerted him that an inmate had attempted to hang himself in the local jail and that Sheriff Baker was already at the scene.

Eccher, who had an office at the small jail and lived nearby, "lit the car up and came flying in," he said. According to his recollection of that evening, the jail trusties were picking up trays after a meal had been served to the prisoners, when with no forewarning, Sheriff Baker heard the clanking of cups on the jail bars, a signal from inmates alerting him to the gurgling and the groaning noises sounding from Walden's cell.

Baker was already inside the cell by the time Eccher arrived to assist him. Walden had removed the military-issue wool blanket from his bunk, loosened the threading on the edges where it had been hemmed, then tore it into a six-inch-wide strip which he weaved through the bars on the jail cell, fashioning a noose. "He wasn't hanging from a ceiling," Eccher recalled, "but it was on the bars high enough that he could get it around his throat and slowly sink down to a sitting position." Eccher and Baker cut the noose off Walden's throat, and the sheriff immediately administered CPR. Eccher assisted in the resuscitation. "Walden darn near got himself done," said Eccher. "His lips were blue, his fingernails were blue. But it was just that fast enough a situation to get that blanket cut down and that the sheriff had done, then he and I both struggled to get the damn thing from around his neck. He had it right up to his Adam's apple."

What possessed Walden to try hanging himself just hours before the arrival of Detectives Hunter and Toth? A guilty conscience? A desperate attempt to forestall the lie detector test? Approximately two days following Walden's failed suicide attempt, he consented to sit for the polygraph exam with the New Jersey authorities after first clearing a medical evaluation certifying him as able to submit to the test, "even though he had a hell of a time talking, because he had squeezed his Adam's apple so bad he had constricted his vocal chords," Eccher recalled.

For numerous reasons, Eccher can remember watching New Jersey State Police detectives administer the test to Walden. The undersheriff was a recent FBI Academy graduate who'd always been avidly interested in the science behind polygraphy. Until then, the tests were given exclusively in Grand Junction, as the Glenwood Springs Sheriff's Office hadn't yet been issued a reliable machine. Furthermore, the test was administered in Eccher's office, a naturally lit room with a scenic view of the roaring Colorado River, and of the Grand Avenue Bridge crossing it. However, he mostly remembers the incident not because he helped rescue Walden from near death, but because this was the same cell from which serial killer Ted Bundy would escape eight years later, shimmying through a hole in the ceiling on a snowy December night in 1977. In what would be the first of several odd coincidences connecting the world's most notorious serial killer to the Garden State Parkway murders of 1969, Bundy spoke glowingly of the manic high he felt that night as he shimmied his lanky frame up though an eighteen-inch diameter hole, dropped down into a vacant jailer's office, and strode unnoticed into a blinding Rocky Mountain blizzard.

Recalling that night for journalists Hugh Aynesworth and Stephen Michaud as he sat on Florida's death row, Bundy said, "I felt that way when I popped out of jail in Glenwood Springs. I had the feeling that things were just *happening*. Everything was just going my way. The stars were right! How can I explain it? My karma was good! I mean, *nothing* went wrong. If something did go wrong, the next thing that happened was so good it compensated."

Bundy recalled the same picturesque view of the Colorado River evoked by New Jersey detectives when they settled upon Eccher's office to conduct their examination of Walden. The former undersheriff does not, however, recall the outcome of Walden's polygraph exam. Neither does he recall discussing the results with the New Jersey detectives sent to question Walden As to whether he killed Davis and

Perry, Walden allegedly stated to Detective Hunter, "Ladies are for loving, not killing."

According to a report in the *Philadelphia Daily News,* however, Walden tried to kill himself *after* he'd been cleared in the lie detector tests. *Coed Suspect Cleared, Tries Suicide* the headline read. "He had just been cleared of the Memorial Day murders of two 19-year-old coeds," the article read, "but Thomas R. Walden had something else haunting him as he fashioned his blanket into a noose and tried to end his life..." The article further mentioned that Lt. Brennan said the tests had "entirely eliminated" Walden as a suspect. The *Daily News* also reported that Walden was wanted for questioning in the disappearance of a Florida girl with whom he'd left that state. Tennessee authorities were also interested in questioning him about a recent murder in Nashville.

A report of the hanging incident in the *Glenwood Springs (CO) Sage-Reminder* corroborates Eccher's version of events from that evening. The article stated that Sheriff Baker "foiled the attempt, gave [Walden] artificial respiration and called a doctor who pronounced him in good health. The lie detector test went off without further mishap, and the New Jersey authorities left assured that Walden was not their man." A photograph beneath the byline shows Walden, clad in a pair of funky checkerboard-patterned bellbottoms, grinning mockingly into the photographer's lens as he is escorted out of the sheriff's office and toward a waiting cruiser by Chief Robert Husted, Sheriff Baker, and Undersheriff Eccher.

After being released on bail in Colorado after his suicide attempt, and before returning to face sentencing on interstate auto theft charges, Walden moved back to Georgia. He moved in temporarily with his brother Roy and sister-in-law Kathy, who at that time were co-managers of Greenbriar Apartments in Valdosta.

On July 20, 1969, Georgia high school teacher Hope Boswell received a call from Kathy. Boswell, a blonde, petite woman who lived in the same apartment complex with two other roommates, was asked if she might like to come over that night to watch the Apollo 11 moon landing and "meet my weird brother-in-law." Though she was dating an airline pilot at the time, like many other unsuspecting young women before her, Boswell was immediately smitten with Ronnie Walden. Though the four sat riveted to the screen that Sunday night, from time to time she couldn't help glancing Walden's way. She had heard stories of his troubles but also knew that Kathy trusted her brother-in-law enough to allow him to babysit their six-month-old child.

Walden didn't hide any secrets from Boswell, at least not where the New Jersey murders were concerned. To prove it, that night he showed her the Colorado newspaper photo of him stepping out of the front doors of Garfield County Jail, flanked by his captors. "We talked about these murders, because when I met him, that's what he had been accused of. He said, 'That's so ridiculous, I didn't know those girls.'"

She and Walden began dating in October of that year and moved in together over a year later.

On September 19, 1969, Walden returned to Colorado, pleading guilty to federal charges of Interstate Transportation of a Stolen Motor Vehicle. He received sixty days observation and study for federal prisoners in Denver on October 17, 1969. On January 21, 1970, he was sentenced to six years at the Federal Correctional Institution in Tallahassee, Florida, and was paroled in August 1971.

Walden and Boswell were married that year, one of the few periods in his adult life when he was out of jail. She became pregnant with their child in 1973. The advent of fatherhood and the promise of a new life free from the petty crimes and scams that had sustained him until now did little to reform Walden. He fled Georgia before their son was born, making his way west to Texas, where he was charged with possession of a stolen automobile in October that year.

While out on parole, Walden found his way to Pensacola, Florida. Strangely enough, this was the same Gulf Coast beach town where Ted Bundy was finally apprehended six weeks after he escaped from Glenwood Springs but not before bludgeoning to death two Florida State University sorority sisters, and after that, murdering twelve-year-old Kimberly Leach in Lake City, Florida.

Former Skipper's Dive Shop manager Charles McDaniel, who moved to Pensacola after returning from Vietnam, can distinctly remember the young man in tennis whites breezing into his Wright Avenue store one afternoon and spilling a load of used scuba gear upon his counter. Because used diving equipment had little resale value, McDaniel was surprised that the customer actually accepted such a low offer for the goods. This suntanned stranger with sun-lightened hair and clear blue eyes looked familiar to McDaniel. He mentioned as much to Walden, who quickly realized that they'd attended Cairo High School together.

This connection was all Walden needed to exploit McDaniel's trusting nature. He claimed to be a professional tennis player, walking his fellow Georgian to the shop parking lot where he'd parked an RV he claimed to have purchased for touring the country on the pro circuit. He invited McDaniel inside, displaying boxes upon boxes of sneakers piled high against an inside wall. "He must have had over a dozen pairs all in boxes, and what was weird about it was they weren't all his size," McDaniel remembers. "He said, 'shit, they give 'em to me, I'll get you a pair. I'll get you six pair.'"

Although he never recalled Walden being a tennis player, McDaniel was admittedly impressed, and felt it was only proper to extend cordialities to a former classmate from his hometown. He allowed Walden to keep his RV parked in the dive shop lot for a few days and to use their indoor showers.

He introduced him to a local single woman, and within a short time McDaniel learned that Walden had moved in with her. She called a few days later to say that Walden had stolen her father's handgun and several of her belongings before skipping town. McDaniel immediately reported the theft to the Florida Highway Patrol, who arrested Walden before he made it out of the state.

In retrospect, McDaniel can see how he was so easily rooked. "I've seen two con men in my life that are good, and he's one of them," he said. "He was one of the best. He knew a little bit about a lot of things. He had information about that area of Florida that made him sound like a world traveler."

Between 1973 and 1980, Walden served time in state and federal prisons in Florida, Texas, Georgia, Missouri, and Kansas on auto theft and deception charges. The majority of the cars he stole during this time were obtained from classified ads in local papers. He would appear genuinely interested, talk his way into a test drive, then disappear without giving a name or presenting identification. No sooner was he paroled than he'd commit another crime, as if the thrilling lure of the con sustained him, providing his only means of survival. He used his good looks and charm to beguile naive women and take advantage of Good Samaritans at every small town where he'd appear.

An adept manipulator, even from behind bars, on September 1, 1976, Walden escaped from the Decatur County Work Camp in Bainbridge, Georgia, "with the assistance of females," according to a parole evaluation. He was arrested later that month while in possession of a stolen pickup truck in Grand Junction, Colorado, where local authorities suspected Ted Bundy had abducted and murdered twenty-four-year old Denise Lynn Oliverson in 1975. During his thirty days on the run, Walden stole a total of thirteen vehicles, including eleven automobiles and two motorcycles.

Paroled from a federal sentence for auto theft in late June 1980, Walden met a woman from Atlanta named Beth Roberts. He convinced her to buy him a .357 Magnum and a box of Remington cartridges, and also to hand over her estranged husband's Gulf Oil Company credit card. He proceeded to steal her Honda, leaving her stranded at a local motel.

After fleeing to Chattanooga, Tennessee, Walden dumped the Honda and stole a 1979 Porsche. In July he returned again to Colorado. One day he drove the stolen car to the Clear Creek Realty Office in Georgetown, representing himself as interested in buying real estate in the local area.

Sporting a year-round Florida suntan, Kim Pemberton is president of the Ferrari Club in Naples, Florida. In the early 1970s he was a reserve on coaching legend Bobby Knight's Indiana University basketball team. With his deeply set blue eyes, high cheekbones, and athletic gait, he could pass for Walden's twin brother. When he was in his early thirties, the former Hoosier guard lived and worked in Colorado, speculating that land prices would soar.

"I was in the real estate office one day and had floor duty, when a guy walks in and introduces himself as a writer, looking to buy a place in the mountains," Pemberton said. "We talked for a while, and I remember he said he was from Atlanta, and that he had done some writing for the *Atlanta Constitution*. He told me he was in Denver on business, liked the town, and decided to buy a place in the mountains where he could enjoy his serenity."

Escorted by Pemberton, Walden spent the day viewing numerous properties in the local mountains. Walden said he was interested in one particular home, which he asked to see again the following morning. As the local hotels were booked, Pemberton offered him use of an extra bedroom in his apartment that night. The two, who shared a common interest in sports and literature, had dinner together that evening. When Walden didn't show up for his appointment the following morning, Pemberton thought nothing of it. After all, this was the real estate business, and prospective clients canceling appointments was a common occurrence. A couple of days later, Pemberton's roommate, who had been out of town on business, returned and asked if Pemberton had borrowed his cross-country skis. He had some expensive fly-fishing equipment that had also disappeared. Together they searched the house but couldn't locate the missing items. It suddenly dawned on Pemberton that he'd been had and that Walden had also taken off with his wallet containing his Indiana driver's license. Pemberton immediately notified the Georgetown Police Department, who issued an APB on Walden.

In late July of 1980, while perusing the Reno, Nevada, casinos in the weeks after he'd fled Colorado, Walden became involved with Patricia Benson from Eugene, Oregon. Walden represented himself to be a physician, introducing himself as Dr. Kim Pemberton. After Benson returned to Oregon three days later, Walden called to say he would be driving out to Oregon for a visit.

Soon after his arrival, they planned a wedding in Reno. Suspicious of this too-good-to-be-true interloper, a close friend of the betrothed attempted to verify Dr. Pemberton's credentials, along with his claim that he owned real estate in Texas. She phoned the Oregon State Police on the same day Walden drove into town, providing them the Tennessee plate number to the Porsche. A check of the tag revealed that it had been stolen.

The Oregon State Police arrested Walden later that day outside the apartment complex where his fiancée lived. Pemberton's Indiana driver's license was among the items in the fugitive's possession. He also held a stolen gas card and a gun registered to the Roberts from Atlanta. Curiously, police also discovered a prescription bottle filled with phenobarbital, a commonly used anti-convulsive medication Walden said he'd obtained from a hitchhiker.

In October, Walden began a five-year sentence at the Oregon State Penitentiary, where he submitted to a psychometric evaluation known as an Otis Mental Ability test. He scored a 127, placing his intellectual functioning in the "very superior range." He was paroled in November 1984.

Walden escaped from an unsupervised paint crew on May 10, 1984, while on a three-day furlough from the Bledsoe County Regional Corrections Center in Pikeville, Tennessee, where he was serving a six-year sentence for grand larceny. He was picked up by a friend who drove him to Graysville, Tennessee. After stealing his buddy's car, he drove to Mount Pleasant, South Carolina, where he planned to solicit the assistance of friends. However, he was forced to pull off the highway and park at a motel in Summerville, South Carolina, when he ran out of gas.

Between 4:30 and 5 p.m. the following afternoon, Walden sauntered into a real estate office in Summerville, ostensibly to be shown a nearby plot of farmland for sale. He met a local agent, George W. Wells, who brought him to look at some properties west of town. When they arrived at the listed address, Walden aimed a .38 caliber handgun at Wells, demanding his wallet. A struggle ensued. The young man from Cairo, once a promising scholar athlete, and who until this point had been able to rely on guile and persuasion to serve his means, shot the unsuspecting realtor point blank in the back of the head. Walden made off with Wells' car and wallet, as well as his jewelry, credit cards, and blank checks. He dumped the body a quarter mile north from the murder scene, in a wooded area approximately eighty feet from Highway 61, just north of the historic Mateeba Gardens plantation. The victim was discovered the following day by a local property owner. Soon thereafter, his blood-spattered car turned up in a mall parking lot.

A nationwide hunt for Walden began after the friend's car he'd stolen in Tennessee was discovered in the Summerville, South Carolina, motel parking lot where Walden had abandoned it. Warrants were issued charging him with murder, armed robbery, and grand larceny of an automobile. After successfully eluding authorities, then heading west to hide out in his beloved Western mountain ranges, Walden must've thought he'd outwitted his pursuers once again. During this time he is believed to have traveled through Pocatello, Idaho, where he met a woman and robbed her of her jewelry in the same town where Ted Bundy is thought to have abducted and murdered twelve-year-old Lynette Culver in May 1975. But a few weeks after his getaway, a Missoula, Montana, deputy sheriff transporting a prisoner back to Jackson Hole, Wyoming, spotted a stolen 1984 Ford Bronco II pulling away from a restaurant. A foot chase ensued after Walden stopped the car, jumped out, and dashed into a local shopping mall. His speed was no match for a police K-9, who sunk his fangs into the thigh of the fleeing prisoner mid-stride.

Walden waived extradition and was escorted back to South Carolina by Dorchester County authorities. On November 19, 1984, he was sentenced to life in prison for the murder of George Wells. "George Wells had no defense counsel, no judge, no jury," said 1st Circuit Solicitor Joseph Mizzell in his closing arguments. "He was murdered in cold blood."

The same day, Walden entered the Central Correctional Institution (CCI) in Columbia, South Carolina, the first of three penal institutions where he would serve out his sentence. What credit for good behavior Walden earned during his confinement at CCI he promptly squandered in 1986, upon transferring to Kirkland Correctional Institution on the outskirts of Columbia. On October 6, 1987, he stole over $1,000 worth of inventory before staging a break-in to cover up his theft. Consequently, he was placed on a two-hundred-ten day lock up. Sometime after this incident, Walden was transferred again, this time to the McCormick Correctional Institution near the Georgia border. For a person of high intellectual ability, but "manipulative," according to a psychological exam administered at the facility, by now Walden must have grown claustrophobic with the mundane futility of prison life, needing to steal as a means to escape boredom and inject a surge of excitement into his humdrum everyday existence. In June 1988, he conned corrections officials into advancing him two hundred dollars, ostensibly to buy a gun. "Walden came to us and said he heard there was a pistol in the prison that could be bought for two hundred dollars," South Carolina Corrections spokesman Frances Archibald confirmed.

Warden R.S. Lindler authorized the purchase, telling a local reporter, "It's worth two hundred dollars to us to get a gun out of prison."

When Walden didn't make good on his promise to deliver the weapon, he was ordered to return the two hundred dollars advanced to him. The money, however, was gone. "Walden was shaken down completely," said Archibald. "All his body cavities were examined. The entire institution was shaken down, and everybody's personal property." Walden was placed in solitary confinement and lost ninety days good-behavior credit. Prison officials searched up and down the entire facility but couldn't find the pistol. They concluded that Walden had used the two hundred dollars to pay debts, conceding they'd been tricked.

Walden was forty-two-years old on August 9, 1989, a middle-aged convict wearied by institutional bureaucracy. As he rose from his bunk that morning, he must've considered that he would never get out of prison alive. He was in for good this time, at a maximum-security facility, his chances in life behind him, the dream of freedom a meaningless and useless excursion. Incapable of thriving within the confines of the penal system where he was unable to manipulate his way out of a jam, and likely reconciled to his fate, he attained his moment of reckoning that afternoon while inside the prison furniture-making workshop. He brought with him a .25 caliber automatic that he'd kept hidden in a hollowed-out portable radio in his cell. Whether he purchased this gun with the money earlier given to him is uncertain, yet officials stated for the record that he'd smuggled the weapon into prison.

For twelve tense hours, a deliriously manic Walden held shop supervisor Foster S. Robinson and a fellow inmate hostage. After releasing them, he turned the gun on himself. Getting nowhere with negotiations, prison officials permitted Walden to phone his brother Roy at 10 p.m. Wednesday in a futile attempt to defuse his younger brother.

"I asked point-blank, how'd you get the gun?" Roy Walden told the *Augusta (Ga.) Chronicle* the following day. "He just kind of laughed and said, 'To be honest with you, the warden bought it for me.' I said, 'What do you mean?' He said the warden gave him the money."

This was the first time Roy had heard from his younger brother since their father died two years earlier. "He sounded awfully hyper" during their ten-minute conversation, he said. "He was talking just like a man cornered. A lot of things he said didn't make sense, and a lot of things did. He kept reiterating that things were going on that people ought to know about. I told him this was not the way to get it out. He talked about injustices."

Walden was enraged by his forthcoming transfer to Perry Correctional Institution near Greenville, South Carolina, which would be the fourth move since his 1984 conviction. He was further angered by racial tensions in the prison, telling his brother, "black inmates have more control than the guards."

"He said when he first arrived here, he was attacked by some blacks, and nothing was done about it," Roy said. "He thought his life was endangered when he first arrived and had been since he arrived there."

Approximately one hour after they spoke, Thomas "Ronnie" Walden aimed the pistol toward his own head. Whatever secrets he held regarding the parkway slayings were silenced by the bullet he fired through his skull. He rests under an unadorned marble slab beneath the tall Georgia pines at Hawthorne Cemetery in Cairo, a small graveyard set between a cornfield and a cow pasture along Tired Creek Road.

Walden's son is a successful sales executive in the Atlanta area. He is a graduate of the University of Georgia, and the father of a boy of his own. Memories of his dad are few. A prison visit here and there, but for the most part he had little contact with Walden, speaking with him maybe a dozen times before losing touch. "I would see him once a year. He was less like a father, more like a weird uncle," he said. He'd never heard that his father was a violent person, and his discussions with his dad's old friends left him with the impression that he was well liked. His mother never shared much about her son's father. Upon learning that Walden was a suspect in a double murder nearly forty years ago, his son offered, "That just doesn't sound like the person I knew. I would tell you if that fit the bill. My father was not maniacal or a cold-blooded killer."

Walden's former wife is just as adamant of his innocence in the murders of Davis and Perry. "I had heard about these murders, but I never got the idea from him that he had done this," Hope Walden said. "Ronnie was a thief, a con man, but he didn't murder people to get their possessions....I am a pillar of doing the right thing, and how I got involved with him, there's no telling. I was naive, dumb. I was an educated woman, a schoolteacher for forty years. I never thought he killed those girls. I have no proof of that, but that's just my gut feeling. That's not him." She followed, "I never saw any anger in him, and believe me, I pushed him to the limit. Rage wasn't one of his emotions."

When apprised of Walden's connection to the parkway slayings, Cathy Moore said, "I always figured he'd left a string of murders. Ronnie could kill somebody without batting an eye-too cool to be true when he wanted to be. I'd put nothing past him, and I've been saying that my whole life."

"I remember my first response was, 'Good,' said Saress Moye, upon learning Walden had shot himself. "I would wish harm on nobody, I'm a kind person, but I felt this world had been ridden of an evil force."

Francene Latkin remains the only person to positively identify Walden's watch as the same found near the slain corpses of Susan Davis and Elizabeth Perry. Her notes corroborate her memories. She also remembered that the watch she saw Walden wearing, which he said was a model used by skin divers, and which was found without a band in the parkway woods, had been attached to a leather band. As opposed to conventional watchbands, which are secured to the watch by a pair of metal pins, several of these fashionable "Mod bands" from the 1960s were actually leather cuff bracelets where the watch face attached to the bracelet itself by a metal snap that could have easily popped off Walden's wrist as he struggled to subdue Davis and Perry. That Latkin noticed a dive suit at Walden's Fort Lauderdale home, and he pawned his scuba gear at a local dive shop several years later, suggests his affinity for the sport. Contrary to what his family believes, Walden shot an innocent man in the back of the head in what appeared to an execution-style, cold-blooded murder. He dumped the body in the woods off a rural road, similar to how Susan and Elizabeth were found. Marjorie Garwood had ridden on the back seat of Walden's stolen motorcycle, and his tire tracks were purportedly found along the parkway shoulder. His prison record and tenure in a mental facility reflects an unbalanced sociopath adept at escaping. Equally compelling is his suicide attempt at the Glenwood Springs, Colorado, jail. Was it a mere coincidence that this incident occurred within hours before the arrival of two New Jersey detectives prepared to administer a lie-detector test? However, the stolen yellow Oldsmobile that Walden had driven to and from South Jersey from Florida was an entirely different make and model than the dark Pontiac witnesses had seen parked in front of Susan's blue convertible. And if one subscribes to the theory that a hitchhiker murdered both girls, why would Walden thumb a ride at the Somers Point traffic circle when he had his own transportation? And why wouldn't the seasoned thief go ahead and steal the valuable heirlooms that Elizabeth was wearing?

While it is commonly known that Davis and Perry were last seen alive at the Somers Point Diner, the newspapers never reported that they had also visited the diner on Tuesday afternoon, May 27, just before crossing the bridge into Ocean City and checking into their Ninth Street boardinghouse. Bette Filling, a former waitress at the diner, still lives in the Somers Point area. She remembers talking to Susan and Elizabeth, for they were the first customers to be seated in her section of the restaurant when it opened at 11 a.m. "They were in the diner for maybe 40 or 45 minutes," she said. "Fran Brewin and I were setting up the dining room, talking to them, laughing. They were really nice girls, and they were so excited, so happy and jolly. They were just so excited about getting into Ocean City, they could not wait until they got in the ocean." She remembers the last words she spoke to them: "I said, 'take a dip for me. Have a nice time but be careful.'"

Filling never called the police to mention what at the time she figured was an incidental detail, something that has always bothered her since. About a week after the murders, after a passable calm had returned to the shore area, she was working behind the pastry counter at the diner one day when she noticed something unusual about the young man seated in the swivel chair at the end of the counter. "He was blonde, about twenty-two. Nice looking," she said. The young man sat quietly over his meal, saying nothing. His face was laced with red cuts and scratches, as if he'd fought off an attacker. Normally such a person wouldn't have provoked a second thought, but after he upped and left, Filling wondered whether his wounds were actually fingernail scratches, and if he was Susan and Elizabeth's murderer. Could the young man have been Ronnie Walden?

As for Walden's guilt in the murders, Francene Latkin said, "I never felt that strongly about something in my entire life. I haven't wavered. I want the case to be solved."

CHAPTER TEN

The Coed Killer

On the same day that Charles Manson was holed up at Spahn Ranch in California, busily delegating responsibilities for the final stages of his Hollywood Hills massacre, three thousand miles away Ray Perry and Wesley Davis Sr. stood before a large gathering assembled in front of a brick wall outside the Absecon state police barracks. The crowd, comprised mostly of reporters and cameramen, stood patiently within the tropical-like swelter. It was the afternoon of August 8, 1969, and the glaring blaze thudded mercilessly on their sweat-dampened hat brims as they eagerly awaited to hear what the fathers had traveled all this way to tell them, and to learn what authorities had earlier promised would be the release of information "of great interest" that would "disclose a breakthrough" in the case.

Raymond Potter Perry Jr., like Davis a gentleman of regal bearing, was attired in a rep-striped bowtie, button down oxford, and dark sport coat. With his bushy eyebrows arched tensely above the rims of his reading glasses, the former WWII army captain approached the podium. He proclaimed that $20,000 would be rewarded for information leading to the arrest and conviction of Elizabeth and Susan's murderer. The offer was being made "in support of the work which has been done and is continuing on the part of the authorities," he said, "and in no event should be interpreted as indicating lack of confidence in them." Reading from a prepared statement, he continued: "An immense amount of work by authorities has turned up considerable evidence but so far not a sufficient amount to produce an arrest. There are strong indications that all who passed the girls' car on the parkway in the early morning hours of May 30 have not come forward. We should like to hope that these additional people have failed to come forward simply through lack of realization that occurrences they observed, even if briefly, could be of major significance—the missing link in the chain, so to speak."

Perry said that the toll collectors' reports of traffic volume through the Somers Point interchange early Memorial Day reflected that many travelers who might have seen something on or near milepost 31.9 hadn't volunteered their tips to police. Though it was Perry's idea to offer the bounty, both fathers would ante up $5,000 each, with the remaining $10,000 underwritten by Perry's employer. The offer, which Perry promised to keep open for one year, was motivated in part by a "desire to avenge the brutal slaying of our daughters, and by the importance of removing the murderer from circulation to prevent their striking again," he said. Like Detective Saunders, Elizabeth's father appealed to the public's sense of fear. "To each person reached by this appeal, we pose this question: Might you, or one of your loved ones, otherwise be the next victims?"

Lt. Brennan walked to the dais next, distributing copies of a sketch composed by state police artist George Homa. Brennan described the subject as "a white male, in his late teens, slender build, medium brown hair, which was curly and hung down over his forehead." He was seen wearing a white t-shirt, allegedly spotted by two witnesses on the parkway near Susan's convertible approximately two hours after she was murdered. Brennan said that the sketch was prepared on July 23, but wasn't released until this press conference "because we had to check it." Although these two witnesses had offered the description to police several weeks earlier, Brennan said his detectives didn't immediately follow up with them because they were more interested in locating people who'd driven past the convertible nearer the time of the murders. "We're not sure this is the murderer, and I wouldn't call him a prime suspect," said Brennan. "We want to know what he was doing around the car."

Brennan announced that he had a twenty-man team still working on the investigation, a statement whose true meaning was lost in the glare of Perry's reward announcement. That over thirty detectives and troopers were initially assigned to work the case full time, and ten had since been reassigned elsewhere, indicates that the police recognized an increasing likelihood that the case wouldn't be solved. They could no longer afford to devote their full resources toward a two-month old murder probe which to date had produced little physical evidence, few witnesses, and just two suspects Mark Thomas and Ronnie Walden. Brennan and his team didn't need to search long for a third, as another person of interest quickly emerged in their crosshairs, himself the focus of another high-publicity series of murders competing for national attention during the early summer of 1969.

In conjunction with local authorities in the neighboring cities of Ann Arbor and Ypsilanti, the Michigan State Police were investigating a string of grisly murders befuddling their police departments as much as the parkway murders confounded state police in New Jersey. Immediately after news of the Jersey Shore slayings was picked up by national wire services, police detectives in Ann Arbor, Michigan, took note of some striking similarities between the slayings in both states. On June 3, the day after Perry and Davis were found in the woods, Det. Captain Harold Olson of the Ann Arbor Police Department told the *Philadelphia Inquirer*, "We will be contacting the authorities in New Jersey in an effort to ascertain if there is a possibility of any connection between those girls and ours."

Beginning in the summer of 1967, Michigan authorities realized they had a maniacal killer on their hands. The badly decomposed body of Mary Fleszar, a nineteen-year-old accounting student enrolled at Eastern Michigan University, was discovered on August 7, 1967. She'd been stabbed multiple times in the chest, and her fingers had been sliced off. Detectives with the Ypsilanti Police Department theorized that she'd been raped but couldn't be certain due to the condition of her mutilated corpse, found by two boys within a patch of tall weeds approximately three tenths of a mile in from the road, adjacent to a deserted farmhouse. Her autopsy revealed thirty lacerations to the face and abdomen. Twenty of the punctures were made by a knife or other sharp weapon. No murder weapon was found in the vicinity. The abrasions on her chest revealed that in addition to being stabbed, Fleszar had likely been beaten.

Nearly a year later, twenty-year-old Joan Schell, also a student at Eastern Michigan, disappeared from in front of the University's student union on the night of June 30, 1968. Her body was discovered a week later by construction workers in a section of weeds and high grass along the shoulder of a road in a sparsely inhabited section of Ann Arbor, just four miles from where Fleszar had been found. Schell had been stabbed five times and her throat was slashed. She'd been sexually assaulted, her blue mini skirt wrapped around her neck along with her undergarments. The autopsy revealed twenty-five total stab wounds to her torso; twenty-two in the front, and three in her back. The murder weapon was believed to be a small knife with a blade no more than four inches long. Said Lt. Eugene Staudenmaier of the Ann Arbor Police Department, "This is the second case we've had like this in about a year, and there is a strange similarity between the two."

A third, similarly wounded victim was discovered in late March 1969. Maralynn Skelton, sixteen, was found brutally murdered at the bottom of a sloping section of dense wet brush behind an unfinished subdivision in Ann Arbor, only a quarter mile from where Joan Schell had been discovered the previous summer. She had been "beaten unmercifully about the face," according to Ann Arbor Police Chief Walter Krasny. A garter belt was twisted around her neck. Her clothes, consisting of a blue t-shirt, faded hip-hugger dungarees, and a dark-blue, zippered windbreaker, were piled nearby. No undergarments were found, and her torso was lacerated with welts.

News of the "Michigan murders" or "Coed murders," as they were now known, had begun to attract national attention, grabbing headlines across campuses and striking fear in the minds of young women in the Midwest. The "Ypsilanti Ripper," as the tabloids referred to him, was on the loose. In Michigan, local colleges adopted a buddy system whereby women would not leave their dorms at night unless escorted by fellow classmates. They dared not step outside their apartments after the sun went down, and left their porch lights on through the night. "We're not talking about the creature from the Black Lagoon," one Eastern Michigan coed told *Time* magazine. "We're talking about a smooth guy—or guys—who can pick up girls, take them somewhere and kill them."

Next to be butchered was thirteen-year-old Dawn Basom, discovered on April 16, 1969, in Ypsilanti. She was found nude, strangled with an electrical cord and slashed with a knife across her chest and buttocks.

The body of another slain coed, Alice Kalom, was discovered near Ann Arbor on June 9, just six days after Olson's announcement of his plan to investigate a New Jersey connection, and eight days following the murders of Davis and Perry. Kalom, whose body was found near an abandoned barn, had been shot, stabbed twice in the chest, and sexually assaulted.

The last of the Michigan murders was committed on July 23, 1969, when eighteen-year-old Karen Sue Beineman was discovered strangled, nude, and beaten to death in a wooden gully near Riverside Drive in Ann Arbor Township. Ypsilanti Police Department detective Bill Henning, who doubled as a sketch artist, drew a composite of the young man who witnesses had seen giving Beineman a ride on a motorcycle the day she disappeared. Two women recalled seeing her with a "good-looking" and "clean-cut" young male with dark, short-trimmed hair that "fell down over his forehead, sort of casual." They couldn't agree whether the style was straight or curly, so they settled upon "wavy." The features they remembered bore a near match to the composite given by the witnesses who were driving past mile marker 31.9 two hours after the murders along the Garden State Parkway and were nearly identical to the young man described by Lt. Brennan at the August 8 press conference in Absecon.

Ann Arbor Police Department and Washtenaw County Sheriff's Office detectives admitted that the method of murder in the New Jersey cases shared "remarkable similarities" with the Michigan slayings. Much the same weapons—knives with short narrow blades—had been used to murder the victims in New Jersey and Michigan. Each had been stabbed multiple times in the torso and neck area. All the women showed signs they'd been severely beaten. They were between the ages of thirteen and twenty-three, Caucasian, and found nude or partially nude. Each corpse was discovered in a semi-rural area, hidden in the weeds near roadways. In three of the Michigan murders, the killer had tied an article of clothing around his subject's neck, similar to the crime scene in Somers Point. In several instances, the Michigan victims wore blue—the same color outfit Susan Davis was wearing when she was found murdered.

Investigators from both states had located the victims' clothing piled nearby their bodies.

On July 31, 1969, Michigan authorities arrested John Norman Collins, a dark-haired, twenty-two-year-old Eastern Michigan University English major, described by Michigan State Police Sergeant Ken Christensen as "a very handsome, clean-cut, attractive young man who seems to have a magnetic effect on young girls." The former standout defensive end and star pitcher from Center Line, a Detroit suburb, had also been an honors student in high school, similar to Ronnie Walden.

Former Buffalo Bills guard Joe DeLamielleure, a member of the NFL Hall of Fame, was Collins' teammate at St. Clement High School. "He was a great player," DeLamielleure recalled. "He was number 27. I still remember that—that's how good of a player he was."

"John is the second most famous athlete to come through St. Clement behind DeLamielleure," said former St. Clement Athletic Director Victor Michaels.

"John was a hard worker; we never expected anything like this to happen," said his former coach, Al Baumgart. "He had all the ingredients: he was good looking, brilliant, and a nice kid."

But the square-jawed former jock held secret his troubled upbringing. His natural father abandoned him and his mother remarried an abusive alcoholic, divorcing him when Collins was four. His afflictions surfaced soon after his enrollment in college. A member of the Theta Chi house at Eastern Michigan, Collins was booted from his fraternity after he was caught stealing from his brothers, and inexplicably dropped out of classes just twenty-four credits shy of graduation. By the time police caught up with Collins, he was living in a Ypsilanti rooming house with Andrew Manuel and Arnold Smith, two other young men with whom he'd allegedly been stealing cars and burglarizing local homes.

In the month prior to Collins' arrest, Manuel, a linebacker-sized Filipino-American with short-cropped black hair and a swarthy complexion, had made a cross-country excursion with Collins to Salinas, California, in a seventeen-foot cargo trailer Manuel rented in Ypsilanti but never returned. Once in Salinas, he and Collins parked the trailer in the backyard of a home owned by Manuel's grandfather. Soon, police in California were able to connect Collins to the murder of a local woman, Roxie Ann Phillips, when her blood was found in the stolen trailer. Eventually, rental receipts connected Manuel to the trailer. "My personal belief is that Collins did not act alone," said Washtenaw (Mich.) County Sheriff Douglas Harvey. "We hope there will be additional arrests very soon. The pieces in the puzzle seem to be fitting together."

HUNT FOR FUGITIVE: FBI Joins Search in 10 Girls' Murders, the August 5, 1969, *Los Angeles Times* headline read. Manuel, who was now in Arizona, quickly turned himself in. His arrest was reported on the August 6 *ABC Evening News* by co-anchor Howard K. Smith. With his olive-colored skin and jet-black hair, his features were also strikingly similar to the young man in the New Jersey police sketch.

The Wednesday, August 6 edition of the *Owosso (MI) Argus-Press* reported that "the Atlantic County (NJ) prosecutor has scheduled a news conference 'of major importance' today on the Memorial Day murders of two 19-year-old coeds near Somers Point, N.J." The article indicated that two detectives had been sent to Michigan to investigate any connection between the murders in both states. The purpose of their trip, according the Michigan official, was "in effect to put the pieces of the two jigsaw puzzles side-by-side to see if they really are one big jigsaw puzzle."

As the August 9 press conference in Absecon neared a close, Lt. Brennan confirmed that he'd dispatched detectives John Saunders (brother of Detective Robert Saunders) and William J. Hunter to Michigan to work with their state police "to ascertain any connection with their series of murders and this investigation," he said. Brennan was cagey at times as he spoke. When asked whether there was "good reason" to believe that the man in the sketch was involved in both the Michigan and Garden State Parkway murders, he unequivocally answered "yes." However, the customarily dismissive Brennan cautioned reporters "There is no reason to connect or disconnect this case with the murders in Michigan."

"This is more or less standard procedure in investigations of this type," Brennan explained, as if to moderate his audience's enthusiasm. "We have no new developments or hot leads. However, Michigan Police have not been able to pinpoint the whereabouts of Collins during Memorial Day weekend, and we want to explore that." Despite the temperance of Brennan minimizing any nexus with the shore murders, he admitted that even before he'd decided to send Hunter and Saunders to Michigan, his men had been in constant communication with the Michigan State Police, who'd been granted sole jurisdiction over the murders by Governor Milliken in the days before Collins' arrest. As reported by E.J. Hussie of the *Inquirer*, a New Jersey State Police source confirmed that they'd held several lengthy telephone conversations on an almost daily basis with Michigan State Police investigators, cryptically adding, "We have done things for them, and they have done things for us."

Brennan further stated that there was a possibility that members of his investigative team might travel to Phoenix to interview Andrew Manuel "if they find something of interest in Michigan," and that his detectives had taken a composite sketch of the parkway suspect with them to Michigan.

"A vicious killer or killers are roaming the streets and highways," Brennan said as he wrapped up the Friday press conference. "The next victim may be someone you love, someone you love as dearly as Mr. Perry and Mr. Davis and their families loved their daughters." Brennan also announced that the New Jersey State Police were interested in speaking with the driver of a black Cadillac who'd picked up a hitchhiker near the murder scene and drove him to Hammonton. The *Ocean City Sentinel-Ledger* had reported that on Friday, May 30, the owner of a late model black Cadillac sedan had "stopped on Ninth Street and gave a ride to a white hitchhiker. He drove the hitchhiker as far as he was going-to the neighborhood of Hammonton, where the driver may have business interests or friends." The article requested readers with information to contact either the state police or Ocean City Police Chief Benjamin L. Dugan. The *Sentinel-Ledger* article didn't mention, and reporters didn't catch, the apparent connection: since the *Inquirer* earlier reported that the eighteen-year-old suspect had received his first ride while hitchhiking from Ocean City to Blackwood, and since Blackwood is near Hammonton, is it reasonable to infer that suspect Mark Thomas had told police he'd received a ride from a man driving a black Cadillac?

"We in law enforcement believe that many people live under the motto or code of arms that says, 'Don't get involved,'" Brennan said. "We are asking you to get involved."

Whether because of the sudden financial incentive, the release of the composite sketch, or Ray Perry's urgent appeal, on Monday, August 11, the New Jersey State Police reported a spike in calls to their murder hotline. They began interviewing the more witnesses who telephoned the Absecon barracks in response to the publication of a "sharp-chinned youth," as one newspaper now described the dark-haired stranger malingering on the parkway aside Davis' convertible two hours after the murders.

A day earlier, detectives Hunter and Saunders had returned to New Jersey from Ann Arbor. After three days of consultations with Michigan authorities, they told newspapers that they'd failed to find any concrete evidence linking Collins to the murders of Perry and Davis. Collins, however, refused to speak with either detective, for he had retained an attorney, and to this day his whereabouts during Memorial Day weekend are unknown. Eastern Michigan University officials told the *Philadelphia Inquirer* there was no way to check Collins' whereabouts through his school records. The university confirmed that Collins had attended classes that ended in mid-June, but added, "It's not like high school—we don't keep attendance records here."

However, on August 12, in response to a question asked by a reporter for the *Courier (NJ) Post* whether it was possible Collins might have been in New Jersey over the Memorial Day weekend, Detective Robert Saunders said, "I don't want to go into detail on anything regarding Collins. I don't want to supply information that would jeopardize the case for Michigan authorities." He further stated, "We are leaving the door open for a possible link."

It is plausible that Collins might have road tripped East and drawn his knife against Davis and Perry after luring them into the woods. Like Ronnie Walden, he was a good-looking and charismatic, clean-cut jock, just the sort of young man who under the right circumstances might inspire trust in the heart of a pair of young college women kind enough to offer the handsome stranger a lift. His killings weren't confined to a specific geographic location, as evidenced by his alleged murder of Roxie Ann Phillips in Salinas. Interestingly, he never spoke to New Jersey police detectives. What would be his reason for withholding his cooperation and not speaking with either Hunter or Saunders, if he had nothing to hide?

Andrew Manuel, Collins' burglary accomplice, was contacted at his apartment in a dusty southern California town. A self-described "hermit in the desert," he passes most days watching television. Failing kidneys and old age have ravaged his body. He lost a leg to diabetes a few years ago when his limbs were infected with gangrene, and he subsists on government disability checks instead of peddling his wares at local flea markets or panning for gold in the nearby rivers, as how he once earned his living. Manuel was never implicated in any of Collins' murders, and insists the pair never traveled to New Jersey together, let alone murdered any women along its scenic coast. "I was never in New Jersey," he said. "I know the police gave me a lot of polygraph tests, and I passed them all. They gave me truth serum and did hypnosis. I don't recall them asking me about New Jersey." His trip west with Collins was spent mostly robbing houses. Five hundred in total, he recalls, between Michigan and California. Collins was a "happy-go-lucky guy," he recalled, and never gave him any indication of being a person capable of brutally murdering multiple young women.

On August 19, 1970, a Michigan jury of six men and six women found John Norman Collins guilty of the murder of Karen Sue Beineman. Consequently, the New Jersey State Police announced they were temporarily dropping the line of inquiry involving Collins, likely losing interest in him as a possible suspect when he was sentenced to life in prison and no longer a threat to society. He is serving his remaining years at the Marquette Branch Prison, a maximum-security facility on the blustery shores of Lake Superior. A book by Edward Keyes, *The Michigan Murders*, was published in 1976. A major motion picture began filming scenes in Ann Arbor a year later but was never completed. As of this date, the New Jersey State Police have never publicly stated whether John Norman Collins has been officially eliminated as a suspect in the parkway slayings.

CHAPTER ELEVEN

Surveillance

After announcing they were discontinuing their pursuit of John Norman Collins, the New Jersey State Police and Atlantic County Prosecutor's Office revealed scant information to the press, other than reissuing the Absecon barracks hotline number and reiterating their pleas for help from the public. Quickly wearying of these stale offerings, toward the end of August 1969 summer local beat reporters filled the lull with a plethora of sensational competing headlines as autumn neared. There was the surreal drama unfolding at the Manson murder trial in Los Angeles, followed in short order by the U.S. Army's decision to bring murder charges against Lt. William Calley for his role in spearheading the My Lai Massacre. Barreling northward, Hurricane Camille deluged the Appalachian foothills and Shenandoah River in Virginia with soaking rains, lifting homes from their foundations, ferrying toppled trees, corpses, and drowned cattle atop its swiftly rising floodwaters. The carnage invoked fervent hope among Ocean City residents that the remnant winds would swerve out to sea or turn a path elsewhere as the rains weakened overland. Wishes for the capture of Susan and Elizabeth's murderer fell alongside prayers that God might spare the barrier island a similar devastation wrought by the Ash Wednesday Storm of 1962.

Similar to how he'd coordinated with Michigan and Colorado authorities, Lt. Brennan dispatched teams of detectives to visit with law enforcement officials in other states where there had been similar crime scenes, exploring the possibility that those knifings were perpetrated by the same assailant or somehow connected to the double homicide in Egg Harbor Township. There was no shortage of destinations, as the rash of lurid slayings in other jurisdictions didn't subside upon Collins' arrest and imprisonment.

The murders outside Somers Point were but two of several brutal murders that year involving young female victims, with coeds, hitchhikers, and prostitutes systematically abducted, raped, and killed in alarming numbers across the country. In an articled titled "The Bloody Statistics of Murder...." the *Philadelphia Daily News* recognized the Perry and Davis murders as part of a series of baffling unsolved sex crimes afflicting police departments everywhere.

In northern California, a hooded killer calling himself the Zodiac was leaving a trail of bodies in the San Francisco Bay area, taunting *San Francisco Chronicle* readers with intriguing puzzles, cryptograms to uncode, and bloody artifacts mailed to the editorial staff. Kansas City, Missouri, police continued their investigation into the April 30, 1969, murders of roommates Barbara Ann Loughlin and Mary Ann Adler, gashed a total of thirty-eight times at their duplex apartment. Joyce Malecki was found in a creek on an army base in Maryland, stabbed in the throat and strangled, her hands tied behind her back. *Multiple Sex Murders Have Terrorized Five States*, an August 6, 1969, UPI byline read, identifying the inexplicable rash of killings in 1969 as part of larger pattern that began with the Boston Strangler in 1962.

Communicating via phone and teletype from Absecon, the New Jersey State Police exchanged file notes and reports with distant precincts, soon learning that the problems they faced—rampant drug usage, the transient weekend crowd, a convergence of out-of-towners, throngs of teenagers and hippies by the thousands—were not confined to the Jersey Shore.

Although he'd ordered his detectives to confer with police departments as far away as Arizona, back in Atlantic County, Lt. Brennan never lost interest in Mark Thomas. Despite an earlier press briefing where he announced that the state police had no further plans to resume questioning the beguiling teen, Brennan had his team continue to track him. Thomas's carefree attitude seemed at odds with the results of his lie detector tests, befuddling the lieutenant. Was he a legitimate suspect, or truly innocent? Did he relish the notoriety accompanying all the attention, or was he emboldened by the cloak of anonymity offered by the newspapers still withholding his name? Although detectives hadn't found any physical evidence to pin the murders on Thomas or to locate a witness who placed him at the scene, his uneven polygraph charts deemed him worthy of further investigation.

In the days following Thomas's release from the Berlin, New Jersey, state police barracks two months earlier, Brennan covertly deployed a cadre of his best men to Montgomery County, Pennsylvania, with instructions to shadow Thomas and scout the haunts he frequented. The lieutenant's strategy made sense, for if Thomas had allegedly been overheard in a Philadelphia store bragging he was in Ocean City at the time of the murders, and he'd met the victims on the boardwalk, wouldn't it logically follow that he might confide his involvement to his closest friends?

Among those who crossed the bridge into Pennsylvania were Detectives Kreps, Dix, Burns, Patterson, Warner, Barnes, and Hart. They abruptly dropped their assignments in Absecon and checked into a local motel in Blue Bell, a suburb of Norristown near where Thomas's parents lived. Because they were working so feverishly at the barracks and instructed to leave New Jersey at a moment's notice, several of their wives phoned division headquarters when their husbands didn't return home after their shifts ended that evening, fearful something terrible had befallen them in the course of their duties. With so swift a departure, the detectives didn't pack a change of clothes, and several had to buy underwear and toothbrushes upon encamping across the Delaware River.

For several long days in early June they worked ceaselessly to gather information tying Thomas to the murders while their lead was hot. Their fieldwork uncovered that he frequented the Plymouth Meeting Mall in Pennsylvania, consorting with a dastardly assortment of hippies who were around his age. Dix spent several days interviewing and giving lie detector tests to several of Thomas's buddies to learn if he'd confessed to the slayings or boasted of having knowledge of them as he'd so brazenly done in Philadelphia. Dix saw Thomas's cohorts listlessly idling among the shrubbery in front of the mall, where they purportedly sold marijuana. "They were hippies and God knows what else they were doing," he said, recalling how they'd befoul his makeshift interrogation room with their stench, often strolling in with scraggly unkempt hair and grimy bare feet.

While in Thomas's neighborhood, New Jersey detectives made several visits to the Whitpain Township Police Department, meeting on several occasions with Sergeant Joseph Stemple, Detective William R. Pistilli, Corporal Peter Vennera, and Chief Earl Kelly. "Mark was one of our favorite sons," Stemple says wryly, recalling the mischievous youth as a neighborhood prankster who'd already had several brushes with the local police department prior to Memorial Day 1969.

Vennera, the department's head juvenile officer, had already cited Thomas for numerous offenses before his eighteenth birthday. In one such incident, he had hacked down several live trees that he earlier planted alongside the driveway entrance to the Cedarbrook Country Club, where he worked for a time in his teens. There was something more disturbing about this spiteful prank, however, which caused Stemple to recall it so vividly in comparison to Thomas's other petty nuisances. When he and Vennera paid a visit to his parents' house on Thayer Drive, they found among his belongings the machete he'd used to fell the trees. The boy's room was adorned with Swastika flags and other racist paraphernalia in tribute to the Fuhrer. They discovered and confiscated the weapon Thomas had used for his revenge on his former employer, and he admitted his guilt without incident.

Made aware of Thomas's racist leanings, the New Jersey State Police enlisted the aid of their Narcotics Division. Detective Ronald J. Perozzi Jr., an undercover detective within that department in the late Sixties and early Seventies, had enjoyed previous success undercover collaring outlaw biker gang members and making covert drug buys. One of his division superiors, likely Lt. Charles "Chick" Croce, handed him a recent photo of Thomas, along with a calling card from the Invisible Empire Knights of the Ku Klux Klan that had been discovered among his possessions. The size of a business card, its writing was replete with the Klan's insignia, the Blood Drop Cross, known as the fringe group's "Imperial Seal." Next to the red and black markings was printed in bold red letters, *YOU HAVE BEEN PATRONIZED BY THE KKK.* Perozzi received instructions to infiltrate the Norristown area and seek any affiliation between Thomas and the Pennsylvania Klan, hoping to track down an enemy or two eager to spill information not protected by secretive oaths. He was to get as close as he could to Thomas without provoking him or blowing his cover. "My orders were to go and see what I could find out," he said. "They would always give me a tough case when they were having trouble getting information on a guy. I would always be able to bullshit my way into the group." The young detective, who wore fashionably long hair and a scraggly mustache while perusing the inner circles of the crime underworld in his sports car, traveled to various local venues where Thomas and his friends had been known to gather, including a record store where he worked. Though he spent several days lurking in corner lounges and eavesdropping on conversations, Perozzi was unable to infiltrate Thomas's circle of friends or establish contact with anybody purporting to have overheard him speaking about the parkway murders.

Detectives Dix and Kreps also learned that Thomas was allegedly under psychiatric care at an adolescent mental health facility near Trevose, Pennsylvania, in the weeks preceding the murders. Kreps said he met with the psychiatrist who'd been treating the suspect, informing him that his patient was being investigated for the murder of two women. He urged the doctor to request Thomas's permission to inject him with truth serum, but the doctor refused and wouldn't speak with Kreps any further once he learned of the horrific crimes for which his patient had been questioned by the New Jersey State Police and the Philadelphia Police Department.

According to Dix, at some time in the week following the murders, Thomas's attorney, Edward F. Kane, allowed his client to be questioned at his Norristown law office. The suspect consented to submit to another lie detector test, the first to be administered by the New Jersey State Police. Kane's instructions, as Dix recalls, were stern: he and Detective Toth would be permitted only to question, not interrogate, his client about the murders of Davis and Perry. Thomas's willingness to submit to the polygraph raised vexing questions, adding layers of intrigue to his persona. Unless absolutely certain of his own innocence, why would the eighteen-year-old submit to another round of lie detector tests, especially when on the previous occasion, according to the Philadelphia Police Department, he'd given "fuzzy answers" to crucial questions? Kane, already an experienced criminal defense attorney with a sterling reputation, certainly would have cautioned his client of the grave risks inherent in the exam, on this occasion to be conducted by detectives with extensive knowledge of the crime scene evidence. Considering the uncertain results from his earlier charts, one can reasonably infer that Thomas must have met with the detectives against the advice of his lawyer. Was the young man gaming to outwit the New Jersey authorities, aiming to prove his fearlessness, or determined to prove he had nothing to do with the murders? Due to attorney-client confidentiality, Kane refuses to comment on the circumstances of this meeting at his office in 1969 but doesn't deny that Thomas spoke with New Jersey detectives on this occasion.

Dix asserts that while in his attorney's Norristown office, Thomas agreed to submit to a "peak of tension" test. In this variation of the standard polygraph exam, a suspect is presented a number of questions in an easily recognized order. He is informed there is one correct response based upon evidence found at the crime scene, which would be known only between police and the true culprit. For example, in a bank heist investigation where only the detectives and the perpetrator know that $20,000 was stolen, the interviewer will lead up to that figure by presenting a number logically preceding the correct amount. "Was the amount of money that was stolen $5,000? $10,0000? $15,000? $20,000?" If the suspect is lying, the graph needle should fall precipitously after he is asked the correct number, a reaction reflecting the subject's relief to have the question behind him. Dix would have asked Thomas, Are you familiar with the murders of Susan Davis and Elizabeth Perry? Were Davis and Perry driving a blue convertible? Did you tie up either of them up with their own bra? Do you know if the girls were stabbed? If Thomas's response to this last question was reflected on the chart as a drop-off from his previous answer relating to the bra, the result would indicate deception.

After "boxing" (police parlance for questioning a subject attached to the lie detector machine) Thomas in Norristown, Dix and Toth returned to New Jersey, where they reported to Major Victor E. Galassi at Trenton headquarters with the results of their exam. The major asked both detectives, on a scale of 1 to 10, with 10 being guilty, to assess Thomas's culpability based upon the fresh test results and their review of the polygraphs administered by the Philadelphia Police Department.

"An 8," Toth told the major.

Dix was so certain of Thomas's guilt at this point, he flatly stated, "If he was in the chair right now, I'd pull the switch."

Although he wasn't deeply involved in the parkway murder investigation, former New Jersey State Police Major Eugene Olaff, the deputy superintendent, received periodic updates on progress from the field. After speaking with Lt. Toth, the senior polygraph detective, Olaff concluded that Toth was far less certain of Thomas's guilt than Dix.

Despite their lingering suspicions, with no physical evidence connecting Thomas to the murders and no witnesses who could place him at the crime scene, the New Jersey State Police still didn't have a strong enough case to turn over to the Atlantic County Prosecutor's Office. As detectives resumed their hunt for new suspects, Lt. Brennan decided to have his most experienced detective continue after Thomas.

Filling a doorway at six-feet, four inches tall and weighing upwards of two-hundred fifty pounds, John C. Kreps III had straight, silver hair raked straight back off his forehead and a set of hooded eyelids masking a shrewd, penetrating stare. He was a fearsome figure in his day, a giant of a man whose imposing presence could draw out the truth from the most self-assured liar. He joined the New Jersey State Police in 1949 after serving with the Navy during WWII, spending six years aboard aircraft carriers in the Pacific and Mediterranean. He was first stationed out of the Berlin barracks in southern Camden County, where he began his career as a road trooper before being transferred to Absecon, ascending to the rank of Detective Sergeant. Kreps' legend is preceded only by his esteemed reputation. His retired brethren, many of whom began their careers under his command and eventually outranked him, openly concur that Kreps might've reached a higher position if he had greater tolerance for the political gamesmanship often required to attain promotions in the militaresque hierarchy of the New Jersey State Police. To most troopers who worked alongside him, the mere mention of Kreps' name inspires a litany of heartfelt superlatives and glowing accolades. While his superiors butted heads with him, or differed with his oftentimes unconventional methodology, they openly concurred that "Big Jack" Kreps was an outstanding investigator, among the best the force had to offer. Detective Robert Maholland, who worked extensively on the Perry-Davis investigation during its infancy, says, "Jack Kreps was my mentor, and he was one of the best fucking detectives I ever met in my life."

Everything about Kreps was oversized, mirroring his approach to life. Tales of his excesses abound. As one might offer a glass of water to a thirsty landscaper, Kreps would hand quarts of beer—not cans, or regular sized bottles—to fellow troopers when they visited him off duty at his home, remaining lucid after guzzling its contents while his pals grew woozy and faltered. An inveterate speeder in a patrol car, legend has it he was once pulled over for speeding in Petersburg, Virginia, while en route to apprehend a fugitive from New Jersey. Asked to show his identification, Kreps brashly stepped out of his car, announcing that he was on official business for the New Jersey State Police. Recognizing his name from the driver's license and detective's badge, it is said that the awestruck young trooper, who'd heard stories of the senior detective from fellow Virginia troopers sent for training at the New Jersey State Police facility in Sea Girt, asked, "You're *the* Jack Kreps?"

By contrast, Kreps' partner in the Perry-Davis investigation was the more understated James J. Hart. Though on paper the pairing seemed a mismatch, their divergent temperaments complimented one another. Hart was stationed out of division headquarters in Trenton, where fellow detectives and troopers labeled him "Gentleman Jimmy" because of his exquisite manners, and "Hound Dog," a nickname owing to his relentless tenacity and work habits in solving complex investigations. Like Brennan, Kreps, and George Saunders, Hart had also served in the Navy, completing a stint aboard the *U.S.S. New Mexico* during the Second World War. A stocky fellow with a shock of thick white hair he wore parted neatly to the side, Hart was courteous to everybody he met, collecting himself each time he spoke. He was known to scribble copious notes during investigations, scrupulously considering every fact before reaching a conclusion. A former associate who worked for Hart after he was transferred to the Organized Crime Division praised him as a "detective's detective."

Because it remains an open investigation, today several former New Jersey State Police detectives are reluctant to discuss details of the Perry-Davis file. Kreps, an unabashedly outspoken eighty-seven-year old, eagerly shared his thoughts in the months before he died 2011. Of the dozens of homicides he'd worked on over the course of his storied career, this was the only case to eat at him after his retirement from the force in 1974. After all, he was among the first detectives summoned to the crime scene after Susan and Elizabeth were found in the Egg Harbor Township woods and was saddled with the grim task of returning Davis's jewelry to her father after the completion of his daughter's autopsy. Detective Dix had shown Kreps the results of the lie detector tests given by the Philadelphia Police Department, one in a series of revelations that led to his firmly grounded belief as to who murdered Susan Davis and Elizabeth Perry. "So, you want to know who killed those girls?" he asked in a gruff voice, interviewed from his condominium in Largo, Florida, before he was stricken by disease. His answer was delivered with no instance of hesitation: "Mark Thomas."

In the weeks following Thomas's release from custody, Kreps would often venture over the bridge into Philadelphia, driving to the Norristown home where he resided when not at his West Philadelphia crash pad. Often without official orders and on his own time, Kreps shadowed his movements. He was certain he could goad Thomas's wrath and get into his head by closely following him, somehow tap into the uncontrollable fury he was confident the teen possessed. By persistently dogging him, could he rile him enough to wrest a confession, or at least persuade him to sit for another polygraph? Kreps frequently tailed Thomas in his patrol car, followed him into bars, or staked out his parents' home on Thayer Drive. He was often joined by Corporal Vennera of the Whitpain Police Department. The two would talk to neighbors, snoop around outside the property, or sit parked on the street at night, waiting to see who went up the driveway.

Kreps often saw Thomas and his father swilling drafts and shooting billiards at the Swiss Cottage Motel on DeKalb Pike in Centre Square, a dank shot and beer tavern attached to a number of cabins for rent to its patrons at eight dollars per night. The giant detective, conspicuous among the lunch pail regulars at the neighborhood watering hole, would seat himself at a table as if minding his own business, relaxing with a sandwich and beer after a tiring week at the office. In a short time, the tall youth came to recognize him as the nosy cop who'd been following him around town and asking questions of his acquaintances. One day Mark's father, William Thomas, approached Kreps. He confronted the detective as he sat alone at his table, and a heated exchange ensued. "He told me, 'You're harassing my son,'" Kreps recalled. "I said, 'That's what you're going to have to prove.'"

"Mark's father wouldn't talk to me because I accused his son of being a murderer," Kreps said. "Every time I went to that restaurant I'd see Mark and his father would say, 'I'm gonna sign a complaint against you,' and I said, 'What are you going to charge me for?' I didn't give a damn, I saw the boy was in there and his father was in there, so I went in there to get his goat."

"I'll press charges on you if you keep this up," William Thomas once threatened the detective.

"For doing what?" Kreps replied. "I'm here eating."

On another occasion, Thomas turned the tables on Kreps, tailgating the detective before pulling alongside his cruiser and demanding that he stop pestering him. Accompanied by a friend whose name Kreps couldn't recall, Thomas agreed to meet with the detective in a nearby diner parking lot. Kreps, the wily veteran, wasn't the slightest bit intimidated by the prospect of facing the two young men alone in the dark of night. Rather, he viewed this as an opportunity to persuade Thomas that he was being offered another chance to pinpoint where he was the morning Perry and Davis were slain—and if he'd only agree to join the detective in the drive back to New Jersey, this would be a great chance to set the record straight. Manipulatively persuasive, Kreps nearly talked Thomas into returning with him, but his friend was quick to sniff out the detective's ulterior purpose. "His buddy said, 'Mark you don't wanna go back there with him, you're gonna go to jail,'" Kreps recalled, his efforts to haul his suspect back to Absecon thwarted once more.

As the surveillance persisted, Thomas allegedly sought guidance from Penny Dutton-Raffa, a local "hypnotist, parapsychologist, clairvoyant and reincarnation theorist" who lived next door to the Thomases on Thayer Drive. In 1979 Dutton-Raffa founded the International Hypnosis Hall of Fame, and three years later published a book titled *From Psycho to Psychic,* telling a reporter for the *Philadelphia Inquirer* that she acquired her "energy ability" after falling down her stairs and suffering a head injury in 1966. She appeared on evening television shows and hosted seminars at local hotels, filling her guest list with purveyors of the supernatural, card sharks, and carnival hucksters who offered demonstrations to sparsely filled conference rooms on topics such as space travel, hypno-sex, and the powers of levitation. "I have no powers," she proclaimed, "but there seems to be something about me that's different than most people. I know things that are going to happen before they happen."

Dutton-Raffa, who died in 2012, was convinced of Mark Thomas's innocence, according to her daughter, Linda DeMarco. He often visited their house in the weeks following the murders, seeking the psychic's spiritual guidance as both the New Jersey State Police and Whitpain Township detectives continued to keep tight reins on his movements. DeMarco also confirmed that the police had extensively questioned her younger brother Bart Dutton on several different occasions in the weeks following the 1969 parkway murders and that he had been in Ocean City with Thomas over that Memorial Day weekend. "My mom said that Mark didn't kill those girls," her daughter said. "He would come over and talk to my mom, really scared. She told him, 'We'll get this all straightened out.'"

Dutton-Raffa created the Barton John Dutton Memorial Hypnosis Scholarship in memory of her late son, the co-owner of a pool-cleaning company, who died from alcoholism in 1996 at the age of forty-three. Given her daughter's comments, and the fact that Whitpain Police department detectives confirmed that Bart Dutton and Mark Thomas were neighborhood friends, Dutton may likely have been the "friend" who New Jersey State police detectives escorted with Thomas to several diners in Ocean City on the day following his interrogation in Philadelphia, in order to follow up on his alibi that he had been eating in a diner with "a friend from Blue Bell, Pa.," as the newspapers reported, at the time the girls were murdered.

Mark Thomas's father was true to his word of vindicating his eldest son. Returning home to New Jersey late one night after a visit to Centre Square, Jack Kreps received a call from an irate Lt. Brennan, who ordered Kreps into his office the following day. He unequivocally commanded that the senior detective back away from doggedly hounding the teenager, as William Thomas had sought and received a protective order against him. With Captain Paterra present at the meeting, Kreps had little choice but to comply with his orders, and thereafter was relegated to monitoring Thomas's activities from afar. "That Brennan," Kreps mused, glancing back on the history of their estrangement, "was a pain in my ass."

Likely exhausted by the unending scrutiny, Thomas enlisted with the U.S. Army on November 29, 1969, two days before the first Vietnam War draft lottery. His place of entry is officially listed as Philadelphia. Newspaper reports and court documents indicate he was stationed at Ft. Bragg, North Carolina, when in February 1970 (Coincidentally, the same month and year that Army Colonel Jeffrey MacDonald allegedly killed his wife and children at the base, though no reports indicate Thomas was involved in any way.) Thomas deserted to Canada. Shirking explicit instructions to keep away from the boot camp trainee, Kreps drove to the army base, but by the time he arrived his suspect had already fled for the border. He interviewed one hundred fourteen soldiers in Thomas's training class, but none recalled overhearing him confess or otherwise inculpate himself in the Memorial Day slayings of Davis and Perry. Upon his return stateside, he was given an other than honorable discharge after officially separating from the Army at Ft. George, Maryland, on September 9, 1970.

Thomas's release represented a bitter defeat for the New Jersey State Police Criminal Investigative Division, though many of their detectives were wary of him from the beginning. While interest in him heightened after an exhaustive nightlong interrogation in Philadelphia, a corresponding number of homicide investigators sensed all along that he was leading them down false trails, motivated by a desperate yearning for attention. Many in the force suspected they'd likely been rooked by the strange-natured hippy, nevertheless narrowing in on him despite long odds that he'd confess to killing Davis and Perry. Costly man-hours were rendered futile. Facing his worst setback yet, the lieutenant in charge of the case could do little but watch frustratingly as the latest person to occupy the center of his fledgling murder probe set off for a country whose prime minister openly offered U.S. war resisters "a refuge from militarism." With Ronnie Walden and John Collins in prison, and Mark Thomas outside their jurisdiction, the state police were relegated to exploring hunches and poring over the thickening file for clues they might have missed at first glance. While Detective Dix administered more lie detector tests, troopers took additional statements as lab workers in west Trenton sifted through the aging crime scene evidence a third and fourth time. While a judge's order may have prevented Jack Kreps from haranguing his favorite suspect, the detective's opinion wasn't bound by a similar constraint or declared with any fear of reprisal when speaking of Thomas: "He knows right God damn well I know he murdered those girls."

CHAPTER TWELVE

A Cautionary Tale

Throughout the winter of 1970 detectives continued to receive thirty to forty telephone calls per month offering possible leads. Despite the growing number of persons interviewed, with each contact's information stored in a rapidly ballooning card file, the case scarcely budged. Foregoing more traditional investigative techniques, the state police explored the murky world of psychological transcendence as an alternative mode of lassoing the killer.

They began with Dr. S. Donald Babcock, retaining the highly regarded Vineland, New Jersey, psychologist to hypnotize the parkway toll collector on shift Memorial Day morning. While entranced, the collector could only recall that the girls were alone as they drove past his booth at dawn. Two witnesses who'd glimpsed Susan's car were also placed under Babcock's spell. However, they couldn't elaborate any further beyond the image of the short-haired youth in the white t-shirt they'd seen lingering aside the open convertible top nearly two hours after the stabbings.

To gather a psychological profile of the person they sought, police engaged the services of a forensic psychologist from Pittsburgh who'd testified in the trial of infamous mass murderer Richard Speck. The thin drifter with pockmarked cheeks and brylcreemed hair had raped, tortured, and slain fourteen nurses in a Chicago hospital on July 14, 1966.

His defense team argued that Speck carried an extra Y chromosome, which accounted for his unusually aggressive and uncontrollable behavior. The same genetic aberration, proponents of the controversial findings theorized, was prevalent in tall, thin young men with brown hair and severe acne. The psychologist theorized that a similar genotype was carried by Perry and Davis' assailant, whom he surmised to be a carpenter by trade. Detectives also consulted a North Jersey psychic, their willingness to try supernatural phenomena perhaps a reflection of their desperation by this point.

Come April, Kreps and Hart were the only remaining detectives assigned full-time to the double murder investigation. The other twenty-eight men were officially transferred to other cases, though each was periodically called to interview a possible witness or person of interest. Police maintained the hotline in Absecon, but the barracks was restored to the road station it had been before the highly publicized murders changed its place in local history. The investigation was now officially based out of the Troop A headquarters in Hammonton, with Kreps and Hart staying behind in Absecon, working the case nine hours a day, five days per week. What had been among the largest manhunts in state police history a year earlier was now condensed to a small paneled back office in the former World War I munitions factory administration building, brimming with transcripts, investigative reports, and photos. On the barracks wall was taped a mural-size aerial enlargement of the densely wooded murder locus, prepared by the National Aviation Facilities Experimental Center. A yellow map pin identified the precise spot where Susan and Elizabeth were found, and a black pin embossed with a cross pinpointed where their Impala had been parked.

"We go at it aggressively every day," Hart told a *Courier (NJ) Post* reporter. "We read and re-read everything. It's in the back of our minds whatever we do. It could be tomorrow.

It could be two or five years from now. All it takes is one break, one slip, one little piece of evidence." Hart and Kreps continued to check tips from callers who'd had visions from the spirit world, identified patterns in numerology, or detected a questionable shift in their Ouija board. Four hundred of the roughly two thousand people who'd been questioned thus far had submitted to lie-detector tests. Five young men were scheduled to sit for the tests again, the detectives revealed, yet didn't offer names or provide specifics. Kreps estimated that the police search and investigation had cost the state and Atlantic County taxpayers more than a half-million dollars.

Kreps was characteristically frank in his assessment of the investigation, unequivocal when asked what all the work had produced after a year's time. "Maybe a possible good suspect," he said, leaning back in a seat behind his desk. "A cold cigar caught in the corner of his mouth mimicked the meter of his words," wrote the beat reporter seated before him. Referring to the apprehension and release of Mark Thomas, though withholding his identity, Kreps remarked, "We've had this son of a bitch since June 4. We're concentrating a lot of our endeavors on this suspect. Along with a lot of the other leads...which we can't ignore. We're trying to come up with more evidence to put him right in the job. He's been worked on a little, but he's not checked out. Does he know he's a suspect? You're goddamn tootin' he does." Alluding to Thomas, Kreps said "the suspect" had failed more than one lie detector test and was unable to prove his whereabouts at the time of the murders. He described Thomas as a white male, twenty years of age, with a police record. (Thomas was actually nineteen-years old at the time of the article.) Employed by a Canadian construction company, he worked "about 1,000 miles from Absecon," Kreps said, describing the gangly teen as a "roamer" who "hitch-hikes everywhere." He added, "We know everything about him from the time he was born until the present. We know when he goes to the bathroom, how he walks and everything else..." Like Hart, he expressed unbridled confidence, saying that all the state police needed was "one good break."

"Somebody may have been here last Memorial Day and left the area before the girls were found," Det. Sergeant Robert Saunders said near the one-year anniversary of the parkway slayings. "They might have observed something. We're hoping they did." Saunders doubted the killer would remain at large forever. "There's no doubt the case will be solved," he remarked. "It's just a matter of time. We won't be satisfied till it is."

When asked by a reporter for the *Philadelphia Daily News* what inroads his detectives had made, Lt. Brennan candidly offered, "A lot of work, nothing concrete."

"Perhaps the hottest suspect," the article read, "was the 18-year-old from Norristown, described by police as a 'hippie type' who'd provided police with 'fuzzy answers to crucial questions.'" Like Kreps, Brennan let it be known that a year after the investigation, Mark Thomas remained in his sights. "We never really eliminated him," he said.

For the second straight year, state police staffed a trailer at the Somers Point circle all day and night during the Memorial Day weekend. Seated on a wooden chair inside the stifling cavern, Trooper Thomas Mulholland interviewed any tourist or local who knocked on the door with information to share. In front of his desk was a board with recent photographs of the two slain girls and the light-blue Chevy. "Nobody would be happier than me if the guy walked in here today and turned himself in," Mulholland told a reporter.

Detective Kinzer, who relieved Mulholland in the mid-afternoon, held out hope that the sight of the trailer and the display of the hotline number would jog a distant memory. "Lots of people might be afraid of appearing ridiculous," Kinzer said. "But they might just have that one little piece of information that will put the puzzle together for us and will not speak up for fear of appearing foolish." Echoing a familiar mantra, he said, "Somebody must have seen these girls from the diner to the parkway. Even at that time of the morning, this place is like a circus. There are a million people around."

The Davises and Perrys coped as best they were able, coming to terms with the tragedy that had befallen their families. "Right now, I think someone more powerful than us here on earth will have to take care of the punishment of the killer of our girls," said Wesley Davis Sr., one year after his daughter's death. "I still have hope, but it's not as strong as it was." He expressed his continued support of the police investigation but took a softer stand with respect to the murderer. "Hopefully they'll get him off the street and put him away, so it won't happen to someone else's child. But I honestly don't feel the man will ever stand trial; he's probably a mental case." To the thousands of young women who were expected to converge on the Jersey Shore over the forthcoming holiday weekend, Davis offered this warning: "Beware of strangers, keep your door locked and if you're in a convertible, keep the top up."

Robert Bell, son of the Rev. Sheridan Watson Bell Jr., the minister who'd conducted Susan Davis' eulogy, was in San Francisco on summer vacation from Yale University when he heard of the tragedy. Robert was a childhood friend of Susan's and remained friendly with her throughout their teens, participating together in the Youth Fellowship program at their church. He'd also been her ballroom dance partner and escort to her eighth grade Harrisburg Academy formal. "Susan is with God now," Dr. Bell counseled his son, who was at a difficult crossroads in his life when the call came that Susan had been slain. Suicidal, Robert had recently disclosed his homosexuality to his father after returning to Harrisburg for the Christmas holidays in 1969. In the wake of these revelations, his father insisted Robert accompany him to the Davis home. At first he couldn't understand why the

Reverend would have his forlorn son be with him to console the grieving family at this particularly painful time of year, the first Christmas without their daughter. Odder yet, their visit took place in the hours immediately following Robert's admission that he wished to take his own life. Rather than dissuade his forlorn son through heartfelt pleas, Bell believes he was asked to join his father's solemn excursion so he'd understand the harrowing anguish suffered by a family after the loss of a child. Witnessing the Davis' explicit grieving firsthand was instrumental in Bell's decision to live, he says, and he remembers the experience as the most valuable lesson his father imparted on him.

Interviewed from Excelsior, Minnesota, Margaret Perry told a reporter, "What makes us sick is knowing that somewhere out there in society is the mixed-up young man and you can't do anything about it.... But I worry what he might do to somebody else's daughter." She did her best to move on after the tragedy. Where the Davises left Susan's room just as it was before she died, Elizabeth's mother promptly removed her youngest daughter's belongings out of their Lakeview Avenue cottage so as to be shut of the perpetual reminder of her passing. She remained active in church, relying on the support of friends and fellow congregants. Rescuing stray pets also kept her busy as she transformed her basement into a temporary animal shelter. She tried her best to remain optimistic despite the growing realization that the killer might never be apprehended. "I haven't given up hope," she said. "I'm hoping he'll be caught. If he isn't, he might do it again. I definitely want him brought to justice, and I think he should have to give his life. I believe in the death penalty because I've never been shown that it isn't a good thing. One of the things about our society is that it's too permissive. This isn't a good way to keep a majority of the people safe.

"Bitterness is self-defeating," Mrs. Perry said. "Our daughter was a darling child. I feel sorry for the young man who did it." She wasn't critical of the New Jersey State Police. "They haven't had a great deal to go on," she observed. As detectives had surmised from the outset, Elizabeth's mother suggested that the girls had simply offered a ride to the wrong man on the morning they were killed. "I think the girls picked up a boy…and I wouldn't at all be surprised if he carried a sign saying 'Harrisburg' or something. This is a great danger; everybody's bumming rides. You just have to pick up one wrong one or one sick one and you've paid a tremendous price for a very small mistake."

The Perrys met with Dean Marguerite Shewman of Monticello College to establish the Elizabeth Perry Memorial Senior Recognition Award. President Gail Myers presented a medallion to the inaugural recipient at the 1970 commencement ceremonies. "Missing from this year's graduating class is a young woman whose life was snuffed out last spring by a brutal murder in New Jersey," she announced to the hushed gathering. "Elizabeth Perry had just finished her freshman year before the tragedy… a committee of students met with the dean to determine the nature of the award and the criteria for so honoring a member of this class. Their feelings were that Elizabeth was characterized by her hard work for others without any thought to glory or reward. They decided that the award should go to a senior student who has given her time and talents to the college community without great fanfare of recognition."

Ray Perry was unable to draw solace from the passage of seasons or cope with the loss of Elizabeth as capably as his wife. Though his thirst to avenge his daughter's death ebbed in due course, he seemed to bear the agony less stoically than Wesley Davis Sr., time no ally in lightening his soul's affliction. He continued to suffer nightmares offering clear visions of his daughter's mutilated corpse on the coroner's table at Shore Memorial Hospital. "He loved Ibby more than life itself," said Pam Hartwick, Elizabeth's best friend. "He never got over it."

Within two years of the murders, the Bemis Company relocated Ray Perry to Mercer Island, Washington, a wealthy Seattle suburb. Though newspapers reported that his employer transferred him so as to provide him with a fresh change of scenery, Suzanne Masiello, Elizabeth's older sister, recalled differently. Today she has a family of her own and resides in New Hope, Pennsylvania, the searing memory of her sibling's murder no dimmer now than when she first heard the news. "My father was hospitalized with psychological problems about a year after my sister died," she says. "He was demoted in his job. They moved him from Minneapolis out to Seattle because of my sister's death. My father had issues before that, but that put him over the edge."

"Basically, my parents died when my sister did," Masiello says. "My mother should have had a nervous breakdown and didn't. My parents might have been murdered along with my sister. There was a point when my father made mention of in essence taking out a contract on somebody. He was irrational enough to proceed with something like that, and I can imagine everyone trying to convince him that the guilty person had died or that God was going to take vengeance, one or the other, and my father didn't need to pursue it personally because he was capable of doing something really crazy. So it doesn't surprise me that my parents didn't push the police more. I think they felt the police had tried very hard and there just wasn't anything else that could humanly be accomplished.

"Within a couple of years, my parents became much more accepting of what had happened and not as vindictive," she recalls. "Not that they lacked interest; they would've loved to have had who was responsible electrocuted or torn limb from limb, but I think it became less pressing as time went on."

With the killer still at large and no imminent arrests, pressure was mounting on the state police to scapegoat somebody. They targeted Louis Sterr and James Dunbar, the two parkway troopers who had the misfortune of drawing patrol the morning of May 30, 1969. Captain Mario Paterra, in charge of the murder investigation from division headquarters, was interviewed by the *Philadelphia Bulletin* in June 1970. He alleged that the three-day delay in the discovery of the two girls was due to Dunbar and Sterr's failure to follow established procedure and filing a false report. According to Paterra, a subsequent internal investigation into the procedures followed by Trooper Dunbar, together with eyewitness accounts, revealed that three cars, including the girls' convertible, were seen parked within a hundred yards of one another on the northbound side of the parkway. The third car, Paterra said, was believed to have been the black 1956 Pontiac sedan driven by the girls' murderer.

Lt. Brennan told the *Bulletin* that the state police believed that the killer made contact with the two girls at or around milepost 31.9 after they'd pulled onto the parkway shoulder. Paterra further alleged that when Sterr ordered Davis' convertible towed, afterward he should have followed up with local police departments to locate the car's true owner. No contact was made with the Camp Hill Police Department, Paterra said, also blaming Sterr for not checking inside Davis' purse, found on the front seat of her convertible.

Strangely, Paterra and Brennan's remarks were inconsistent with their earlier conclusion that the girls were presumably murdered by a hitchhiker who initially met them at the Somers Point traffic circle. As Mark Thomas didn't have a car while in Ocean City, and was never before connected to the black Pontiac, the new theory also suggested that police were straying farther from him as a possible suspect. Or did the existence of the parked Pontiac, which officials alleged that either Sterr or Dunbar should've noticed when patrolling past milepost 31.9, present top state police officials a convenient target in the two troopers on duty that morning?

The problems for Sterr and Dunbar didn't end with these public accusations. On December 29, 1970, New Jersey State Police instituted secret court-martial proceedings against Sterr, charging him with failing to follow official procedures into the investigation of the Davis and Perry murders. The hearings were held at the Criminal Investigation Division headquarters in Hammonton. Officially, Sterr was charged with "acting improperly in failing to pursue more closely circumstances that preceded the discovery of the bodies." Captain Karl Kloo, commander of the parkway Troop E headquarters to which Sterr was assigned, recommended the charges, and was the only witness to testify against him. The trooper was further accused of failing to report his actions and neglecting to file a teletype message requesting that the automobile's owner be notified. Sterr's attorney, Patrick McGhan of Atlantic City, tried unsuccessfully to have the hearing held open to the public. Sterr was initially offered a five-day suspension rather than a court-martial proceeding but opted for the latter because of his unblemished record as a state trooper.

Testifying in his own defense, Starr stated that the teletype machine at the Avalon barracks was inoperative the day of the slayings and that his report of the car's recovery was provided to at least two state police radio stations. He said that within ten minutes of arriving at the scene, he'd checked the girls' car with the National Criminal Information Center and learned that it hadn't been stolen. He claimed to have logged these facts at the Avalon barracks before going off duty for two days. Curiously, the *Philadelphia Inquirer* made no mention of a malfunctioning teletype machine when they broke the story of the murders.

The New Jersey State Police Fraternal Organization retained Westfield, New Jersey, attorney Thomas J. Savage to represent Dunbar in the appeal of his termination from the force. In a preemptive posture, Savage was also hired to represent Lewis Cavileer, the sergeant in command at the Avalon barracks where Dunbar and Sterr were stationed, and whom, Savage feared, "would be the next court-martial target." There were "signs on all sides" that the state police had "embarked on a cruel and deliberate campaign" to make Dunbar, Sterr, and Cavileer patsies for the department's failure to solve the Memorial Day slayings, Savage said, "even to the extent of losing some valuable tapes needed in evidence." The union lawyer argued that the firing of Dunbar, by way of refusing his re-enlistment after his two-year probationary term ended, violated New Jersey State Police regulations because the termination wasn't precipitated by formal charges against the young trooper. Savage further alleged that the department "wants the public to swallow the theory that Dunbar quit because he committed blunders in the investigation of the murders."

Savage said Dunbar was never told why he was being released, "And we have to assume it was because of the murder probes," the lawyer proclaimed. According to Savage, the refusal to re-enlist Dunbar was "a clear violation of his constitutional rights" and state police regulations requiring formal charges to be brought against the trooper. He claimed that Dunbar followed "every rule in the book" in handling Susan Davis' convertible. "It's tragic enough for the parents of those young women," Savage said, "but it's serving no purpose to wreck the lives of some dedicated state policemen."

McGhan successfully overturned Sterr's two-week suspension, and the trooper was returned to duty and eventually promoted to sergeant. Arguing before the New Jersey Superior Court, Appellate Division, Savage maintained that Dunbar's constitutionally protected due process rights to a fair hearing had been violated. A panel of judges, however, held that the New Jersey State Police Superintendent, Col. David Kelly, was under no legal obligation to re-enlist Dunbar after his two-year probationary period ended.

"It wasn't a happy time in my life," recalls Dunbar, today a successful real estate salesperson still residing in Atlantic County. Recalling that fateful early morning shift, he says that he had just been transferred to the Avalon barracks a few months before the murders. "Actually, I didn't see [the convertible] and Lou Sterr relieved me in the morning. As far as I know, he found it on his first run. He ran the NCIC on the thing. It wasn't reported missing or stolen in Pennsylvania, but everything wasn't computerized then. They didn't have it as missing, and he had it towed in. As far as I know, he did everything that he could have done and found out later." In further defense of his late comrade, he added, "As far as I know, Lou Sterr did everything by the book, what he should've done. I don't know how else he could've followed up on it. If there was one thing to point a finger at, it was the bureaucracy of Pennsylvania."

Dunbar was stoical and understanding upon learning he lost his appeal. He isn't bitter by what transpired, though he remains certain he wasn't re-enlisted because somebody had to fall on the sword, and headquarters decided upon him because of his probationary status. "I don't know if they were pinning the blame on someone, but the powers-that-be at the time were covering their asses." In the months after the murders he saw his performance reviews slip and recalls living with constant threats of being court-martialed. "I was basically in limbo for a year. I wasn't a happy camper. I could have played politics to stay, but my attitude was I have to look at myself in the mirror. Was I a scapegoat? I guess they had to show they disciplined somebody. If I had happened to be there at the right time, I could have been a hero," he says. "It's always stuck to my craw. At the time I would've liked to have been confronted with an accusation of what I did or didn't do. But I'm an eternal optimist; everything works out for the best."

The revelations unearthed during the court martial hearings riled Wesley Davis Sr. In January 1971 he denied a widespread report that he'd been "pressuring the state police because of the failure of the department to develop special leads." The reporting protocol pertaining to abandoned cars on the parkway, it was revealed during the court martial hearings, had been replaced due to the tragic errors of Memorial Day. Davis told Colonel Kelly that he "questioned the efficiency of [his] handling of abandoned cars."

"I cannot fault the state police for its effort," Davis said, "but there sure must have been something wrong with the system when a car filled with personal belongings and identifications could be garaged for three days without anyone coming up with the knowledge that it involved two missing girls who might well have been murdered." He further stated, "I can't in any way claim the state police haven't expended a lot of time and effort on this case, but I'm doubtful about some of the procedures." Davis said that Ray Perry had also expressed "considerable dissatisfaction" with the overall progress of the murder investigation.

Little was reported after the state police hearings until early March 1971, when detectives announced plans to question William Charles Mosbach Jr. A twenty-two-year old Sony record company plant employee from Pitman, New Jersey, Mosbach had recently been arrested for the alleged rape and strangulation of Kathleen Janet Doughty, a Pitman High School sophomore. Detective Dix, who questioned Mosbach in his jail cell in Gloucester County, New Jersey, remembers that he easily passed a lie detector test and was never questioned any further.

New leads trickled in at a much slower rate. A May 30, 1971, newspaper article reminded the public that the special hotline was still open, but the $20,000 reward had been withdrawn in February. The police had investigated more than three thousand persons without an arrest, yet publicly expressed their optimism. Detectives Hart and Kreps were still working the case full time, now two years later. They'd covered between California and Florida, scouring the Northeast and Canada in search of their man. Brennan told a reporter that for the first time since the weeks following the murders, the state police trailer would no longer be parked at the Somers Point circle. "It really didn't pay off that much last year," he admitted.

While Wesley Davis Sr. and Margaret Perry willingly obliged columnists seeking their take on the emotional injuries wrought upon their families, behind the scenes Ray Perry continued to advocate the slain girls' cause. He made certain Elizabeth and Susan hadn't passed in vain, keeping true to his wishes that other girls like them take precautions to ensure they not share the same dark fate. In April 1972, days before Governor Dan Evans of Washington signed legislation legalizing hitchhiking, Perry registered his objection to Evans, State Patrol Chief O.C. Furseth, and to the bill's sponsor, State Rep. Jeff Doutwaite. Perry warned that the bill's passage would remove vital enforcement powers from the Washington State Police, hampering their ability to "weed out bad characters." Doutwaite addressed Perry's concerns by callously responding, "I basically don't believe that people in a free country should be told whether or not they may allow another person to enter their private car....If anyone thinks it is too dangerous to offer another one a ride, he need not ever do it. Likewise, if anyone thinks it is too dangerous to practice hitchhiking, he need not ever do it." That same year, a spokesman for the New Jersey State Police told *Philadelphia Inquirer* reporter Kathy Begley that due to the similarities between the cases, his department intended to investigate any possible connection between the parkway slayings and a string of twenty-two murders thought attributable to the Sherman McCrary clan of California, a roving family of cross-country murderers whose young female victims had been abducted, bound and beaten, and found miles from where they were last seen.

Another five hundred persons had been questioned as of 1973. Tips, which a year earlier had continued to pour into the Absecon barracks hotline, slowed to a scant three to four every few weeks. Lt. John J. Toth, who'd polygraphed Ronnie Walden, was appointed to head the newly formed New Jersey State Police Major Crime Unit. He spoke of the matter with sorry resignation, his words emblematic of the regret felt by all. "It's one case we won't forget."

"They were two darling little girls," Margaret Perry said from her new home in Seattle that winter. "It's got to be somebody not mentally stable to do a thing like that. Sooner or later, he or they will be punished one way or another." She added that the families were eager to see the case solved "if for no other reason than to save someone else. Talking about it still makes me cry."

Davis, interviewed by telephone from his bottling company in Harrisburg, said, "Somewhere up and down the line the killer may be caught and punished. There's still a chance some clue may come up or someone may start talking."

Four years later, detectives admitted being farther from solving the case than since the first days after the slayings. "Somewhere there has to be somebody with information that will help us," said Detective Kinzer. He gestured at the filing cabinet in his office at the Hammonton station, its drawers teeming with reports and fruitless leads the police had chased. "We haven't turned up anything so far," he confessed. They searched for similarities between the parkway murders and the unsolved deaths of Gary Deal and his family, brutally slain in their Folsom, New Jersey, home in Atlantic County in 1978. Leak and wife were shot to death, and their three-year-old son had his throat slit in his upstairs bedroom. State police couldn't match the suspects in that case to the parkway slayings, however, despite help from investigators for the Atlantic County Prosecutor's Office.

There were instances of false confessions in the succeeding years. Detectives were once called to the Tuckerton state police barracks when a man called purporting to have knowledge of the slayings. His veracity was undermined when he badly flunked a lie detector test. On another occasion, parkway trooper John Petracca was hurriedly summoned to the Wildwood Police Department by Detective Kinzer, who had him question a middle-aged man being held at the station on an unrelated charge. Petracca, who hadn't reviewed the file, was hastily debriefed on the case and apprised of a vital holdback—that one of the victims had been bound to a tree with her bra. The trooper soon discovered that the drunken detainee was no different than other braggers before him, a mentally unbalanced man needful of attention.

Wesley Davis Sr. seemed much more pessimistic about bringing the killer to justice: "At some point he'll be caught, but probably only when he goes to meet his Maker," he said. The fathers checked with detectives two or three times a year, the erasure of time slaking somewhat their thirst for revenge, easing the bitter frustration and stewing resentment they held against the police for their initial delay in locating their girls and failing to arrest a suspect. Police artist George Homa's composite sketch, based on the description of a woman who saw a slender teen lingering by the blue convertible on the morning of the murders, was of little help in apprehending the killer, despite the inundation of calls received at the Absecon barracks in the days following its release. Interestingly, state police now disclosed snippets of this witness' account, whereas eight years earlier they were reluctant to even admit her gender. She said she'd slowed down to look at the young man standing beside the car because she thought he resembled her nephew, a source revealed to *Philadelphia Bulletin* reporter Lawrence

Light. However, she changed the description of his hair several times. She first recalled for police that the young man combed his curly hair straight across his forehead. She later remembered seeing a widow's peak. She was certain, however, that his hair was short, prompting detectives to check with local military bases.

"Unfortunately, we think all we have is a picture of her nephew, not the killer," a detective told Light.

Police interrogated a joy rider who'd stolen a car and plunged it into a pond in the vicinity of the murder scene. George Dix flew to San Francisco and Arizona with Thomas Kinzer interviewing suspects held for similar crimes. Detective James Cuzzupe trekked to the Benrus Company headquarters in Ridgefield, Connecticut, where he rifled through old storage boxes for receipts, files, papers, anything useful in narrowing the point of purchase of the Belforte Sea Diver watch left behind at the crime scene. Jack Kreps continued to make periodic visits to the Whitpain Township Police Department. Their men had been keeping an eye on Mark Thomas, who'd relocated to the Allentown, Pennsylvania, area upon returning from Canada.

"Two years after the crime, my wife got a call from a young man," boardinghouse landlord Walter Syben recalled. "The young man said, 'I killed those girls. And they haven't caught me.' Then he hung up."

By 1980, Detective Sgt. Thomas Kinzer had been named in charge of criminal investigations at the state police barracks in Hammonton, including the unsolved murders of Davis and Perry. Lt. Brennan had retired several years earlier, along with Detectives Kreps, Hart, and Dix. "We've kept it open all these years and every once in a while we get calls and tips which we check out," Kinzer said. "We have suspects whom we interviewed who still have not been totally eliminated."

"I felt bad about that case. I still do," says former Lt. Colonel Jeffrey Barnes. As the second ranking policeman in New Jersey, he once held twelve hundred detectives under his command and was one of the troopers assigned to guard Mark Thomas the night he was escorted to the Berlin barracks. "I don't think any investigator, I don't care how long he worked it, would tell you any different. I don't think you'll talk to anybody who worked on that investigation who wouldn't have given a piece of their pension to solve it."

The families communicated less frequently, Ray Perry said. "We exchanged Christmas cards and kept in touch, and then after a time, less so." Every few years on the anniversary of the tragedy local columnists would write nostalgic pieces, dusting off similar retellings of the troubling mystery. Although these articles appeared more infrequently with the passing years, the alluring narrative never lost its mystique within the beach communities along the downward bend of the Jersey Shore. To this day theories flutter across dining room tables in Ocean City and Somers Point. Versions of what happened to the two young women within the hour after they drove off for home are debated among surf fishermen slinging bunker heads at the inlet in October, waiting for the striped bass to begin their annual southward migration. From mothers who were teenagers themselves in 1969, the cautionary tale is passed to their daughters over hearths on starry winter nights, like a legacy of pioneer wisdom. Among the unemployed and retired whiling away the gusty spring afternoons at the bars near the Point Diner, every May 30th inspires rampant conjuring among those who've tracked the case closest:

Those two girls back in '69? They ran into Ted Bundy is what happened. He was here, did you know that? Nope, he didn't do it, it was a hitchhiker hiding in the backseat of their car outside of the diner, waiting for 'em. There was another serial killer in the area back then, wasn't there? I heard it was a local crazy who got killed in Viet Nam. Whoever did that flagged them down on the side of the road, pretending to be hurt and then lured them into the woods. He was long gone by the time that cop found their car. What a shame. Really, what a shame. I wonder if they'll ever find who did that.

For those who were driving past mile marker 31.9 of the Garden State Parkway early that morning and glimpsed a light-blue convertible parked along the shoulder, an image of whom they witnessed ducking into the murky wooded depths, or might've noticed lingering beneath the oak trees shadowing the forest's edge, remains incomplete. Instead of signaling the advent of summer, each Memorial Day is a haunting reminder of a memory whose missing episodes continue to elude them. Reluctantly accepting their dismal prospects of ever solving the cold case, until 1982 the retired detectives of the Absecon and Hammonton barracks anguished similarly over the chances that had escaped them. That is until one day in October that year, when representatives of the Major Crime Unit heard from authorities in Florida that a notorious criminal, a young man whom they'd sought to question two years earlier, had made a stunning revelation.

CHAPTER THIRTEEN

Bad Seed

Mostly he cruised after nightfall, avoiding the sunny Daytona Beach skies. It was not that he feared detection as he prowled the beachfront avenues, squinting into the noon brightness and blinding glare of the aquamarine surf. Instead he preferred to select from the more susceptible prostitutes slinking about the foggy boardwalk area after dusk, with its palm treed walkways darkened into a gloomily illuminated underworld of tattoo parlors, corner saloons, and faltering neon motel signs. He made exceptions, of course, deviating from his usual pattern if a fortuitous sequence of events randomly presented itself, like driving past a pretty girl stranded on the side of the road midday, gazing worriedly down the open hood of a broken-down car. Or if he crossed paths with a coed seated alone at a Holiday Inn bar, desperate for a lift home. The pastoral serenity of contented families sunning themselves by hotel pool sides and the youthful camaraderie of spring breakers fueled his loathsome contempt toward all varieties of women. Like the hookers he targeted, he felt they were equally deserving of the punishment he craved to inflict.

A pudgy man with thinning black hair, he wore tinted, ill-fitting eyeglasses that fell crookedly upon his temple. A coarse pelt of chest hair spouted from under the open buttons of the flowery polyester shirts and leisure suits he donned while scanning young women leaning against street signs. As he pulled alongside them in his cherry red AMC Gremlin, adorned with a front bumper tag which read, "No Riders Except Redheads, Blondes, and Brunettes," he appeared little different from a typical john roving the oceanfront, perhaps a desk worker in search of a tawdry excursion from his solitude. But it soon became apparent- both to the unfortunate victims who failed to escape him and the few lucky souls who managed to claw free from his grasp-that the hapless character with the showy set of wheels was anything but a mere eccentric seeking a kinky interlude, or someone who would scurry home shamefully after a quick blowjob in his front seat.

Gerald Eugene Stano was the deviant predator lurking in the mind of each teenaged runaway who takes to the streets, the binge-drinking psychopath working gals warn one another about. Relying upon a cunning instinct for avoiding detection, he forged a bloody swath through Florida's Atlantic coast during the mid to late 1970s. He claimed to have murdered forty-one women in all, a figure too low by some estimates, yet seen as falsely exaggerated by those unable to settle on a precise count. It was his routine to guzzle scotch and lurk the waterfront, training his eye upon the girls who appeared desperate enough to trade sex for drug money. As he would confide to a reporter while in prison, beer and whiskey would "help relieve one part of my mind, and the other part of my mind, the subconscious, would take over. I'd just start off, going for a ride, just to relieve some of the tension for myself...just see if I could boil it off by driving somewhere. It didn't work that way. Instead, it would be directed at the young ladies in my car." He rationalized his actions as a means of avenging his own shortcomings. "What made me kill, and kill again, I can't really answer that, except like this: I would be drinking and lonely, and thinking about all the couples having fun together, and here I am single having no fun at all. Then I would go riding around, and I would find a girl walking, and hopefully she would get into my car…"

According to survivors of his wrath, the initial perception of Stano wasn't dispelled within the first moments after he coaxed them into his meticulously kept vehicle, as he compensated for his slow-witted intellect with a peculiarly innocent charm. Soon after luring them inside the Gremlin, its cavern rank with vaporous breath, was when the true horror began. Normally a comment about his weight set him off, or the merest reminder of his ex-wife, perhaps a request to lower the blaring disco music thumping with bass. He'd internalize the slights momentarily, allowing them to simmer. Under pretense of consummating the trick, he'd drive to a secluded location nearby before stunning his unsuspecting prey with a quick blow to the face. So hasty were these unprovoked explosions, even hardened prostitutes who'd prepared themselves for such erratically behaved customers were unable to counter the swiftness of his vengeance with a spray of mace and couldn't escape in time to make a getaway. Most were stabbed to death or strangled within a half hour of their abduction. He discarded their partly nude bodies in wooded ravines, camouflaging them from the roadways with carefully arrayed sticks and leaves. Robbery wasn't Stano's main purpose, for his victims were found with all their jewelry and mementos intact. Nor did he rape them, further perplexing psychologists struggling to decipher his motives. Delivering unto each unsuspecting woman the sorry fate they undoubtedly understood in their fleeting last moments, he never expressed the minutest regard for the suffering he'd caused. As one Florida detective remarked about the killer's unrepentant attitude, "he felt like he had just stamped out a cockroach."

Stano's comeuppance arrived unexpectedly early one morning in March 1980, as he drove up alongside prostitute Donna Hensley on Atlantic Avenue in Daytona Beach. Stoned on Quaaludes, Hensley accepted twenty dollars from the boozy patron and had him drive her to the seedy motel where she was living at the time. After they finished, and Hensley was dressing, a switch fired off in Stano's head. Livid, he rose from the bed and threw on a pair of gloves, searching frantically about the room for a weapon. His brown eyes lit aglow with delusional rage, he slashed at Hensley's bare legs with whatever random instruments were within arm's reach-nail file, knife, can opener, a pair of scissors-ranting how he'd been ripped off and demanding his money back. As he sauntered toward her swishing a jug of burning chemical acid, Hensley dashed through a back door, shattering the pre-dawn quiet. Bloodied by attack wounds, she staggered into the motel lobby screaming for her life.

Based upon Hensley's description of a red car, Daytona Beach Police Department Detective James Gadberry tracked her twenty-eight-year-old assailant to a local Hampton Inn restaurant, where Stano toiled as a short-order cook. The arrest warrant was also based on a similar description offered by other prostitutes in the area, each of whom recalled a similarly unsettling encounter. One after another, Gadberry heard similar tales of the chubby, dark haired man with shaded glasses who transformed into a raving madman after he got off, ranting how he'd been gypped, as if suffering a pervertedly violent buyer's remorse.

Gadberry shared his findings with Chief Marvin Powers, who directed Sergeant Paul Crow to join Gadberry in the questioning of Stano. A senior detective who'd started out with the department in 1966 after a tour of duty in Vietnam, the former Air Force policeman with the bristly mustache and balding pate was a recent graduate of the FBI Academy in Quantico, Virginia, where he'd studied the newfound law enforcement technique known as psychological profiling.

A calm, self-assured presence belied the detective's bulky, powerlifter's frame. Crow was a seasoned investigator with a southern gentleman's demeanor, adept at rooting out the truth from the likes of the fidgety suspect seated before him. At the time of Stano's arrest he'd been studying the unsolved killing of Mary Carol Maher. A former swimming star at Mainland High School in nearby Ormond Beach, the twenty-year old with chlorine-streaked, shoulder-length blonde hair had disappeared while hitchhiking along Atlantic Avenue on January 28. Her body was discovered February 17, 1980, beside a desolate road near the Daytona Beach Regional Airport. She'd been stabbed repeatedly, her corpse sprinkled with sticks and fronds gathered from nearby palmetto bushes, the clothes she'd been stripped of tucked neatly beneath her. Noting the distinct similarities between the thigh wounds suffered by Hensley and those found on Maher, Crow decided to further explore the connection first brought to light by Gadberry. "I knew I was looking for a very neat person, a real Felix Unger, if you will," Crow later remarked.

An exceptionally skilled interrogator, Crow went about questioning his suspect in methodical fashion, allowing a joke about the uneven trim of the seasoned detective's mustache to pass between them with the familiar ease of two old friends trading jabs. He didn't intimidate Stano with swaggering posture or threaten him with the prospect of a lengthy jail sentence if he didn't immediately divulge all he knew. Instead, he deftly forged an alliance within moments of their introduction, forming the basis of a relationship Stano misinterpreted as genuine and trusting.

Within hours after booking him, Crow presented Stano a color photograph of Maher. As if anticipating this moment, Stano admitted knowing her. To the astonishment of his captors, with brazen audacity he stood and gestured Maher's approximate height, specifying the jeans and top she was wearing when he'd killed her. Stano explained that he'd offered Maher a ride for the purpose of soliciting sex from her when an argument ensued. As to what unfolded next, he later described the encounter for a psychiatrist: "I reached under the seat, grabbed the knife, and let her have it one time in the chest...then she slumped over and I stabbed her in the back." Remorselessly he divulged gruesome details of the victim's last moments as she grew delirious with shock, perhaps gagging on her own blood. "She just started, you know, fluttering a little bit...She was muttering some stuff. But it was garbled, really." To test the truthfulness of Stano's confession, Crow, Gadberry, and two other police officers had Stano direct them to the precise location where he'd dumped Maher's body.

On the same day Gerald confessed, Crow contacted his parents, Eugene and Norma Stano. After informing the Ormond Beach couple that their oldest son had confessed to killing Maher, Crow asked for some insight into the troubled young man. Could they pry open a window onto Gerald's personality, perhaps shed some light as to where else he might have killed? As the history of their son slowly unraveled, a crucial portion of his distraught parents' narrative offered a possible connection to the 1969 murders of Susan Davis and Elizabeth Perry.

Gerald's story began in Schenectady, New York, on September 12, 1951, when he was born Paul Zeininger to an abusive alcoholic who'd birthed four children before him. He suffered a horrid infancy, neglected so severely he was forced to subsist on his own feces before being rescued by state officials when was six months old. One psychological report revealed that his birth mother had used a knife to slice open and peel back the tip of his penis, and that he might've suffered from organic brain disease as a consequence of malnourishment. A child placement agency, noting the circumstances of his first months, characterized him as "unadoptable," in those days a cruel euphemism reserved for children born retarded, or possessing other irredeemable maladies too distasteful for upscale couples to overlook. But Norma and Eugene Stano, unable to conceive, were willing to gamble on the troubled thirteen-month-old despite stern recommendations urging them to select otherwise. Like an inherently aggressive breed of dog, it was only a matter of time before his neurological impairments manifested. Amply warned, the couple fell for the damaged child notwithstanding futile attempts to discourage them, finally persuading the city of Schenectady to allow the adoption to proceed.

Within a relatively short time the Stanos took notice of their eldest son's oddities, reaffirming the grim diagnosis they'd chosen to ignore. Two years after Gerald was born, they adopted a second boy, Roger. His inclusion was said to have stoked a fiery rage within his older brother. Gerald once snuck into Roger's room and clobbered him when he was ill, actions stemming from a jealousy which sowed the seeds, a psychologist later theorized, for Gerald's latent savagery. In grade school he bullied classmates and slaughtered chickens with his bare hands. He stole regularly, earned poor grades, and was getting into mischief regularly by the time he was in middle school, once dropping a manhole cover off a highway bridge, smashing the hood of a car beneath him.

It was around this time that Eugene Stano, a public relations executive for El Producto cigars, moved his family from upstate New York to Florida for a spell before returning north again, relocating with his wife and two boys to the Philadelphia suburbs in 1967, purchasing a large split level dwelling at on Arch Street Road in Blue Bell, less than two miles from the home of parkway murder suspect Mark Thomas.

Gerald was a poor student at Shady Grove Elementary School and Wissahickon High School, lonely and without friends. Former classmate Eric Dull, who graduated the same year, remembers a peculiar incident from 1969, during their sophomore year science class. Gerald, teased about his younger brother, who'd been missing from school for about a week, grew frantic in the wake of the tormenting.

"He started getting upset," Dull recalled, "and he said, 'My brother's dead. My brother's dead, 'How would you like to find your brother dead in a ditch? I found my brother dead in a ditch.'" Roger returned to school a week later unharmed. "Gerald was just a kid…strange in general," Dull said. "No one ever feared anything about him. He was just the strange kid on the block."

In hopes of instilling discipline within their incorrigible son, the Stanos enrolled Gerald at Hargrave Military School in Virginia. The experiment was an unmitigated disaster, for before long he was caught stealing money from his fellow cadets. Returned to the halls of his old high school near Norristown following his expulsion, he graduated at age twenty in 1971. He lingered in Montgomery County several years afterward and impregnated a mentally retarded young woman, obligating his parents to pay for her abortion. For a brief time he worked at Bryn Mawr Hospital and Burroughs Corporation in Paoli, but was promptly dismissed from both jobs for petty theft and chronic absenteeism.

Before he sunk into thorough degeneracy, Gerald's parents hoped a change in scenery in Florida might do him good, perhaps stave off his inevitable demise. He moved in with his grandmother in Ormond Beach, where the Stanos owned several properties. The lure of stealing continued to sway their wayward son, as his employment records reflect termination for thievery in each menial job he held thereafter. In a 1975 he married a local hairdresser in Daytona Beach, only to have her file for divorce a year later for beating her, attempting to strangle her dog, and shooting a horse she owned. All the while his drinking problem worsened.

Listening with horror as Detective Crow alleged that Gerald had confessed to savagely murdering Maher, and that he'd led authorities to the precise location where he concealed her body, Eugene Stano retained renowned Daytona Beach criminal defense attorney Donald Jacobson to represent his son.

Crow continued checking into Gerald's background while he remained incarcerated at the Daytona Beach jail. He'd admitted to assaulting Hensley, and cavalierly confessed to murdering Maher. A number of prostitutes had reported confronting a man fitting his description. Soon Crow learned of several local teenage girls who'd gone missing. Noticing an emerging pattern, he expanded the scope of his inquiry and learned there were a plethora of similar unsolved murders in the other states where Stano had resided. These included the outskirts of Philadelphia, in the city's surrounding counties, where aging autopsy photos from unsolved murder cases revealed stabbed corpses hidden among near roadways, each neatly covered with forest underbrush. Apprised by Crow of the uncanny likeness between the crime scenes in Daytona Beach and the 1969 parkway murders, the New Jersey State Police were among the outside agencies most eagerly awaiting the chance to question him.

Eugene Stano urged Jacobsen to plea bargain for his son's life at all costs. The attorney hired local psychologist Ann McMillan to evaluate his client, with the end goal of formulating an insanity defense to rescue him from Florida's vaunted electric chair. But Dr. McMillan found the outcast fully capable of thinking for himself, easily surpassing the legal threshold of distinguishing right from wrong. "Jerry is the closest thing I have ever seen to a bad seed," she told a reporter. "Mary and Joseph wouldn't have saved him."

In the weeks following Stano's confession to the Maher murder, an arrangement was struck among Jacobsen, Crow, and assistant state attorney Larry Nixon. Stano would be offered immunity for murders he'd committed in the Seventh Judicial District of Florida. In exchange he'd receive a life sentence for Maher's murder, spared the electric chair so long as he continued to assist authorities by disclosing where he'd disposed of his victims. The informal agreement only extended to the boundaries of Volusia County, however. If Stano admitted to any murders outside this jurisdiction, the deal was off and neighboring authorities were free to pursue the death penalty. It would be seventeen months, however, before the terms of understanding were entered on record before a judge. Crow continued questioning Stano, allowing himself ample latitude to venture outside Jacobsen's strictly defined parameters.

On April 6, 1980, a twelve-year-old boy discovered the dismembered corpse of prostitute Toni Van Haddocks. Her partly devoured skeleton, scattered by animals, was found in the dense palmetto scrub at the south end of Primrose Lane in the Daytona Beach neighborhood of Holly Hill, five doors down from where Stano's brother Roger was living at the time. The police were aware Gerald had a poor relationship with his brother. Considering the proximity of the victim to Roger, and that Van Haddocks, like Maher, had multiple stab wounds and her body was sprinkled with nearby debris, Crow decided to explore a connection.

On May 9, Gerald confessed to murdering Van Haddocks, later explaining to a reporter that he'd purposely placed the body near his brother's house because "I felt that maybe I could get back at him by doing it over there." In the ensuing weeks, Crow questioned Stano at the Volusia County Sheriff's Office along with Detectives Steven Lehman and Dave Hudson. Ostensibly trying to elicit details of the Van Haddocks murder, truthfully they wanted to confirm their suspicions that he was guilty of several capital offenses both in and outside their state. Craftily persuading the gullible prisoner into believing that the three detectives had his best interests in mind, they cautioned him that other jurisdictions also wanted him for murder, but it wasn't likely they'd bother pursuing him, and perhaps seek the death penalty, if Stano was serving a life term in Florida. Why not clear his conscience? Crow warned Stano that if he didn't divulge more information, he might be whisked away to a jurisdiction where he wasn't under Crow's protection. Stano was clearly flummoxed by this confusing dilemma. Rather than limit the scope of his interrogation to victims within Volusia County, Crow continued to use the looming threat of his execution—Stano's greatest fear—to narrow in on murders in other areas of the country, suspecting he'd nabbed a killer with far vaster boundaries. At the top of the list was New Jersey, followed by Pennsylvania.

While conducting further investigation into Stano's past, on May 14, 1980, the Volusia County Sheriff' Office contacted Sgt. Joseph Stemple of the Whitpain Township (PA) Police Department. Stemple offered to complete a thorough background check on Stano and locate his school records, for Stano's former Blue Bell address was within Stemple's patrol area. Coincidentally, Stemple is the same official who years earlier noticed a trove of Nazi paraphernalia in suspect Mark Thomas's room and coordinated with the New Jersey State Police in the summer of '69 as they tracked his movements in the weeks following the parkway murders.

At some point during the weeks following Stano's arrest in Florida, the New Jersey State Police learned, and withheld from newspapers, that in 1969 Stano lived approximately one mile from Mark Thomas. According to Sgt. Stemple, Corporal Vennera of Whitpain Township, and two other highly placed sources within the Pennsylvania State Police, Thomas and Stano knew one another during their teens, but the terms of their relationship are less clear. The police sources, both with knowledge of the Perry-Davis investigation, characterized the teenagers as friends. Stemple and Vennera recall Stano and Thomas as acquaintances seldom seen in one another's company. Gerald, they concur, was a quiet, strange misfit while living in Blue Bell, mostly keeping to himself.

In 1969 Gerald's younger brother Roger had also been questioned by New Jersey State Police regarding the parkway murders, as Stemple recalls. A teenager also, Roger, who died in 2016, was much friendlier with Thomas than his older brother, according to Vennera. Both men distinctly recall that New Jersey authorities had an interest in speaking to Roger due to his alleged neighborhood association with Thomas.

As neighborhood teens with juvenile records, might Mark Thomas, Gerald Stano, and his younger brother Roger have joined forces, conspiring to make a road trip to Ocean City that ended in murder? In the course of their investigation into Mark Thomas's acquaintances in 1969, did New Jersey State Police detectives question the future serial murderer and release him without any follow-up investigation?

While interrogating Stano again on May 19, 1980, Crow warned Stano that New Jersey detectives were keen on questioning him about a pair of young women stabbed to death near Ocean City when he was a sophomore in high school and living in Blue Bell. New Jersey officials, anxious to fly down to Florida, had a "pretty strong case" against Stano, Crow told him, adding, "they put something of you at that scene." Scenting what apprehensions this topic kindled, the detectives freely exercised their advantage, beginning a game of wits between confessor and captor.

Stano tensely asked his inquisitors to specify which state had been itching to send detectives to meet with him. "Pennsylvania or Jersey?"

"Jersey," Lehman answered.

"Oh, great, that's all I need."

"Oh yeah," Lehman agreed. "A bunch of meat ass Polacks. You know them as well as I know them. You know, they got a couple of lieutenants who were ready to fly down here Friday afternoon. They talked to Paul, and Paul called me and I said, well you know, let's call up and tell them hey look."

"Frankly we're scared. Because they're gonna come down and take you," Crow warned.

"You're scared. Shit. I hate to see what my shorts look like when I get back up there."

"Well, this is what you have to expect because they have strong evidence for you," Crow responded.

"Oh, that's nice."

"Well, that's why we've been asking these questions today trying to get some answers from you," Crow said. "Well, let's back up now and come back to here. We gotta get some clout, so we can keep you in the state. We got the Van Haddocks girl and the Maher girl…you best get yourself ready to talk some more, okay?"

Fixated on the imminent visit from the New Jersey State Police, and by what archaic methods these cops from up north might use to wrangle a confession, Stano remained unfazed as he was presented with grisly crime scene photos of Van Haddocks' severed head. "I'm worried about New Jersey and Pennsylvania coming down here," he admitted.

"Well, so are we, okay?" Lehman added.

"You are? Hey, it's my tail, not yours. You guys go home at night, I don't," Gerald responded.

Later the same night, while describing the knife he'd selected to kill Van Haddocks, Stano shifted the topic back to New Jersey and Pennsylvania, where authorities were anxious to tie him to several unsolved murders in the eastern third of the state.

"Gerald, you want to go ahead and let it rest on just two cases?" Crow asked, referring to Maher and Van Haddock.

"That's all I can do, Paul, 'cause that's all I know of. If I get fried, I get fried. Depending on what the doggone doctors have to say. I'd like to know what Pennsylvania had to say. You can say to some extent without letting the cat out of the bag."

As would soon become obvious during the course of this conversation, Crow was clearly referring to the New Jersey State Police instead of Pennsylvania when he replied, "They've got a pretty, I shouldn't say a pretty good case, but they, you know we've talked at some length about the case they got up there. They connected your good friend to it, mainly." His reference to this unidentified person is significant not so much for the intrigue such a 'friend' imports, as for the response this unexpectedly drew from Stano.

"Do you know his name?" Stano asked.

"Yeah, well I can't tell you," Crow responded.

"Oh thanks."

Feigning worry, Crow warned, "They are probably going to be coming down here in the next week or the week after and place formal charges against you."

"That's nice," Stano replied.

"Not really," Crow retorted, the seriousness of his tone certain to exact any levity from their conversation. "Don [Jacobson] is really upset about it."

"Does he know about this now? Will you call him this morning?" Stano asked.

"I can call him...see what the hell he's got on his mind." Once more Crow tested to see if Stano might divulge specific details of the double homicide in New Jersey. If he was patently fearful of meeting with their state police, what could he be hiding? "I'm curious," Crow began. "The style's a little bit different.

"In what line?"

"Well, they were stabbed to death, too, but there were two girls not just one. One was tied up which was different."

Perhaps on the verge of solving the parkway murders, Lehman interrupted Stano, preventing his suspect from possibly incriminating himself. Later in the same conversation, however, he circled back: "And part of the way we're going to keep you down here is just like Sergeant Crow said, Pennsylvania and Jersey, man, they're chompin' at the bit.

"They think I did..."

Again, Stano's response was cut short by Lehman, once more steering Stano toward the unsolved murders in Volusia County.

Stano refused to cooperate with authorities from New Jersey when they flew down to interview him in 1980, in the days after Crow and Lehman questioned him about the parkway slayings. The Volusia County Sheriff's Office investigation log reveals a number of conversations held between their agency and authorities from both New Jersey and Whitpain Township, Pennsylvania, one day following Crow and Lehman's interrogation of Stano. Specifically, the handwritten notes from May 20, 1980, indicate that Volusia County detectives spoke with Lt. Louis Taranto and other senior officials within the New Jersey State Police Major Crime Unit: "*Cont. Det. Sgt. Thomas Kinzer, or Det. Sgt. Robert Maholland...1969-Camp Hill 2 Girls...Down Shore. Missing from [Somers] Point ...Suspect Mark Thomas.*" This entry, composed the day *after* Crow and Hudson had already divulged specifics of the parkway slayings to Stano, confirms that the New Jersey State Police was the first agency contacted by the Volusia County detectives immediately after interrogating Stano, and that his evasive responses to their pointed questions about the holdback—that one of the coeds had been bound to a tree—were cause for concern. The fact that Thomas was the only other suspect mentioned in the investigation logs further implies that the lanky Norristown teen may have been the "good friend" Crow and Lehman said the New Jersey State Police had purportedly "connected" to the murders of Davis and Perry.

Why would Stano nonchalantly describe murdering two young women in Florida, yet dodge questions when confronted with details of the 1969 parkway slayings, especially when Crow and Lehman offered him numerous opportunities to assert his innocence? What prompted

Stano's sudden interest in the identity of his mysterious "good friend" Crow told him was linked to the double homicide at the Jersey Shore? If he had no knowledge concerning the Davis and Perry murders, why did Stano refuse to speak to the New Jersey State Police in 1980?

These questions went unanswered for the next year as Crow continued to build a foundation of trust with Stano, fielding letters sent from prison. His writings hinted of more victims in fervent hope the senior detective might secure authorization to have him transported back to the Daytona Beach jail, where Stano could relax uncuffed in Crow's inner sanctum. After receiving clearance from Jacobsen, Crow had Stano lead him and Detective Hudson to the bodies of two more victims, Nancy Heard and Ramona Neal. On September 2, 1981, Stano formally entered a plea of guilty to the Volusia County murders of Maher, Vann Haddocks, and Heard in exchange for a life sentence.

Needful of companionship, Stano continued to write and call Crow from Florida State Prison. Pursuant to an order of the state court, he was again escorted back to the Daytona Beach Jail during the week of August 10, 1982, promising to tell more. Two days later, Stano signed a waiver of rights form before confessing to the murder of Cathy Scharf, a seventeen-year-old Port Orange, Florida, hitchhiker he'd choked and stabbed to death in 1977, dumping her body near a roadside gully. As this homicide took place outside county lines, Stano's admission formed the basis of a grand jury indictment for first-degree murder.

In the year before the trial, a procedure was implemented allowing all requests for interviews by other law enforcement agencies to be channeled through Crow's office. His cozy quarters had been a restful haven for Stano, the chair across from the detective's typewriter a shrink's sofa where he was coaxed to divulge his deepest secrets, allowed ample freedom to digress from the topic at hand. Uninhibited, at length he'd babble of souped-up custom cars, his primary infatuation, with the reverent enthusiasm of an Indiana farm boy pridefully removing the dust cover from his gleaming '57 Chevy. Stano's penchant for clothing occupied their discussions also. And of course he'd speak of girls, those he longed for yet detested, prompting him to quip, "I can't stand a bitchy chick." Crow endured his distracting chatter, mining beneath the cathartic impulses and narcissistic ramblings for the identities of more victims. "One day's conversation would be about all I could take for a week," Crow said. "It's like taking a six-hour exam. When it's over, you're distant, empty."

Among the additional girls Stano claimed to have murdered was Barbara Bauer, a doctor's daughter and cheerleader from New Smyrna Beach, Florida. Her death proved that Stano's tastes were more eclectic and varied, not limited to prostitutes and troubled runaways as earlier presumed. "There will probably be some more," the suspect tantalized an *Orlando Sentinel* reporter. "Ninety-eight percent of the cards are on the table now for Florida," he said. "I'm hoping that it will all be over within a month to two months." In early autumn 1982, he offered the following signed statement to Crow:

> " *September 22, 1982.*
> *Going through New Jersey. It was 1972 or 1973. AC Expressway. Small sports car, convertible top Chevrolet. College girls. Custom-grey vinyl top.*
>
> *Gerald Eugene Stano*

In the wake of Stano's somewhat obscure revelation, Crow immediately notified the New Jersey State Police as well as the Pennsylvania State Police, who were investigating the unsolved deaths of four young women found similarly murdered in Montgomery County between 1969 and 1973. Bucks County District Attorney Michael J. Kane also deployed two county detectives to Florida to question Stano about the murders of several women there in the 1970s.

Shortly after Crow advised the New Jersey State Police that Stano had alluded to killing two girls driving in a convertible on a Jersey Shore highway, Lt. Herbert Orth, head of the Major Crime Unit, dispatched detectives Robert Maholland and Thomas Kinzer to Daytona Beach. Kinzer was the logical choice, as he remained in charge of the Perry-Davis investigation out of the Troop A barracks in Hammonton. Before earning his detective stripes, Maholland toiled many sleepless nights in the heady days after the murders in 1969, following new leads and interviewing countless witnesses as a young trooper stationed in the Absecon barracks. As reflected in the Volusia County Sheriff's Office notes, both detectives had detailed conversations with Crow in 1980 and were obviously still intrigued by the circumspect remarks made by Stano at the time. News of their impending arrival was first reported on October 14, 1982. Crow told the *Palm Beach Post* he was withholding details of their forthcoming visit at the request of New Jersey officials: "Investigators from New Jersey are expected at the end of this week or the beginning of next week, and maybe after that we can say more."

"Numberwise, I couldn't say roughly how many," Stano told the *Orlando Sentinel.* " It's rough to answer it…there's two in New Jersey and four to six in Pennsylvania." A glint of hope resurfaced in the long dormant Jersey Shore murder investigation. After all this time, following years of disappointing promise and false hope, did the New Jersey State Police finally have the right man?

Maholland and Kinzer met with Stano at Crow's Daytona Beach office. Though guardedly optimistic, Maholland had learned to temper his enthusiasm over the years, disappointment a constant companion to his overeager hopefulness. He felt a familiar discouragement once he spied a hypnotist's certificate hanging from the wall behind

Crow's chair. He wasn't a believer in psychics, healers, or any other purveyors of the supernatural, especially when practiced by those wearing a badge. "That for me sent up a red flag right away," he says.

Maholland and Kinzer grilled Stano for nearly four hours that morning, sifting through one dodgy response after another. All the while they sensed he wasn't telling everything he knew. As they broke for lunch, Maholland intuited he and Kinzer were being duped, that something was a bit too cozy between Crow and Stano. Maholland "pulled out every stop in the book," he says, allowing every possible inference that the man before him had abducted Davis and Perry and angrily gashed them with his pocketknife in the woods just north of Ocean City, stashing their partly nude bodies underneath a pile of sticks as they lay bleeding to death.

"This Gerald Stano wasn't the tallest tree in the forest," says Maholland. Today a happily retired sport fisherman along the Jersey Shore, Maholland recalls Stano was "totally confused," and "couldn't tell me anything to convince me he was involved in these murders."

Maholland and Kinzer conferred outside Crow's office, debating what strategy to implement that might confirm their suspicions. "I said to Kinzer, 'Tom, this guy is full of shit. He's getting fed something." Maholland decided to test his theory. Before returning to Crow's office that afternoon, the New Jersey detective allegedly disclosed a false piece of information to Crow—the discovery of a bloody blouse he said was located near the crime scene—to see if Crow would turn around and reveal these facts to his prisoner. "I said, 'this was what she was wearing, right?' I told [Crow] that, not the suspect," says Maholland. "I just made it up. Sure as shit, when we went back after lunch we interviewed Stano, and he [mentioned] the same clothes I told the detective about. That detective went and told him," he says. "I was convinced right then and there this was all bullshit."

Maholland adds, "I felt Gerald Stano was just reading shit in the paper, telling this [Crow] that he killed them. I was pretty clever in sniffing shit out back then. I had a bad feeling from the beginning down there. I went through all the motions. I tried to keep an open mind, but when we tell a detective that these girls are wearing something and this Stano comes right back and tells us this an hour later, you know, the guy's full of shit because he's being told what to say."

Stano continued confessing to Crow, despite mounting skepticism. Wire services picked up the feed from local Florida newspapers, and the story caught fire. All eyes were on the former Daytona Beach fry cook. Stano relished his portrayal as a misogynistic knife-wielding maniac, sitting for countless media interviews. Though he admitted to targeting prostitutes walking the streets, "some of them were even just in college, maybe one or two college girls, one or two in high school," he bragged to one journalist. On October 12, Tom Brokaw reported the story for the *NBC Evening News,* as Dan Rather did on the *CBS Evening News* the night before. *Stano Nears Murder Record,* proclaimed *Lakeland (FL) Ledger* writer Robin Williams, speculating that his spiraling body count might surpass Chicago child murderer John Wayne Gacy. According to another newspaper story, Stano told Crow that he'd committed four to six killings each year since his first, the double murders near Somers Point when he was in high school.

Detective Maholland was among the first of several state officials to publicly express grave doubts about Stano's truthfulness. "At this point, we don't believe he's our man. I'm not convinced at all," he told the *Philadelphia Inquirer* nearly a week after his return from Florida.

"He tried to convince us that he killed those girls," Detective Kinzer told the *Atlantic City Press.* "But he couldn't come close to what actually happened...There were enough details about that the crime that he didn't know. He wasn't even close."

Pennsylvania authorities were similarly dubious. Trooper Mike Williams of the Pennsylvania State Police had questioned Stano in Daytona Beach contemporaneously with the arrival of Maholland and Kinzer. Stano told Williams that he'd murdered four young women in the Montgomery County, Pennsylvania, area between 1969 and 1972, pointing out on a map the precise locations where the crimes occurred. A dozen local and state police officers excavated three sites for any traces of the victims. These included the heavily traveled grounds between the road and fence surrounding the U.S. Naval Air Station in Horsham Township, where Stano said he'd dumped the bodies of two women. Behind the screen of the Route 309 drive-in movie theater, near the intersection of Welsh and Evans Roads, was where he allegedly stabbed to death a young woman in 1972. He also claimed to have slain someone wearing a "white nurse's type uniform" after picking her up at the Astor Diner, abandoning her corpse in the woods near the intersection of Horsham and Upper State Roads in Montgomery Township after he was through with her. Searchers spent four hours at each location but found no evidence that anyone had been murdered there.

"We're pretty much closing the books on the guy until he shows us something concrete," Pennsylvania State Police Corporal John McGeehan told the *Inquirer*.

Toward the winter of 1983, Stano began to recant his murder confessions, which by now had reached thirty-nine. According to Graydon McCoy, a Crime Intelligence Analyst for the Florida Department of Law Enforcement, the 1969 double slayings in Egg Harbor Township were among the unsolved cases for which he denied any culpability. However, Stano continued to maintain that he'd killed two women in Pennsylvania.

As to why Stano began withdrawing his confessions with almost the same speed he initially made them was due to the influence of his new team of pro bono attorneys. Mark Olive, a public defender with Florida's Office of the Capital Collateral, argued that Stano's confessions were directly attributable to the coercive influence of Paul Crow. Aware of Stano's gullibility and marginal intelligence, Crow had opportunistically dangled the hope of protection from state prison and death row to persuade him to talk more freely, Olive alleged. His appellate briefs cited numerous instances where attorney Donald Jacobsen had purportedly violated Stano's constitutionally protected right to effective assistance of counsel by allowing him to incriminate himself without an attorney present. Both Crow and Jacobsen harbored an ulterior agenda, Olive explained, with each aspiring toward fame and the prospect of a lucrative book deal.

"Everybody paints a picture of Gerald Stano the happy confessor," Olive said. "It didn't happen that way. The confessions were wrought by psychological abuse."

Given his randomly coincidental emergence within the narrative threads of parkway murder suspect Ronnie Walden, it should come as no surprise to followers of the Perry-Davis case that a more infamous serial killer was housed alongside Stano in 1986, with a forty-foot stroll separating each condemned inmate from the electric chair. Not only did Ted Bundy and Gerald Stano occupy adjacent cells for a time at the Florida State Penitentiary, their death warrants were signed the same day by Florida Governor Bob Graham, who often invoked execution "themes" for publicity's sake. Bundy, when interviewed by Washington State officials seeking his help in solving a string of baffling cases involving murdered prostitutes in that state, likened Stano to the culprit known in the Pacific Northwest as "The Green River Killer."

Referring to Stano, Bundy offered, "I mean, as far as I know, he's one of the nicest, pleasantest individuals I've ever run across." Bundy reasoned that Stano's multiple confessions owed to a mixture of Paul Crow's persistence and Stano's desire to clear his conscience. "It was his skill in bringing Stano along to the point where Stano said, 'Sure, I'll just tell you everything.' But I think it may be a combination of Stano wanting to tell, and somebody knowing how to get it out of him....But now I think Jerry is saying, 'Hey, I really didn't mean all that stuff I told you about. I don't know anything about it.' And that's the position you put someone in, if you bring the full weight of the state down on them."

What reverence Stano held for Crow quickly dissipated as his Day of Judgment drew near. In his final statement, composed the day before his electrocution, he wrote, "I am innocent....Many police officers have come forward and said that I was put on death row by a police officer who lies under oath. This is true....Sgt. Paul Crow created the story....Crow should be held accountable."

Raymond Neal, whose twin sister Ramona had been murdered by Stano, was one of several family members invited to witness the execution. Selected members of the press watched transfixed alongside Neal from behind a glass partition while two corrections officers fastened a leather headpiece atop Stano's shaved skull, attaching a wet ocean sponge before the switch was thrown. "Die, monster, die," Neal uttered as the voltage coursed through the doomed convict's shuddering limbs. At 7:15 a.m. on March 23, 1998, Gerald Eugene Stano was pronounced dead.

"It's a wonderful day," Neal proclaimed later that morning, before throwing back two snortfuls of whiskey. "I'm the happiest man on Earth."

Often adrift in his imagination, Stano told the truth as often as he lied. He didn't begin withdrawing his confessions until the prospect of his death became real, and by that time he'd already implicated himself, leading authorities to the precise locations of twenty victims in all. The likelihood of his culpability in the murders of Susan Davis and Elizabeth Perry hinges upon a careful examination of his tendencies, together with an analysis of the crimes directly attributable to him.

Dr. McMillan warned investigators that Stano might offer up several "red herrings" and "false trails" during interrogations in order to satisfy a craving for attention. While several psychiatrists who'd testified in his two murder trials (the first ended in a mistrial) differed with their diagnosis that Stano suffered from paranoid schizophrenia, they concurred he was a compulsive liar, a common behavioral trait in someone afflicted with antisocial personality disorder. According to the fourth edition of the *Diagnostic and Statistical Manual of Mental Disorders*, the disorder, more commonly known as sociopathy, is characterized by "a pervasive pattern of disregard for and violation of the rights of others." Deception, in the form of repeatedly lying, is a recognized character trait in sociopaths, along with lack of remorse, irritability, and aggressiveness. "It would be nice to have Stano admit to everything," Pennsylvania State Police Cpl. McGeehan told the *Inquirer*, "but Stano is a pathological liar."

His crime scenes tell a different story, however, rebutting commonly held doubts concerning Stano's veracity. Similar to how police investigators detected a pattern left by Michigan serial killer John Norman Collins, Stano's murders were characterized by a distinctive *modus operandi*, a term used by law enforcement agencies to describe an identifiable "method of operation" used by a criminal over a period of time. This repetitive behavior suggests that a series of similar crimes have been committed by the same offender.

Stano habitually lured girls into his cars before subduing them with brute force. He stabbed them with a knife stowed under his driver's seat for quick retrieval, each attack accomplished in a fit of sudden rage that took his victims by surprise. His victims were discovered in rural thickets aside major highways near where they'd been slain, with each body carefully concealed with sticks and brush. He scouted for girls in resort communities like Somers Point and Daytona Beach, towns with a prevalence of bars frequented in large number by college students and young females, offering large seasonal crowds that provided him the cover needed to lurk unnoticed.

As Detective Crow observed, most of Stano's attacks were accomplished within the first fifteen minutes after meeting his victim, fitting within the timeline of the swift abduction and murder of Davis and Perry fewer than two miles from the Somers Point traffic circle, consistent also with the coroner's estimation that their deaths occurred within forty-five minutes of their last meal.

When fleeing the scene of a crime, Stano often pitched his victims' belongings out his car window. The keys to Susan Davis' Chevrolet were discovered one-tenth of a mile north of the crime scene, along the shoulder of the Garden State Parkway, suggesting her assailant flung them in the course of his escape. Stano never left behind a weapon, and the knife used to slay Davis and Perry was never found.

Fueled by violent rage and an intense hatred toward women, Stano stabbed his victims multiple times in the frontal region, often strangling them with his bare hands for added pleasure. These gratuitous measures, which go beyond what is necessary to complete the crime, are classified as "overkill" by criminal psychological profilers, signature behavioral traits often seen in serial offenders to express anger toward their victims. Stano never raped the girls he accosted and made sure to leave them partially clothed, with their private areas exposed. Before strangling Barbara Ann Bauers in September 1973, Stano bound her with a length of nylon rope, securing her tightly with a style of nautical knot he learned to tie when on his parents' houseboat.

In an August 24, 1985, letter he wrote to journalist Kathy Kelly while languishing on death row, Stano admitted a fondness for the Jersey Shore while griping about his domineering parents, confirming he'd spent time there on more than one occasion: "They never [gave] me a chance at anything. It was always what they wanted me to do. If I wanted to take my girlfriends to the shore (N.J.) I had to have their parents talk to mine and confirm it."

Though Stano's confession to the parkway murders was off by at least three years, Crow justifies its reliability based upon a distinct flaw in Stano's peculiar psychology. Though the murderer often possessed an uncanny recollection for the specifics of each murder, he had trouble recalling names and correct dates. "Gerald was always off on time," Crow says today, understanding that Stano's brief statement from 1982 differed in temporal proximity from Davis and Perry's deaths. Having previously questioned him regarding the parkway murders, Detective Crow was unequivocal when first asked his opinion as to who killed the coeds in 1969: "It was Stano." Interviewed a second time nearly a year later, the former detective seemed less adamant.

By his own admission, included among Stano's victims were "one or two college girls," a description befitting Davis and Perry. When speaking to Crow, Stano recalled their murders perfunctorily, a mere afterthought assigned low priority within the bloody corridors of his selective memory. He noted the make of Davis' car and the approximate color of her convertible top, a style of confession eerily similar to his others—that is, the admission of the crime ensconced within a description of the car he owned at the time, or that his victim was driving when they encountered him.

A 1976 Stano mugshot, taken after his arrest by the Daytona Beach Police Department for check fraud charges, reflects a thinner, gaunt complexion, shaggy black hair and suntan, youthful features and dark, almond shaped eyes. His image bears a resemblance to the New Jersey State Police composite released publicly in August 1969, fitting with Lt. Brennan's description of a "a white male, in his late teens, slender build, medium brown hair, which was curly and hung down over his forehead."

At five-feet-eight inches tall, Stano was the approximate height of the man that Albert Hickey witnessed entering a light-blue convertible outside the Somers Point traffic circle. Before his crown thinned with the onset of middle age, Stano had a full head of wavy brown hair, similar to the description of a "shaggy-haired" youth offered by the former Point Diner security guard. Though prostitutes and runways were among his most convenient targets, he also selected more conventional young women from affluent families.

A roamer, Stano wouldn't have thought twice about a spontaneous jaunt to Somers Point. As Florida Department of Law Enforcement official Edward B. Williams commented, "He was the kind of guy who would jump in his car and drive 1,200 miles just to see how long it takes."

Susan Davis was wearing a blue dress and blue jacket when she left the Syben's boardinghouse. The same outfit, piled neatly beside her when she was found three days later, reflects the behavior trait of a fastidious, compulsively neat perpetrator, another of Stano's identifying "calling cards." If one subscribes to Dr. McMillan's theory that Stano purposely stalked victims wearing blue, his brother's favorite color, to avenge a bitter jealousy toward his younger sibling, a reasonable argument can be made that he claimed his first two victims at the Jersey Shore in 1969.

If Crow routinely baited Stano with suggestive prodding, as his doubters allege, why didn't he spoon-feed Stano accurate details of the parkway murders when he confessed to them in 1982? If the renowned detective was disingenuous, wouldn't he have coaxed Stano to change the dates from 1973 to 1969, and lead him to name the correct highway so that the confession would appear a near perfect match to the crime?

Marvin Powers, former Chief of Detectives for the Daytona Beach Police Department, first ordered Sgt. Crow to join in the questioning of Stano immediately following his arrest for the assault against Donna Hensley. Powers remained in the Daytona Beach area after his retirement from the force and today runs a private investigation firm in central Florida. Few others have a greater understanding of Gerald Stano's pathologies. He is unswayed by the suggestion that Stano wasn't a serial murderer and scoffs at the notion he was overly susceptible to Crow's shifty maneuverings. If he didn't murder thirty-nine women, Stano approached a number close to that, Powers is certain. Apprised of details about the parkway murders, Powers says, "If you could put him in the area, he'd be the number one suspect. That sure sounds like him."

David Hudson, a former detective under Powers, questioned Stano "hour after hour, day after day" in the months following his initial arrest. Starting out with the force in 1975, Hudson completed thirty-one years of service with the Daytona Beach Police Department, retiring as Captain of Investigative Services in 2006. Like Powers, he chose to stay in the central Florida area after his career ended, working part-time as a private investigator. "One of Gerald's marks was covering the bodies with brush and sticks," Hudson says, informed of the double murders near milepost 31.9 of the Garden State Parkway. "This leads me to believe he may be involved. Sounds like it very well could be him. That's how he used to do it." Hudson doesn't subscribe to the prevailing wisdom among disbelievers who contend Stano's confessions were nothing more than extravagant creations shaped by Crow's guidance. "Gerald was the truest sociopath I've ever met," Hudson says. He remembers a man who could recite the make, model, engine, and body type of a vehicle before he'd remember the color of a victim's hair, or the exact date he'd killed her. "I am 100% convinced that every murder he confessed to he did. No doubt in my mind."

A host of factors point toward Gerald Stano's involvement in the 1969 murders of Susan Davis and Elizabeth Perry. On paper he seems like the ideal candidate for so horrific a deed, despite his questionable credibility. He fits the general physical description offered by witnesses. He resided a short drive from the Jersey Shore and offered a cryptic admission to the murders of Davis and Perry. The crime site near milepost 31.9 reflected a near perfect match with other murders attributable to him. When pieced together, the abundance of circumstantial evidence explains why the Major Crime Unit went to the expense of flying senior troopers to Florida on two separate occasions to investigate a connection, no matter how tenuous it seemed. And although Detective Kinzer returned from Florida wary of Stano's truthfulness, a year later he admitted to Florida journalist Leslie Kemp that his interrogation of Stano was "inconclusive...we have nothing to connect him to the murders, but we can't eliminate him." Because the state police still had no murder weapon, or witnesses who could positively identify him as the youth seen loitering near milepost 31.9, the consensus remained that the killer was still at large.

Were it not for the enigma surrounding Stano, the Davis-Perry file boxes would've resumed their station among the shelves at the West Trenton storage facility. But due to the vast publicity generated by the serial killer's lurid tale, several months after their disappointing foray to Daytona Beach, the New Jersey State Police heard from an Atlantic County man compelled by his own conscience to share his secret. He said he'd spotted a man near the crime scene fourteen years earlier and stood ready to identify him.

CHAPTER FOURTEEN

The Gospel According to Mark

On May 29, 1983, nearly fourteen years to the day from when Susan Davis and Elizabeth Perry were murdered, the *Philadelphia Inquirer* reported that an Atlantic County, New Jersey, man had provided the New Jersey State Police with crucial information about the 1969 parkway slayings. According to a state police source, the witness had been driving a truck near his home in Egg Harbor Township, near mile marker 31.9, at approximately 6:30 a.m. on the day both women were killed. He'd spotted a man walking briskly along the opposite side of Mt. Airy Avenue, and as the witness slowed his truck to have a look at him, the man ducked suspiciously into the woods alongside the road. His conscience had begun to bother him earlier in the year, the witness said, after he read in various newspaper accounts where Gerald Stano had confessed to the murders of Davis and Perry. He was quite certain the Florida serial killer wasn't the man he'd seen that Memorial Day. According to *Inquirer* reporters Robert J. Terry and Robert Fowler, "The man the witness selected has been a suspect in the slayings almost from the beginning."

South Mt. Airy Avenue extends in a southeast-northwest direction, perpendicular to the Garden State Parkway and Black Horse Pike. It ends at an intersection with Steelmanville Road, several hundred feet from the overpass tunnels crossing under the southbound lanes of the parkway, approximately a quarter mile from where the bodies of Elizabeth Perry and Susan Davis were found.

Behind Stephen Hauck's one-story roadside cottage at 28 South Mt. Airy Avenue is a vast dirt lot surrounded by a forest of scrub pine and oak. Hauck, originally from Pomona, New Jersey, purchased the property in 2011 as headquarters for his booming house relocation business. Today the cottage is used as a den where workers rest between shifts. During weekdays the sandy off-road lot behind it is a billowing haze of dust clouds kicked up by roving pickup trucks and flatbeds toting bulldozers. Forklifts and cranes, used to lift homes from their foundations, are stored beside rows and rows of storage trailers. But when Hauck purchased this land several years ago, the vast expanse had become a decaying junkyard scattered with half-submerged truck frames, old hydraulic lifts, copper strippers, and rusty flatbed trailers, with the cottage facing Mt. Airy Road and forty-two acres behind it belonging to his close friend, an eccentric junk dealer named Robert D'Amore.

Until his death in 2011, D'Amore lived at the cottage and used his vast acreage as home to his once-thriving scrap metal business, National Salvage Company. He earned his living primarily by purchasing high voltage transformers from Atlantic City Electric, stripping down their useful parts, then hauling the meltable scraps to Reading Metals Refining Company in Pennsylvania. By then it had been years since the business had prospered, and the faint hum of parkway traffic echoed distantly through his silent expanse, resembling an abandoned construction camp in a desert boomtown run out of money. The warped axle rod of an eighteen-wheeler rested near one side of the home, beneath a NO TRESPASSING sign. Similar notices were stapled conspicuously to telephone poles in the vicinity, a warning to deer hunters and opportunistic trash pickers seeking to scavenge a few sections of aluminum piping. An aging

Mercedes sedan was parked out front on a dirt driveway, its interior scattered with balled store receipts and Styrofoam cups. From under an eave a pet rooster crowed achingly beside the front door, pecking at his cage.

In his eighties, long since retired and reliant on a walker in his final years, D'Amore passed his time watching late show reruns while comfortably ensconced in his La-Z-Boy, a row of pill bottles within arm's reach. Though able to, he didn't bother getting up to welcome visitors at his door or turn to greet them as they knocked. Bald, with deeply set blue eyes, he was congenial toward guests despite a gruff manner of speaking, nonchalantly beckoning their entry as if they were a neighbor come to borrow a socket wrench. What havoc exhaustion and heavy machinery had wrought on the old man's body, the Lord compensated for with a keen intellect mostly unscathed by the ravages of time, and an ample sex drive satiated by visits from a steady stream of Atlantic City prostitutes who, according to Hauck, "robbed him blind." Interviewed one hot, dry July afternoon in 2010, D'Amore clearly recalled the day in 1983 when New Jersey State Police Det. Sgt. Robert Maholland paid him a visit, some six months after questioning Gerald Stano in Daytona Beach.

Maholland had heard from a fellow New Jersey State Police trooper who'd taken a call from an Atlantic County junk dealer claiming he had knowledge about the co-ed murders of '69. Having nothing to lose and everything to gain by this point, with faint expectations Maholland paid a visit to D'Amore, then fifty-seven years old, at his Egg Harbor Township home. "He said, 'I saw a guy walking up here that morning,'" Maholland recalls. "He described his clothes. I said, 'Why the fuck didn't you tell somebody?' He said he did tell somebody, but he couldn't remember who he told. I said, 'Do you think you could pick this guy out if I showed you a lineup?' He said I think I can, so I got six of the closest pictures I could come up with and he picked that fucking guy out in about three seconds."

"It was early," D'Amore said, leaning forward in his chair, speaking loudly to hear his voice above the studio audience laughter from a *Tonight Show* rerun playing on his TV set. He eagerly recounted the episode from that Memorial Day, which occurred within moments of turning left out his driveway early that morning. He was driving a tow truck, on his way toward Somers Point to "scrap some cars" with a hired laborer who was seated beside him. There had been a spate of break-ins in the neighborhood recently, and D'Amore had begun viewing strangers askance. "I'm driving down the street here, on Mt. Airy Avenue. So now, this guy, he's walking up the street, the opposite direction. First, I remember exactly how he walked." With both elbows tucked to his sides, D'Amore aped the gestures of an evasive figure walking hurriedly in a straight direction, as if constrained, yet poised to burst into full sprint. "He was tall, and as I pass him, he ducks into the woods real fast. I jumped out of the truck, and I thought maybe he robbed somebody. He was wearing dark clothes and walked just as straight as an arrow. And at a good pace. Before I got to him, he was in the woods. I was a short distance, about ten yards from him. I didn't even pass him, and he was already in the woods, I knew he did something, but I didn't think it was a murder because his clothes weren't messed up." Nor did D'Amore see any blood on the stranger's clothing or other signs he'd been in a tussle. The worker seated beside him, described by D'Amore as "kooky and unreliable," wasn't able to describe the man seen slipping into the shadowed foliage.

"These two girls, they didn't deserve to get murdered the way they did," says D'Amore. "I wanted so bad for him to get caught because I felt sorry for the parents of these children. I tell you one thing, if I'd a caught him, he wouldn't have gotten away. I was a tough son of a bitch. In them days I could've picked up the back end of a car. When you're ducking away from something, there's something that you did." As if anxious to prove his veracity, D'Amore rose from his recliner, eased out the front door toward his car and proceeded toward the precise location on the eastern divide of the road where the incident occurred. Heading down Mt. Airy Road, he gazed out his driver side window, slowing at an approaching intersection. "Right...there!" he exclaimed, jabbing a finger toward the stand of trees just steps north from the turn onto Old Zion Road.

"You know, he didn't look exactly the same, but I picked him out," D'Amore said as he returned home, referring to the moment when Sgt. Maholland arrayed a half-dozen close-ups before him, asking him to choose the man he'd seen ducking into the woods that Memorial Day morning. Without hesitation, he pointed to Mark Thomas.

The state police presented their findings to the Atlantic County Prosecutor's Office for possible indictment by a grand jury. Before he was appointed lead prosecutor, Jeffrey Blitz headed the office's criminal investigation section. A hard-nosed, well-regarded attorney possessing little tolerance for meddling reporters, Blitz refused to elaborate on any new information in the parkways slayings beyond the standard reply, "We will neither confirm nor deny whether the state police have turned over any new evidence. We do not comment on cases being actively investigated."

On December 8, 1983, despite a statement from the first eyewitness to place Thomas a mere two hundred yards from the crime scene, Atlantic County Prosecutor Joseph Fusco announced that his office had ended their latest inquiry into the 1969 Memorial Day murders. "All available evidence concerning this case has been evaluated, and, to this date, no evidence exists to charge any person in connection with the murders," Fusco said, identifying Thomas as "a long-distance truck driver in the Norristown area."

Mark Thomas was born in Philadelphia, Pennsylvania on October 16, 1950, to William and Alvera Thomas. The family lived in York, Pennsylvania, for a time before his father, a Dun & Bradstreet salesman, moved his brood to their spacious two-story home on Thayer Drive in Whitpain Township.

Tall, with a rangy frame and large protruding ears, as a boy Thomas was taunted by classmates who noted his resemblance to the Ichabod Crane character from *The Legend of Sleepy Hollow*. The eldest of three children, he was neither quiet nor shy, despite the skinny awkwardness he portrayed. Former neighbors recalled a glib, towering boy impressed by own his quirky behavior, such as crawling through the sewer tunnels beneath Thayer Drive and expertly tying complicated string knots. His eccentricities drew a devoted following of neighborhood peers, though an equal number kept their distance from the mercurial youngster.

He dropped out of school after his eighth-grade year at Shady Grove Junior High School in Ambler, where Gerald Stano had attended before shipping off to military school. Given their closeness in age, with Thomas less than a year older, the two likely roamed the halls at the same time, even if their relationship remains somewhat of a mystery.

Long after he had become a well-known figure in civil rights groups such as the Anti-Defamation League and Southern Poverty Law Center, Thomas was asked about his background by several reporters in the wake of his surging notoriety. Interviewed by reporter Vince Rause in an August 1994 *Philadelphia* magazine feature article, he said "I knew then that schools are BS, that they're just places where they turn people into sheep." Instead of attending high school, his teenage years in the late 1960s were spent wandering the East Coast, he explained, working odd jobs and protesting the Vietnam War as a member of the militant organization Students for a Democratic Society. "I hit the road," the former hippie mused, "did my Jack Kerouac thing."

Thomas told *Morning (PA) Call* reporter John Martin that he'd fled basic training in North Carolina after speaking at length with returning combat veterans who were bitter toward Uncle Sam. "I would have nothing to do with the Army after I realized what was going on," he said, ironically admitting to Martin that he often invoked the U.S. Armed Forces Constitutional Oath. Jack Kreps, however, steadfastly maintained that Thomas shot for the border when he learned that the tenacious detective was on his way down to question him again, not due to any ideological objection.

He undertook an odd assortment of jobs to sustain his itinerant wanderings about North America, consumed vast quantities of peyote, and shared quarters with a Native American woman in Ottawa. For a while Thomas joined the crew of a traveling carnival and worked as a cook in a Canadian logging camp, the latter admission eerily echoing Detective Kreps' disclosures in a 1970 *Courier (NJ) Post* newspaper interview.

His immersion in the liberal counterculture also included stints loitering in Philadelphia's Rittenhouse Square and fraternizing with beat poets in Greenwich Village. It was in New York City, according to Indiana State University Professor of Criminology Mark Hamm, where Thomas underwent a life-altering epiphany upon randomly encountering Jim Morrison at a downtown bar in 1969. According to Hamm, Thomas claimed he "spoke briefly" with the Doors' mordant lead singer, who offered up dark wisdom about the meaning of life, the first of several men to cast a bewitching spiritual influence over the impressionable teen and help shape his views in the coming years.

Missing from Thomas's wistful tales of self-exploration, which he offered freely in various permutations to local and national reporters during the Eighties and Nineties, was any reference to the Garden State Parkway murders. Conspicuously absent, too, were any recollections harkening back to Kreps and the New Jersey State Police, how they incessantly monitored the young man's movements after he crossed the border into Canada and later re-entered the states sometime in the early 1970s.

Thomas remained in the Norristown area after returning to Pennsylvania from Canada, finding work as a truck driver and day laborer. In 1977 he married Barbara Tipton, who gave birth to the first of their three children. In 1980, with his part in the parkway murder probe a shared secret between him and law enforcement officials, Thomas moved his wife and kids into a ramshackle stone farmhouse on twenty-three acres of Pennsylvania Dutch country in Macungie, a borough outside Allentown in Lehigh County. Situated in Longswamp Township, amid a patch of roadside woods several miles from the Bear Creek ski resort, the former junkyard was littered with rotting tires, rusted appliances, and disabled automobiles. In exchange for rent of one dollar a month, Thomas pledged to rebuild the Walker Road property for its owner, Donald Neilson, a Montgomery County developer. Thomas reneged on his commitment, however, allowing the premises to wallow in disrepair.

During the early 1980s Thomas took a job as a driver for George Kemner, the controversial owner of KEM Transportation & Equipment Company in Limerick, Pennsylvania. Kemner was a devout follower of Christian Identity, a religious ideology whose core faith holds that white persons of Anglo-Saxon, Celtic, Scandinavian, and similar northern European ancestry are descendants of the Lost Tribes of Israel, therefore God's chosen people. Fervent anti-Semites, Identity adherents believe Jews are the spawn of Eve and the Serpent. A shady character who'd been investigated by the state police for hiring unqualified drivers and using rigs with faulty brakes, he preached at length to his acolyte, with the young study listening closely at his heels. Similar to his brush with Jim Morrison, Thomas was spellbound by his elder prophet, as if awakened to a profound revelation. "It was as if I'd somehow known these truths all my life," Thomas told Rause. "I firmly believed Christ was a Jew...I believed the Jews were the chosen people of God." Raised as an Episcopalian, Thomas said he flirted with agnosticism and born-again Christianity before seeing the light. "I found that [Christian Identity] was a spiritual understanding of a racial truth, that God's covenant was peculiar to the Aryan race."

As Thomas started up his own small trucking business after Kemner died, he found himself drawn even closer to extreme-right Christian fundamentalism. Each week he brought his wife and children to the Salem Bible Church in Macungie, where he taught Sunday school, calling and writing fellow congregants in a crusade to proselytize them. As his rhetoric turned more provocative, with weekly tirades aimed toward Jews and Blacks, church leaders denounced him.

As if taking his cue from the spirited revolutionaries he'd seen rallying youthful throngs at the parks and streets of Philadelphia, Thomas began ranting publicly about the illegality of taxation. His views reflected the teachings of the Christian Posse Comatitus, an offshoot survivalist movement begun in 1970 by Californian William Potter Gale. Latin for "power of the county," its adherents, most of whom are white supremacists and Christian Identity members themselves, believe the U.S. Constitution does not grant law enforcement powers above the county level, and that state and federal governments are part of a vast conspiracy to undermine their Second Amendment rights. They refer to Washington, D.C., as the Zionist Occupational Government ("ZOG"). The Book of Revelations is interpreted as a manual for a looming battle pitting Aryan warriors against Jews, Blacks, and other "mud people" who've diluted the purity of the Caucasian race. Heavily armed, Posse members hoard canned food and stash ammunition in their underground bunkers in preparation for the final Holy war.

Pastor Thomas trumpeted his brand of separatism at a local shopping mall, where he worked part-time as an instructor at the George Gordon Barrister's Inn School of Common Law. Founded by a former waterbed manufacturer from Boise, Idaho, who died in 2014, Gordon's website touted him as "the nation's foremost teacher of pro se courtroom strategy and procedure, a pioneer who taught himself the ins and outs of defending himself in court when Big Brother put him out of business." Readily assuming the role of neighborhood provocateur, Thomas held himself out as a self-taught lawyer eager to assist the common man against his government oppressor. When a local judge disallowed him from appearing as counsel on behalf of a defendant fighting a traffic ticket, Thomas led a protest outside the courthouse steps after the proceedings ended, sporting a t-shirt that read, "The Lord giveth and the government taketh away...but only if you let it." He chimed to a reporter, "The only way to change the law is to challenge it. We're not being antagonistic or anything. We just want our freedom." On another occasion he tried to represent his wife Barbara before The Hon. Calvin Lieberman of the Berks County Court. Appealing her fine for driving his unregistered car, Thomas argued that she was his property, and thus his servant under the theory of English Common Law. "The issue is basically no different than cattle being in the public right-of-way," Thomas argued. "It's not that I am a chauvinist, but that's just the way the law works in this case." Judge Lieberman was none too amused by his theatrics and threatened to toss Thomas in jail for practicing law without a license.

Acting on complaints from neighbors, on multiple occasions Longswamp Township ticketed Thomas for violations of its junk-removal ordinance, with orders to clean up the automobile parts strewn about his yard. For the most part he ignored the citations and refused to pay his taxes, taunting local officials by posting anti-government signs for passersby to see. He fed his daughter milk from the goats roaming freely about his land, and his wild geese often disrupted traffic as they crossed Walker Road. The township was reluctant to approach the towering figure with the sallow complexion, dank black hair, and dark brooding eyes, undoubtedly intimidated at some level by his brash defiance.

Pennsylvania State Police Detective Stanley Levengood, stationed out of the Reading barracks during those years, was among the local troopers called to Walker Road on several occasions to investigate allegations of automatic gunfire echoing from the woods behind the farmhouse. Little could be done to tame Thomas's flagrancy, for all his firearms were duly registered and legally obtained. "He was a strange character," says Levengood. On one occasion, as he was speaking to Thomas in his driveway, a pit bull began humping the rear fender of his police cruiser, rocking the entire chassis. "The township wouldn't go after him because they were afraid of him. He was a scary looking guy, reminded me of someone right out of the mountains of West Virginia."

Behind his farmhouse Thomas set up a trailer that served as a makeshift chapel, dedicating it to Albert Lentz, onetime leader of the racist White Unity Party in York County, Pennsylvania. Inside, Aryan Nations flags adorned walls shelved with works such as *Mein Kampf*, and mercenary fare like *Combat* and *Soldier of Fortune*. Copies of *Guns & Ammo* were stacked in boxes, beside rows of folding chairs.

Enticing bedraggled white men back to his church with the promise of free food and coffee, Thomas cruised the local country roads in a dilapidated blue school bus kept parked in his backyard. At first he corralled but a smattering of curious onlookers, sharing his message with anyone who'd listen. "I went to truck stops, taverns, anywhere I could think of, and sought out decent working men who were serious, two-fisted people. Where I went I found an audience." His

Identity sermons were derived from a mélange of sources including the Old and New Testaments, Carl Jung, the U.S. Constitution, and Jim Morrison. The Lizard King's darkly surreal poetry and apocalyptic lyrics, heard in such songs as "The End," dovetailed with Thomas's own version of the doomsday prophecy. According to his take on Armageddon, the Posse Comatitus warriors will overcome the forces of evil, cleanse the earth of inferior races, and create an eternal Kingdom of Christ on Earth in the aftermath of their triumph. Blacks, Hispanics, and other non-whites would be relocated to their land of origin. The Jews, as understood by Thomas's reading of the Bible, "must be cast into hell."

Traditionally, a large percentage of Christian Identity followers have also belonged to the Ku Klux Klan. Thomas told a reporter that he first joined the secretive organization in the late 1980s. As a rising star within their hierarchy, he presided over a number of local rallies as part of his effort to change the Klan's image as a violent faction better known for tree lynchings and cross burnings in the Deep South, and was seen wearing a white robe and hood at traffic intersections, holding out a can for donations. "I found that many people in the Klan were prejudiced," he explained to a reporter. "They wanted to sit in bars, read Playboy and bitch about the 'niggahs.' But I worked hard to lead them away from that kind of thinking, which is counterproductive, and helped them to think about the things that are important: to understand the true origins of the white race, to identify the real source of our social problems." His mission: spread the belief that racial integration was a Jewish conspiracy formed to eradicate Christianity. "Racial segregation is God's law. And it's the duty of the Anglo-Saxon people to see that those laws are followed...." Continuing to offer only a selective interpretation of his past, Thomas conveniently neglected to mention his previous affiliation with the hate group, investigated by an undercover detective with the New Jersey

State Police in the weeks after the parkway murders, and seen on vivid display in his bedroom on Thayer Drive.

At a march he led at Valley Forge National Park in 1988, thirty or so Klansmen in white-hooded regalia gathered at the historic battlefield as a crowd estimated at four hundred watched the spectacle unfold. "People say that because I'm in the Ku Klux Klan, I hate people," Thomas began. "Let me say right here, I love every black person in this country. And I love my own white people a little bit more. That isn't hate." The main thrust of his lecture he aimed toward the true enemy. "Every black person here has an ancestor that was kidnapped, taken from his family and his homeland and brought here in the hellhole of a Jewish ship," Thomas bellowed from onstage as several disgusted onlookers flung spit at his robed brethren distributing literature. "Open any textbook and you'll see the publisher was a Jew. Every television station you watch, everything is controlled by Jews." He snidely added, "The black people here might be interested to know that Malcolm X was killed by the Jews and replaced by Martin Luther King, who was a traitor to his people. Now he's supposed to be a hero?"

By the time of a local Independence Day rally in 1989, Thomas had been named Grand Chaplain for the state of Pennsylvania Invisible Empire of the Knights of the Ku Klux Klan. "What our founding fathers had intended for this country is a far cry from what we've got today," he cried out to the rain-soaked crowd. "The Jew is running this country like Benjamin Franklin said he would, and he's destroying all the races…and, it's going to get worse. Our people are going to turn this country around and it's going to begin right here.

"What's the matter with America," Thomas went on, "we have a Jewish problem. We don't have a black problem. Who do you think brought the blacks here? The Jews did."

"Kill the fuckers!" a man hollered from the crowd.

"You're not going to kill them," Thomas replied, "you're going to send them back....If you don't do something soon, you're going to be slaves in your own country. It's time for you to wake up for your children's sake."

Thomas's Walker Road homestead drew reporters from all over the Lehigh Valley, eager to learn more about the "father, minister, journalist, philosopher," as Thomas once described himself. Greater numbers flocked to his sermons, seeking a pathway to salvation. Aware of his connection to the 1969 Perry-Davis homicide investigation, the Pennsylvania State Police, who'd already tightened aerial surveillance over him, joined forces with the New Jersey State Police. Together they hatched a covert plan to remind Thomas that his antics hadn't gone unnoticed, and that he'd remained on their radar all along.

According to Captain John McGeehan of the Pennsylvania State Police, the same man who led an investigation into Gerald Stano's confessions to a number of unsolved Pennsylvania slayings, on an anniversary of the parkway murders an undercover trooper purportedly sent Thomas an envelope containing a greeting card, using a local post office to drop the mail so the return address would remain unidentifiable. Enclosed in the card were photographs of Susan Davis and Elizabeth Perry. From a distance, intelligence detectives allegedly spied through high-powered binoculars as another undercover trooper with the Pennsylvania State Police, posing as a postman, delivered the mail to the Walker Road property. A third, assuming the identity of a young Thomas follower, had been placed inside the main dwelling to gauge his reaction as he read what was inside. According to McGeehan, Thomas was visibly shaken as he viewed the pictures of the Memorial Day murder victims, "as if he'd just seen a ghost." He immediately stormed out of the main farmhouse and stalked toward an outbuilding, allegedly reappearing fifteen minutes later without the envelope in his possession.

Ambushing him with demons from the past didn't send Thomas scurrying into the shadows, as police had hoped. As the suspicious activity at Walker Road continued, his wife Barbara left him, taking their three children with her. Disabled as a result of a 1989 truck accident, he subsisted on welfare payments and other governmental provisions. To help put food on the table he created *The Watchman* newsletter, resuscitating an old printing press located next to his chapel. Requesting a small donation for a subscription, he posted its incendiary contents on *Stormfront*, a white supremacist website affording him the ideal vehicle to spread his word of hate to a growing legion of the nation's young neo-Nazi movement. In 1990 Thomas traveled to Richard Butler's Aryan Nations headquarters in Hayden Lake, Idaho, where he spoke at the Aryan Nations World Congress and was ordained as a Christian Identity preacher. He shared the stage with Tom Metzger of the California-based White Aryan Resistance, and Robert Millar, the mainstay of a large Identity community in eastern Oklahoma known as Elohim City. Before he lit out for home, Thomas pledged to Pastor Butler that he'd make his farm the Aryan Nations compound of the East. (According to a *Klanwatch Intelligence Report*, however, Thomas was booted from the lakeside "white homeland" due to his "philandering with skinhead girls.")

After returning from the Idaho panhandle, for the next several years Thomas hosted weekend galas out behind his Macungie spread, teaching white Christian rule to members of the Klan, neo-Nazis, and Aryan Nations brotherhood. Their leaders, accustomed to hearing bumbling hillbillies struggle to be understood at the podium, listened enthusiastically to this flamboyant orator masterfully articulate the source of their white rage. His firm grasp of syntax and flair for the eloquently impassioned delivery contributed toward his swift rise through the racist underground network, belying his middle-school education. In 1991 he assumed the reins as national head of the Posse Comitatus after its leader, James

Wickstrom, was convicted of plotting to distribute $100,000 in counterfeit bills. A number of ardent disciples moved in with Thomas, raising concerns he was transforming the farmstead into a training academy for Hitler youth. On any given weekend carloads of Pennsylvania skinheads traveled from distant counties to hear their guru hold forth at his outings, joining him beneath a large military-green tent stored in his church trailer.

"They go up there each week and get their batteries charged," remarked Richard Anliott, then director of education and community service for the Pennsylvania Human Relations Commission. "Thomas sees himself as a father figure to all these guys." His neighbors, among them horse breeders and owners of historic inns, suspected he was using the property for survivalist training that included target practice with live rounds. Police inspected his firing range, however, and deemed it safe. A sizeable contingent of local authorities continued to view Thomas as an egotistical crackpot rather than a ticking time bomb. It was as if he understood all too well the balancing act played by law enforcement officials and politicians, which ordinances they were willing to enforce, and what violations they'd let slide as a waste of their manpower. He routinely pressed these ill-defined boundaries, as though challenging the cops to cuff him so he could make a grand spectacle of the occasion, twist the message, and eagerly assume his role as leader of the oppressed everyman.

Thomas's fortunes changed most notably in the winter of 1993. Remarried by now, he sired two more children with his new bride, Donna Marazoff. That same season he invited Fox television crews onto his land to film a segment for a syndicated program, "Face the Hate," hosted by *Beverly Hills 90210* actress and current SAG President Gabrielle Carteris. The video began at a kitchen table, with the petite young woman who once portrayed plucky high school newspaper editor Andrea Zuckerman bravely facing an entourage of tattooed thugs garbed in camouflage gear and swastika bands. She was confronted by burly Identity member August Kreis, a renowned Klan brother from Pennsylvania who would figure prominently in the white-power movement for years to come. "Are you a kike or just married to one?" he challenged the nighttime soap star. After confirming she was Jewish, and married to a man of similar faith, Carteris asked the group, "What do you feel is the only way to get rid of the Jews?"

"Kill 'em all," someone muttered. Others called out, "Six million more! Death! Genocide!"

Later in the broadcast, as Carteris stood amid clumps of grimy snowmelt outside the mobile home church, from mere steps away Kreis gestured toward the holstered semi-automatic clipped to his waist and said, "If God was commanding me, I'd reach down right now and just take care of business."

Masked foot soldiers clad in paramilitary wear and berets stood guard close by, bearing AK-47 rifles. As the camera turned to Thomas, he declared from the shadows, "My Bible does say that the Jews are the people of Satan and our God commanded us to exterminate them."

In an interview with local newspaper writer Chuck Ayers of the *Morning (PA) Call* in June 1993, given on the day the program aired, Thomas quickly dispelled the notion he was stockpiling munitions for an inevitable confrontation with the government, like the showdown that had ended tragically at the Branch Davidian compound outside Waco, Texas, in April that year. "Those people who were carrying firearms [on the television show] were not from here. We're not a heavily armed compound. I'll tell you that. It's a home. We have no illegal weapons here. It's not a fortification of any kind."

The show served as a turning point, despite Pastor Thomas's futile attempts at damage control. The viewing public didn't see an eccentric racist leader entertaining a television crew, or merely seeking a forum to espouse his agenda. They witnessed instead a small army of racists wielding semi-automatic weapons, commanded by an apparent genocidal demagogue who in no uncertain terms had uttered the directive to "exterminate" an entire race of people. They were looking for a reason, and they found one to fear him.

After "Face the Hate" aired, Thomas forbade all media from his property. State police, till now no more than a bothersome nuisance, made Thomas paranoid under their constant watch. "They keep us under regular surveillance," he complained to a reporter. "I'm sure they've tapped my phone. They systematically photograph people who come here. I've heard their helicopter fly over us so low that it blew down the tent we were meeting in and interrupted a Bible study."

Among Thomas's most vocal opponents during this time was Floyd Cochran. The two met during their stay at Aryan Nations headquarters in 1990, when Cochran was director of propaganda and youth recruitment for the Aryan Nations, the fifth-highest post in the organization. He relinquished his position and defected from the white-power movement after leaders insisted he euthanize his son, who was born with a cleft palate. "Now I'm not saying that Mark Thomas will tell these kids to go blow up a building, or go do this or that," Thomas's arch nemesis reflected, "but when you fill a kid's head with militant texts from the Bible, when you tell them over and over that they're warriors of God, then it's only a matter of time before some of them decide to trigger the race war by going out to commit racist crimes."

The comparisons were unavoidable. "From the beginning that's what strikes you, the parallels between David Koresh and this guy," said Richard Anliott. Thomas, he concluded, was "setting himself up as Pennsylvania's pope in a religion of hatred."

By 1994, Thomas was arguably the most recognizable white supremacist in Pennsylvania. Now forty-four years old, he married for a third time and impregnated his nineteen-year-old bride, Wendy, soon after his second wife left him. While a guest on an episode of *The Maury Povich Show* that aired on June 22, 1994, Thomas quoted scripture as a stage full of young white supremacists shouted in unison, "White Power!" Simultaneously, the viewing audience watched footage of a cross-burning ceremony at his farm. As for why he appeared on these tabloid programs (his debut on *Geraldo* would soon follow) and continued to pursue the unforgiving glare of notoriety, he cockily explained to *Morning Call* reporter John Martin, "Somebody's got to do it....I am a public figure."

Thomas would often distribute flyers for the numerous rallies he hosted at his farm, replete with live performances by heavy metal bands. One of these two-day-long extravaganzas, celebrated in October 1994, he billed as an "Aryan Nations Gathering," with the topic for discussion "National Socialism, Identity, and Odinism, Choices in a Changing World." At first glance the invitation appears like a newspaper insert for a local flea market, perhaps a summons to a Pentecostal retreat. Only upon closer inspection is its sinister message revealed: "Please observe: This is a 'WHITE UNITY' Gathering....We Reserve the Right to Refuse Admittance to Anyone....Refreshments and snacks will be available....Volunteers needed in the kitchen.... Bring a container of food to share with your comrades.... absolutely no drinking. Save the partying for after the gathering...." Leaf-peepers taking in the autumn foliage were likely stunned to drive past a large cross ablaze under a harvest moon that evening, casting fire-lit shadows across the tattered swastika flag hanging from an upstairs window ledge.

Had any of these onlookers sneaked past Thomas's security detail, they might have encountered seventeen-year-old Bryan Freeman of Allentown and his fifteen-year-old brother, David. Less than four months after visiting Walker Road that fall weekend, the brothers, students at Salisbury High School in Pennsylvania, murdered their parents, stabbing their mother numerous times and slitting their father's throat. They also bludgeoned the skull of their twelve-year-old brother, Erik, with a baseball bat. According to Floyd Cochran, in the weeks before her death, Brenda Freeman had reached out to him several times. "She started calling me about a month and a half ago, seeking anything she could to get them away from Mark," Cochran said.

Thomas admitted that the boys had attended concerts at his farm, but denied knowing them personally, scoffing at allegations he'd somehow influenced their motives. "You really think that teaching that a God who wants races to stay separate would incite two German boys to murder their German parents?" he questioned *New York Daily News* reporter Linda Yglesias. In a column for *The Watchman* he titled "Natural Born Killers," Thomas addressed the tragedy, deflecting blame: "The Freeman family were devout Jehovah's Witnesses and raised their children in that faith, yet no one in the media dared suggest that it was that cult which was the cause of their actions. I have a close personal friend who was raised in that same sick 'church' who was molested by her mother and stepfather all her life with the full knowledge of the entire church and they did nothing but forbid her to go to the police....If the allegations I heard (and I did hear them before the killings) are true, then the parents got what they deserved."

He continued to covet controversy while keeping reporters at bay, withstanding the barrage of negative publicity. Despite increased police reconnaissance, Thomas managed to adroitly sidestep significant legal trouble until 1995, when Donna Marazoff won a protection-from-abuse order filed in a Berks County, Pennsylvania, court. "He has stated several times that if I ever get involved with anyone who tried to be a father to the kids he will kill them," Marazoff alleged. "He has threatened to burn down our barn on several occasions." She told the judge that Thomas bragged of connections that would allow him to "disappear without a trace." As a condition of the protection-from-abuse order, Thomas was forbidden to possess any weapons. By now he'd shorn his hair tight along the sides, plastering his longer front locks straight across his brow. With his shortly clipped mustache, his image came to resemble the infamous leader of the Third Reich, though he bristled when asked if he'd intended the comparison.

While immersed in women troubles, and navigating a barrage of increasingly negative press coverage, in early 1993 Thomas took in fifteen-year-old skinhead Kevin McCarthy from northeast Philadelphia, a troubled kid who'd heard first met Thomas at a Bible study class in Philadelphia, then watched Thomas lecture at his trailer chapel. McCarthy was the first of several neo-Nazi teens who fell under the preacher's influence at a formative crossroads in their lives. Thomas allegedly provided McCarthy paramilitary training, with lessons in marksmanship using shotguns, pistols, and assault rifles. He also explained how to subvert security systems, create diversions, and thwart government communications systems. Much as Thomas had looked to George Kemner for wisdom and guidance, "I came to look up to him as a father figure," McCarthy would say of Thomas.

In the summer of 1993 Thomas escorted McCarthy to Elohim City in Oklahoma, the dusty separatist religious community aptly described by journalists Andrew Gumbel and Roger G. Charles as "an assortment of caravans, squat houses, and makeshift structures made of ammo crates and bright orange polyurethane." A refuge of sorts for white supremacists across the country, the encampment was ruled by seventy-year-old Robert "Grandpa" Millar, then considered by some to be the most influential Christian Identity preacher in America. Given to wearing kilts and clerical tunics, and rumored to possess magical powers, he'd welcomed Thomas to his four-hundred-acre settlement on numerous occasions. "Mark and I go back a long way," Millar said of his buddy. "Any friend of Mark's is a friend of mine." Upon his return east from "religious training" at Elohim City, McCarthy met twenty-four-year old Scott Stedeford, a Camden, New Jersey, drummer who'd recently formed the heavy metal band Cyanide. After asking him to take over as the group's bassist, Stedeford introduced McCarthy to their lead guitarist, former Eagle Scout Michael Brescia. Shortly after the formation of the new trio, McCarthy introduced Stedeford to Thomas, who offered to help overhaul the blown engine in his Chevy. Like McCarthy, Stedeford soon succumbed to Thomas's charm after discovering their common ground: Though of a different era, he, too, was a Doors worshipper, hypnotized by the entrancing beat of percussionist John Densmore.

Thomas encouraged Brescia's westward pilgrimage as well. Heeding the call, the LaSalle University dropout struck out for the Ozark foothills sometime in the fall of 1993. In what was quick becoming a right of passage for Thomas's youthful inner circle, McCarthy in turn introduced Stedeford to Millar's hilly enclave near the Arkansas border. Upon returning home, Stedeford contacted Thomas, who invited him to crash at his farm for a while. On October 5, 1994, as the two were nailing shingles on the new roof at Walker Road, a blue car turned into the driveway, carrying white supremacists Richard Lee Guthrie and Peter Langan. An outlaw, cross-dressing biker described by Guthrie as "a raving psychopath, a cross between Ted Bundy and Ted Kaczynski," Langan, like Thomas, had been ordained an Identity minister. The visitors arrived in search of recruits to assist in the string of bank robberies they'd recently undertaken in the Midwest to help fund their cause of overthrowing the U.S. government. Guthrie commented later, "We could care less who they were, as long as they agreed with the same things we did: to plunder with extreme prejudice."

Seated around Thomas's kitchen table that autumn evening, the three older men reached an understanding: Stedeford would join their crew, but only if known by a code name. He was thereby anointed "Tuco," an homage to revolutionary William Harris of the Symbionese Liberation Army, the group responsible for kidnapping Patty Hearst. With Thomas remaining behind in Pennsylvania, "Wild Bill" Guthrie, "Commander Pedro" Langan, and Scott "Tuco" Stedeford knocked off the Columbus National Bank on October 25, 1994. They fled to Thomas's soon after the heist, dispersing their take.

Langan and Guthrie next struck a Des Moines, Iowa, bank, making off with $29,000. Thomas rendezvoused with Stedeford, Guthrie, and Langan at a Waffle House in Van Buren, Arkansas on November 14, at which time Thomas introduced Langan and Guthrie to his protégé, Kevin McCarthy. Seventeen at the time, McCarthy was now a full-fledged comrade in arms, assigned the nickname "Newt" after Newt Gingrich. Collectively, the gang resolved to divvy the loot equally among them, with a portion of the proceeds funneled toward other covert missions to be decided by Mark Thomas.

Thomas drove back to Pennsylvania after the meeting in Arkansas, chairing operations from a safe distance. With their war chest now totaling upwards of $95,000, Langan, McCarthy, and Guthrie knocked off the Third Federal Savings and Loan in Middleburg Heights, Ohio, on December 9. Donning Santa Claus masks, they made off with $7,400. A local article chronicling the event dubbed them "The Midwestern Bank Bandits," but they soon chose to be known as the Aryan Republican Army. "We call ourselves the Aryan Republican Army because in some of our tactics, and some of our goals, we have modeled the organization after the Irish Republican Army," Langan boasted on a recruitment videotape obtained by the *Sunday Telegraph*, a London paper. Disguised in President's masks while brandishing fake bombs to terrorize their captives, they adopted their style from the surfer gang in the 1991 movie *Point Break*, starring Patrick Swayze and Keanu Reeves.

Though behind the scenes his operations were running smoothly, Thomas was losing badly in the court of public opinion. There had been an unflattering piece written about him in the *New York Daily News*, and in a March 6, 1995, article Keith Schneider of the *New York Times* suggested that his compound had become the focus of widening scrutiny. Bent on clearing his name and portraying himself as an unfairly persecuted victim, Thomas embarked on a misguided campaign to alter his persona. Often dressing in a black Jim Morrison t-shirt, he took to open meetings of the Boyertown (PA) Unity Coalition, a grass-roots organization created to stem the rising tide of hate crimes in Pennsylvania. "I have been cited and scandalized by the media in the past two weeks," he announced at a school board hearing, addressing accusations that he'd help brainwash the Freeman boys. To emphasize his point, he held up a copy of Vincent Rause's scathing *Philadelphia* magazine expose, titled "The State of Hate." He claimed he was no longer affiliated with the white supremacist movement, "on sabbatical" from his beliefs.

But Thomas's overtures toward community leaders often contradicted the messages expressed by his writings. His commentary on the Oklahoma City bombings evinced a festering hatred toward the federal government, a call to strike against ZOG. The horrific massacre at the Murrah Federal Building, which claimed one-hundred sixty-eight lives on April 19, 1995, elicited his halfhearted sympathy. In a chapter from the July issue of *The Watchman*, "Oklahoma, Whodunnit?" he wrote, "If one thing has been demonstrated in Oklahoma, it is that the people can strike back at ZOG with or without 'assault weapons.' ...I mourn the untimely loss of all innocent life but I also acknowledge that the sick and twisted 'establishment' of this wicked land must be smashed whatever the cost. ...We were all born to die in the struggle to throw down the kingdom of Satan, even as our God himself had to do..." Seething with righteous indignation, he further composed, "If we are indeed all equal, perhaps we should begin a campaign to elect Tim McVeigh to the White House." In November of the same year he wrote, "With every day that passes unless the White Race rises up against their tormenters in a consuming fury, we will instead be consumed by them....It is increasingly apparent to even the most indifferent of Whites that our government is the enemy of our race and as such is a treasonous fraud. The penalty for treason is, and always has been, death because there is no other crime so dangerous to a civilization."

The string of robberies ended in January 1996 when "Wild Bill" Guthrie was apprehended in a Cincinnati restaurant. The FBI collared "Commander Pedro" three days later, and the arrest of McCarthy followed soon thereafter. Guthrie began singing in March 1996, telling investigators that Thomas had introduced him to other members of their crew. The feds seized a cache of weapons and ammunition Thomas had stashed in a friend's garage when he learned that the feds were securing warrants to search his property. While visiting McCarthy in prison, he said, "If we conspire, it's the same as if you did it and I could spend the rest of my life in jail." His pleadings went unheeded, however, for his former apprentice soon turned state's witness.

On January 30, 1997, Mark Thomas, now forty-six-years old, was indicted by a federal grand jury in Philadelphia for conspiracy to commit bank robbery and receiving stolen bank money, in violation of 18 U.S.C. Sections 371 and

2113(c). The indictment alleged that he'd "recruited young people to his residence …to rob banks and commit other crimes on behalf of the Aryan Republican Army." That same day a federal magistrate judge issued a bench warrant for his arrest.

As the thundering blades of a chopper echoed through the frigid dawn gloom on January 30, Mark Thomas hunkered down in his kitchen and called the FBI. "Do you have a warrant for my arrest?" he asked an agent from the local Allentown field office.

"Yes," he replied.

Thomas knew the endgame was nearing. Anticipating this moment, he'd sandbagged the windows of his office in preparation for a shootout. He began phoning members of the media, notifying them that authorities were preparing a raid. "Frankly, I think they want my hide," he told the *Morning Call.* Thomas's pregnant wife was huddled inside their kitchen along with the couple's two-year-old daughter as pandemonium ensued. Fearful for their lives, she couldn't shake the harrowing images of Ruby Ridge and the incinerating Waco compound so graphically depicted on television. The FBI and U.S. Marshall Service soon converged, swarming the perimeters and sealing off exits in expectation of a fiery standoff. Regrets alone were insufficient to thwart the forces aligned against Thomas, armless resistance a futile defense against the advancing numbers. The showdown with the government that he'd prophesied, a call to arms he'd led in expectation for the bloody final act of the biblical apocalypse, found him outmanned as agents closed in.

CHAPTER FIFTEEN

A Piece That's Missing

Before his luck turned, such abundant publicity might have presented Mark Thomas with an opportune moment to reach for a catchphrase culled from the prophecies of the Old Testament. At last, a substantial media presence to witness firsthand the federal government's manifest violations of his civil rights, validating his extensive writings on the matter. For the first several hours that Thomas was confined to his home, however, existential musings escaped the erstwhile glib preacher. Though he'd foretold of this moment for some time now and had ample time to prepare his remarks, he lost hold of his flinty demeanor during the tense standstill, blubbering shamefully as siren lights lit upon his first floor windows.

Matt Stevens, from Philadelphia NBC affiliate WCAU, was among the reporters sent to cover the standoff. From 6 a.m. till 12:30 p.m., Thomas held company with various news crews, Stevens noted, and never left his kitchen. He remarked at how vulnerable Thomas seemed as his world toppled, not the fearless revolutionary who'd once valiantly proclaimed, "Unless the White Race rises up against their tormentors in a consuming fury, we will instead be consumed by them."

"I know I was not afraid of being in any danger of any kind," Stevens remarked. "I don't think the guy even owns a pop gun. It was just [reporters] and him and his one-and-a-half year old daughter and his pregnant wife in the kitchen."

At some point while held at bay that morning, Thomas phoned Reading, Pennsylvania, criminal defense attorney Peter David Maynard. He brokered a stalemate before his client's preserve was dismantled, arranging to drive Thomas to the local FBI field office in Allentown where he would surrender without further confrontation. Outfitted in an infantry cap, black jeans, and his trademark Aryan belt buckle, Thomas was seen walking out of his home early in the afternoon, leaving in his lawyer's Mercedes. At the same time, the FBI and federal prosecutors called a news conference in Philadelphia, announcing the indictment of Thomas and his four conspirators.

A flurry of bureau agents in black combat gear scoured junk piles and sifted through heaps of dug earth in the wake of Thomas's departure. Sidestepping fresh mounds of goat shit, they trooped through barns and abutting outbuildings, snapping photos, removing computers and floppy disks. Several hours later, evidence specialists lugged away two cardboard boxes to examine for incriminating contents. By and by the commotion subsided once agents, expecting to confiscate a sizeable haul of explosives and automatic weaponry, found little that was useful or of possible danger to them other than a pistol buried in the backyard. Bureau officials were livid at WCAU news director Steve Doerr. They insinuated that a source within his staff had leaked word to Thomas in advance of the raid, providing him the opportunity to destroy evidence before their arrival.

Thomas was jailed that same night in the Lehigh County Prison, pleading not guilty to all counts of conspiracy at his February 5, 1997, arraignment. The following day he was released to the FBI for questioning. For the first time since the heady days following the 1969 parkway murders, he sat squarely in the crosshairs of a major criminal investigation. "We are pleased that he has been indicted," announced Barry

Morrison, regional director of the Anti-Defamation League. "We've been monitoring his activities for many years. He had a spellbinding influence on some" and had done damage "to hundreds of young people" whom he had recruited and "infected with his racist, anti-Semitic demagoguery."

"I think he's getting railroaded," declared Woody Woodley, head of the Pennsylvania KKK. "I don't think Mark had anything to do with it... I don't think Mark is a thief or a gangster or anything like that." He was quick to assure there would be a replacement for Thomas. "When one leader steps down, another one steps up. There will be another one to carry the flag, I'm sure of that."

Richard Butler, firebrand patriarch of the Aryan Nations, was equally defiant. "Mark just doesn't do that kind of stuff. He's just a militant pro-white activist. We support him one hundred percent. He's just a pro-white activist, and they're trying to intimidate him. I think they just made Mark a target."

Unlike with the parkway murders, this time Thomas recognized that the evidence against him was overwhelming. From the outset, the FBI let him know what formidable leverage they possessed in the form of taped conversations, witness statements, and testimony from accomplices. His unyielding resolve cooled in the face of the voluminous material that had been amassed. As the sentencing guidelines for federal bank robbery recommended a term from eleven to fourteen years, Thomas promptly expressed a willingness to cooperate once he realized what was at stake.

Appearing haggard and unshaven, the former Aryan Nations East Coast ambassador and KKK chaplain stood flanked by a bevy of U.S. marshals at his February 18 hearing at U.S. District Court in Philadelphia. He pleaded guilty to seven of twenty-two federal conspiracy charges and to receiving proceeds from the Midwest bank heists. In a signed eight-page plea agreement, Thomas promised to disclose information about the robberies and "any other crimes about which he has knowledge." In return for Thomas's testimony against his co-conspirators and pledge to assist a Justice Department bent on fracturing the nation's white supremacist firmament, U.S. prosecutor Michael Schwartz said he'd request the sentencing judge to impose less than the maximum allowable term. Under the arrangement, Thomas's sentence would be "postponed until his cooperation is complete."

How much would the pastor tell? Who would he name? Word of Thomas's treachery spread feverishly through clandestine mountainside hollows, where Klan folk gathered to discuss the flagrant betrayal of oaths. Brian Levin, a civil rights attorney and former director of the Center on Hate and Extremism at Stockton State College in New Jersey, termed Thomas's vow to tell all "by far the most significant catch of this decade. It's hard to overstate just how trusted and respected Thomas is in the white supremacist world." As for Thomas's expansive network of underworld contacts, Levin exulted, "He is a virtual Rolodex...one of the most trusted and influential leaders in this movement."

His once enthusiastically supportive kinsmen swiftly turned their backs on Thomas. "This is very significant. I'm shocked to hear this," said Richard Butler, who'd assured unflagging loyalty to his forsaken Pennsylvania adjutant a week earlier, likening him to a colonial patriot. "I don't know what they had on him. I certainly don't understand it." He'd once ordained Thomas as a Christian Identity minister but now sought to distance himself, as if the two were only casually acquainted through yearly gatherings. "He was never really that closely associated with us...He turned traitor, I guess. I never thought he would do something like that."

Over the course of the next year, as he was shuffled among a host of state and federal correctional facilities in the

Delaware Valley, Thomas reluctantly divulged the names of key players in his vast syndicate. Because his ascension in the extremist movement dovetailed with recent bloody showdowns in Ruby Ridge, Idaho, and the Branch Davidian inferno in Texas, Thomas and his crew were already subject to federal scrutiny into subversive activities nationwide when focus intensified as to their possible link to the 1995 Oklahoma City bombings.

Before the arrival of his lawyer on the morning authorities overtook his compound, Thomas sat in his kitchen, sipping tea and holding forth with local journalists once regaining his composure. He'd been holding a trump card, and now must've seemed as good a time as any to play it if he was to cut a deal. Likely motivated by revenge, his insatiable craving for attention, or a desire to divert federal investigators seeking to implicate him in the ever-widening Oklahoma City inquiry, Thomas proceeded to sandbag the young man who'd testified against him at a pre-trial hearing in Ohio as part of his own plea arrangement, former protégé Kevin McCarthy. Just as in 1969, when he'd boasted to a clothing store clerk that he'd been in Ocean City at the time of the Davis and Perry murders, another statement he likely wished to have back, Thomas's vengeful retaliation on the morning of his arrest would meet with unintended consequences and fateful repercussions. To a *Morning Call* reporter, one of several to whom he granted interviews the day he turned himself in, Thomas confided that in July 1995 fellow ARA member Richard Guthrie told him that Guthrie and McCarthy were complicit in the Oklahoma City bombing. "He implied that he had something to do with it, that he had knowledge of who had [something] to do with it," Thomas told the reporter, "and he said that McCarthy took part in the bombing, in either building it or setting it off. His exact words were, 'your young Mr. Wizard took out the Murrah Building.'"

Apart from a shortsighted desire to discredit McCarthy's testimony as a government witness, and avenge his disloyalty, what else could Thomas hope to accomplish by uttering such remarks just before turning himself in? Arguably, this was a clever ploy designed to entice the public into believing he was withholding vital intelligence about a bombing conspiracy, information he could dangle before investigators in hopes of pressuring them into dismissing the charges against him or offering a reduced sentence. Whatever his designs, the preemptive strike soon backfired, for his harmful allegations against McCarthy (Thomas soon withdrew his remarks when pressed to substantiate them) were consistent with other incriminating information the FBI learned about Thomas on April 5, 1997, the day they interviewed Donna Marazoff.

According to an FBI report (known as a "302"), Thomas's estranged former girlfriend told an agent that in early 1995, while he was at her Alburtis, Pennsylvania, residence visiting with their two children, Thomas angrily confided, "We are going to get them. We are going to hit one of their buildings during the middle of the day. It's going to be a federal building. We will get sympathy if we bomb the building. That's when there will be the most casualties. They will know what it is to lose their loved one, how it feels." Marazoff also alleged that Thomas was in Oklahoma on April 19, 1995, the date of the bombings, calling her upon his return to Pennsylvania that night. Thomas vehemently denied making these statements, providing investigators a number of alibis who confirmed he was home in Pennsylvania with family members, watching live television coverage on the morning of the explosion. Satisfied by his explanation, agents let the matter rest for the time being, reasonably assured that Thomas had no direct involvement in the catastrophe.

The suggestion of latent homicidal tendencies stirring within Thomas drew a faint chuckle from Paul "Gil" Hendrickson. The lead FBI agent in the bank robbery investigation that resulted in Thomas's arrest, Hendrickson orchestrated the pre-dawn siege of his Walker Road stronghold. In order to secure a conviction for the federal conspiracy rap, Hendrickson needed to make sure he had everything on Thomas and began probing farther into the troubled man's past in the weeks following his apprehension in 1997. In the course of his investigation, he was apprised of the Perry and Davis murders. The veteran agent pored over the New Jersey State Police files, studying their inconclusive findings. "I wanted leverage," he recalled, making certain the vanquished Aryan guru spilled forth all his contacts in the neo-Nazi community, and wasn't withholding information in violation of his bargain.

Hendrickson listened to hours upon hours of aged tape reels from the June 4, 1969, nighttime interrogation by New Jersey State Police Detectives Dix and Patterson. Over the course of several weeks between 1997 and 1998 he met with detectives from the New Jersey State Police Major Crime Unit at the Philadelphia Police Department headquarters at Eighth and Race streets, the same administration building where Thomas had been grilled throughout the night twenty-eight-years earlier. Hendrickson hoped to trip him on an inconsistency, perhaps hear mention of a previously undisclosed material fact. But after weeks of scrutinizing the recordings offered him by the New Jersey State Police, he was unable to resurrect any incriminating material. "He adamantly denied the murders…There was nothing he said that I could use to get him to talk to me….I spent days going after the murder thing," he recalls. "There just wasn't anything to tie him to them. I said to him, 'It's best to come clean now with everything you've done, because if I find out there's something you haven't told me, all deals are off.'" As he'd done so often in the past, Thomas steadfastly maintained his innocence in the parkway slayings. "Mark Thomas was a wimp who had others do his dirty work," says Hendrickson. He speaks in a tone mixed with incredulity and self-deprecating lightheartedness in recalling Thomas, as if describing a blowhard used car salesman who'd once sold him a lemon. "He hasn't got the guts to commit those murders."

Shorn of his glib façade, Thomas appeared at his March 19, 1998, sentencing hearing before U.S. District Judge Ronald Buckwalter. Wendy, Thomas's second wife, offered character testimony on his behalf. "Well, I would like to state that Mark is a very loving and caring husband to me. He always has been. I've known him for five years now. We have two children together, and he's a wonderful father."

Thomas's former wife Barbara, also in attendance, sought leniency for her forlorn ex as well. "I've known Mark for over twenty years. I was married to him for eighteen, and we have three children by that marriage. I just know that he's a good person, he's a good father, and I'd just like to tell the court that."

As if comprehending the magnitude of his predicament, Thomas stood humbled in reverent silence before his sentence was read. Facing stern rebuke before a federal government he'd decried on innumerable occasions as a terrorist organization, he was forthright with self-appraisal in his plea for mercy. "What can I say?" he solemnly asked the judge. "What I would express today is my remorse... There's no way that I can set guidelines for the destruction of three young people's lives, and that's what I'm guilty of morally....Through my own personal life, which is a reflection of my own depravity that led me to this place, I have brought lives into this world that I'm unable to support...I do renounce racism, especially anti-Semitism that I have preached for many years. It's the very root of what's been wrong with my life.... It is pathological, and I did it in God's name. How can that be forgiven? I ask that of Him every night." During the proceedings, Thomas told of the chest pains he'd suffered while incarcerated for a stint at the Curran-Fromhold Correctional Facility in Philadelphia.

His serious condition had prompted a transport to a Salem County, New Jersey, hospital.

Persuaded by Thomas's candid remorsefulness, Judge Buckwalter reluctantly reduced his term to eight years, to be served at the Federal Correctional Institution in Fort Dix, New Jersey, followed by a three-year supervised release thereafter. His ruling was reached despite tepid endorsement from assistant U.S. attorney Ronald E. Goldman, who noted that Thomas hadn't fully disclosed his role as the gang's shadow warrior. Assistant U.S. Attorney Michael Schwartz, unmoved by the defendant's mea culpa, remarked, "Anyone who is caught and is in jail is going to express remorse."

Published in 2002, criminologist Mark Hamm's book *In Bad Company: America's Terrorist Underground* postulated that several of the ARA, among them Thomas, had been in the vicinity of Oklahoma City as the federal building collapsed. Not only was Michael Brescia complicit in the atrocity, Hamm theorized, he was the same swarthy, twenty-something Caucasian wearing a baseball cap, portrayed in a police composite sketch as the "John Doe #2" allegedly witnessed alongside McVeigh the morning he detonated his homemade fertilizer bomb. Mark Potok, a Senior Fellow with the Southern Poverty Law Center, dismissed Hamm's findings as highly circumstantial in his organization's spring 2002 Intelligence Report. But in the months following Thomas's release from Fort Dix Correctional Institution in 2004, after he returned to Pennsylvania to serve the remaining three years of his sentence, Hamm's conclusions were cast in a different light.

Interviewed from federal prison, where he was serving a far lengthier sentence for his role in the bank robberies than his co-conspirators, an embittered Peter Langan told the Associated Press that after his arrest in 1996 he'd offered the FBI information connecting the Midwest bank robbers to the Oklahoma City bombing. Succumbing to an avalanche of public record requests by the news organization, the

FBI was pressured to declassify reports establishing that Thomas had allegedly visited Elohim City one week prior to the bombing. So had several other ARA soldiers, thereby validating some of Hamm's claims. Phone logs revealed that McVeigh, at one point lionized by Thomas in his newsletter columns, had attempted to call a German national named Andreas Strassmeir just twelve days before the detonation. An Elohim City, Oklahoma, security guard and firearms instructor of murky origins, Strassmeir had allegedly met McVeigh at a local gun show in 1993, and the two were seen speaking to one another at parties. McVeigh had unsuccessfully tried to reach Strassmeir at the Ozarks compound, where he'd been rooming with Thomas's former cohort, Michael Brescia. It also came to light that McVeigh's call to Elohim City was the first he placed after contacting the Ryder Truck facility where he'd rented the vehicle used in the deadly blast.

USA Today reported that the FBI had destroyed videotapes and other incriminating material purportedly revealing that McVeigh, who was executed in 2001, had more contact with the ARA than originally suspected, and that the blasting caps uncovered in the rubble were similar to those kept at an ARA safe house in Ohio. The inference of a government cover-up, which drew the attention of the *New York Times* and other national media outlets, prompted bombing suspect Terry Nichols' defense attorneys to subpoena Thomas as a witness to establish that Nichols and McVeigh had numerous accomplices. McVeigh's former attorney, Stephen Jones, said the disclosures confirmed what he'd suspected all along. "I think these pieces close the circle, and they clearly show the bombing conspiracy consisted probably of ten conspirators…. "They [government officials] simply turned their backs on a group of people for which there is credible evidence suggesting they were involved in the murder of 160 people."

On April 23, 2004, however, Oklahoma District Court Judge Steven Taylor, presiding over the Nichols murder trial, prevented defense lawyers from calling Thomas to testify. "As to the Midwest bank robbers...this is a dry hole," Judge Taylor ruled. "There is absolutely no evidence of any overt act by the bank robbers in bombing the Murrah Building... nothing at all to link the bank robbers to the crime that is being charged before this court."

The inconsistencies reflected in his lie detector tests, along with junk dealer Robert D'Amore's identification of him near the murder scene, hint that Mark Thomas may have known more than he was letting on about the deaths of Susan Davis and Elizabeth Perry. Nevertheless, substantial doubts continue to plague the case against him, supporting his claim of innocence in the brutal slayings of the two coeds. Although the two major crimes for which he was investigated span nearly thirty years, Thomas's pattern of behavior over this time period falls along a discernible continuum dating back to his teens, making it plainly apparent why the Atlantic City Prosecutor's Office never sought to indict him.

A Pennsylvania social worker assigned to evaluate ex-wife Donna Marazoff and Thomas in 1996 concluded that Thomas suffered from antisocial personality disorder. "That kind of personality dynamic can emerge in many different ways," Thomas told John Martin of the *Morning Call* in February 1996, dismissing his diagnosis as mere narcissism. "Excessive attempts to attract and be the focus of the attention of others," among the diagnostic criteria set forth in the *Diagnostic and Statistical Manual for Mental Disorders* were glaringly evident prior to Thomas's incarceration in 1997, offering context for his self-destructive lapses in judgment. As a bright, mischievous teen who'd acquired a juvenile record before he was interrogated at length by the New Jersey State Police in Philadelphia, Thomas could have easily stopped detectives at any point by asserting his *Miranda* rights, rather than allowing the process to continue until dawn without the assistance of an attorney. His indiscriminate remarks at the outset of the parkway investigation, when he was allegedly overheard in a Philadelphia clothing store brashly proclaiming he was in Ocean City when Davis and Perry were murdered, reflect a wily youth afflicted by rampant conceit, not a calculating sociopath.

The charges that Thomas had puppeteered a devoted band of miscreants into committing crimes intended to cripple the U.S. government also accord with the social worker's evaluation. Defined by the Mayo Clinic as "a mental disorder in which people have an inflated sense of their own importance and a deep need for admiration," narcissism is a condition common among all cult evangelists, according to author Len Oakes. In *Prophetic Charisma: The Psychology of Revolutionary Religious Personalities*, Oakes presented a complex study based upon his experiences as a former cult follower, with years spent researching common personality traits afflicting religious gurus. His book documents the psychological underpinnings of those perceived by their devout congregants as one of God's messengers. Such leaders, Oakes explains, share "their opposition to convention and their ability to inspire others with their visions," utilizing their persuasive skills to preach what God has spoken to them, no matter how controversial or offensive their message. Nearly all of these self-proclaimed prophets claim to have experienced an "awakening" at a crucial point in their lives. Thomas's moments of divine inspiration, as he'd explained to numerous reporters, were split into two clarifying occurrences-when he met Jim Morrison in New York City, and later, the day he was introduced to the teachings of Christian Identity by his boss and spiritual mentor, George Kemner. Thomas manifested his calling by proselytizing scores of dispossessed, embittered white men and offering them a pathway to salvation led by white rule, then leading astray the vulnerable skinhead youths he'd sheltered. Oakes, however, took pains to distinguish the less harmful, more charismatic figures like Thomas from messianic leaders such as David Koresh and Jim Jones. Delusional with power, these fanatics were ultimately consumed by their own paranoid excesses, revealing their own murderous inclinations by forcibly inducing their flocks toward mass suicides.

Though publicly he continued to espouse scriptural justification for the superiority of the white race, Thomas's unfaltering stance on racial purity showed signs of weakening long before his arrest on conspiracy charges. As if desperate to be understood, in June 1996 he called Ann Van Dyke, then the assistant to the executive director of the Pennsylvania Human Relations Commission, an organization that had publicly lambasted Thomas's activities in the past and warned of his rising stature in the Pennsylvania's proliferating hate movement. Hardly an ally, over the course of ten days and several lengthy exchanges, Van Dyke listened as Thomas unburdened himself, assuming blame for what psychological harm he'd wrought upon the boys he'd mentored, remorse he'd later express to his sentencing judge. "I'm under a lot of emotional turmoil," he frantically told Van Dyke, his tone stripped of all pretensions. "I never thought those young fellas would do that stuff," he confided, comments that Van Dyke understood as robbing banks. He explained that the paternal influences comprising the Christian Identity hierarchy had "filled an empty hole in my life. I met a series of men who were my surrogate fathers." What guidance he'd received from the likes of George Kemner and Robert "Grandpa" Millar, Thomas passed down to Kevin McCarthy, Scott Stedeford, and Michael Brescia to compensate for his estrangement from his own father.

Were these sincere expressions of moral uncertainty, or a ruse to earn an enemy's trust and sympathy? During their conversations, Thomas was careful to refrain from any mention of the Perry-Davis investigation, neglecting to disclose that he and William Thomas were often seen playing pool with one another at a local bar as the police shadowed his son in 1969. His father summoned a lawyer in the middle of the night, with both parents accompanying him to Berlin, New Jersey, to halt the questioning of their son at the White Way Hotel. The closeness that Thomas inferred was lacking between his father and him is inconsistent with what Detective Kreps recalled of the afternoon he was confronted at lunch by the protective father, demanding he cease "harassing my son."

Although the New Jersey State Police and officials connected with the Oklahoma City bombing investigation leveled serious accusations against Thomas, neither inquiry yielded any substantive proof that he'd ever physically harmed someone. While it is true that Donna Marazoff claimed he'd threatened her, the accusations were slung in the midst of a divorce, and family law squabbles are inherently spiteful and subject to interpretation. Despite their stormy history, when she was interviewed by the FBI regarding the incriminating remarks she'd purportedly heard Thomas utter, Marazoff admitted that although he was "very manipulative," Thomas "lacked [the] courage" to undertake an act of violence such as was perpetrated in Oklahoma City. Nevertheless, she steadfastly maintained he had the ability to persuade others to commit such a terroristic act on his behalf.

Given Thomas's intelligence and relatively passive comportment, it seems illogical that he would murder two young women in 1969, flee the country, and then actively court publicity as a local rabble-rouser upon returning to Pennsylvania. Nor would he accept numerous leadership posts within notorious separatist organizations if he'd had such a dark secret to hide. More likely, the incessant attention bestowed upon him by New Jersey and

Pennsylvania authorities, both tantalized by the prospect of a guilty plea in the parkway murders, provided Thomas a source of amusement as he thrillingly immersed himself within these precarious situations, confidently protected behind an empowering fortress of innocence. Perhaps due in part to an elemental distrust of government, his innate psychology, or a desire to be a courtroom lawyer, from his teenage years until his arrest in 1997 Thomas enjoyed gaming the authorities whenever such an opportunity arose, slyly suggesting he possessed incriminating information of great value to them. Playing this to his advantage at every turn, he enticed them into believing he knew more than he actually did, with foolish indifference toward the dangerous implications. His conversations with Van Dyke are telling in this regard. While some might question the timing of his calls to her—after all, Thomas's anguishing bouts of self-loathing at the harm he'd wrought upon his underlings took place only *after* he realized that his apprehension in the bank robbery investigation was a *fait accompli*—his reaction is in keeping with past behavior. Shame at one's own conduct is symptomatic of a narcissist, "…a response to the narcissistic wound *and* a stimulus to narcissistic self-aggrandizement," a group of psychologists recently theorized, categorizing the emotional response as a "coping mechanism" to assuage deflated pride and compensate for low self-esteem.

Former state police detectives who worked closely on the Perry-Davis case remain sharply divided on the topic of Mark Thomas, unable to form a consensus. Until he died, Jack Kreps was convinced Thomas had slain the coeds. Given the fervency of his steadfast conviction, however, it was difficult for Kreps to remain objective. While his devotion to the case was admirable, his dogmatism must be considered relative to his single-mindedness, for his conclusion was drawn upon his own frustrations in obsessively pursuing the footloose eighteen-year-old, resulting in the issuance of a protective order against him. Along with the other detectives who worked round-the-clock in the days and weeks after the coed murders, Kreps was eventually assigned to other matters after the investigation turned cold. Although decades passed before Thomas's name surfaced publicly in connection with the Pennsylvania white supremacist movement, the New Jersey State Police never lost track of him. Kreps, however, wasn't privy to a review of the file after being taken off the case, denied access by the Division of Criminal Justice long after he'd retired. Had he traced Thomas's trajectory over the years and been witness to his theatrical escapades, perhaps he would've noted the clearly discernible consistencies befitting the social worker's diagnosis and reconsidered his position in light of the puzzling contradictions.

A former high-ranking major with the New Jersey State Police Major Crime Unit, who worked extensively on the case out of the Criminal Investigation Headquarters in Hammonton, spoke on the condition of anonymity. Like other detectives who'd periodically reviewed the Perry-Davis file every few years, at some point he was informed of Thomas's burgeoning public profile. He concurs that Thomas was a shrewd, exceptionally bright teenager needful of attention, who "enjoyed the notoriety" that comes with being a person of interest in a major criminal investigation. "If I felt that [Thomas] did it, he'd be in jail right now," he said.

Another former detective's view is especially illuminating to this point. Along with George Dix, former Detective Harry Patterson of the New Jersey State Police pressed Thomas throughout the night of June 4, 1969, as his subject was held for questioning in Philadelphia. "I don't see how that kid—one solid punch and he would disappear into little pieces—how he could have controlled both of those girls," Patterson remembered. "There was always a question in my mind about him. I was never totally convinced." Patterson, who resided in Atlantic County, New Jersey, until he died in 2019, subscribed to the notion that with suspects such as

Ronnie Walden already in prison, and John Norman Collins serving a life term in Michigan, the New Jersey State Police clung to Thomas because they had no other viable leads to pursue in the weeks following the murders. "Every lead was run down, and the only real tangible possibility or likelihood was this kid....He would infer like he knew something. This kid liked to give that impression. He was a little wacky." Practically speaking, it would have been nearly impossible for a scrawny eighteen-year-old like Thomas to overtake two tall, sturdy young women like Davis and Perry, Patterson was certain. "When I talked to him he was a hundred twenty-five pounds. A strong girl could grab him by the neck."

Patterson remembered being "nose to nose" with Thomas as the night wore on and frustration simmered among his inquisitors as they were ordered to charge or release him. "He agreed to come back to Jersey with us. Now, does that make sense? If he had done that, the stress would have been horrific. I know, because I was interrogating him *hard*. I was six inches from his face. I could see the tears coming down. I can't believe that he would volunteer to come back to New Jersey with these cops if he had done it. A normal human being would jump at the first opportunity to get away from these guys.

"I don't think he knows anything," Patterson was certain. "He would put forward that impression just to stay in the limelight. I think he knew it couldn't be proved that he did it because he knew he didn't do it....He was a moderately warm lead. Nobody was jumping up and down. His actions and everything he did led me to believe we didn't have the right guy....this kid had no menace in him. I had many pretty strong arguments with Jim Brennan. Brennan figured he did it. Kreps was adamant.

"I don't know anyone who was closer to getting inside that kid's head than me, and I don't think he did it," said Patterson. "Harvey Burns and I interviewed a lot of people. We talked to all of his friends. But Jim [Brennan] wasn't going to back us off because Jim, almost as bad as Kreps, felt that this was the kid….he just struck me as a pimply faced eighteen-year-old skinny kid who wanted attention, and that was consistent with my impression from the Roundhouse."

Likely delusional with sleeplessness, Thomas let forth a harangue of confusing drivel between the time he was at police headquarters in Philadelphia and driven across the bridge to South Jersey thereafter. "At Berlin he described visions, leading us to believe he saw something and ran away," said Patterson. "He said he dreamed he had a knife in his hand, and he buried it at the edge of a lake," Patterson recalled, though he admitted having difficulty discerning a coherent narrative thread to what Thomas blathered while in custody. "He was so full of shit I didn't even memorialize it or commit it to memory; it was that silly.

"By the time everybody got through questioning this kid, he probably knew a lot about the crime such that he could throw out suspicious leads," Patterson concluded. He is of the mind that the murderer was either a transient serial killer, or an angry serviceman on leave who had followed the two girls out the diner after they spurned his advances-in either scenario, somebody who fled town quickly long before the bodies were found.

"There's a piece of Mark Thomas that's missing," said retired New Jersey State Police Lt. Colonel Jeffrey Barnes. A plainclothes detective in 1969, Barnes and Leland Sharpe were assigned to guard Thomas while he rested in a room at the White Way Hotel, his first stop after being escorted from Philadelphia by New Jersey State Police detectives. (Sharpe didn't recall being at the White Way Hotel; another source, in addition to Barnes, confirmed his presence.) "Mark Thomas was absolutely not terrified about being in police custody, I can tell you that," Barnes said. "He wasn't comfortable, but he wasn't panicked by any means. Imagine, in 1969, somebody picking you up and telling you you're the chief suspect in a double homicide? I don't know what he learned from our interrogators before I talked to him, or what he learned from Philadelphia PD, but definitely, he had some facts. I don't know what happened when he was in their custody, he may have been given some information, but some of the things he said pointed to the fact that he had knowledge of this thing. I'm not sure where he got that, firsthand or whatever. Thomas certainly had enough knowledge to fail a polygraph, let's put it that way.

"If there were fifty guys that worked on that case, twenty of them are going to tell you Thomas didn't do it," said Barnes. "There was no agreement. I would never go into court and swear that's the guy who killed those two girls."

Gone is the narrow toothbrush mustache many said he'd styled to resemble the Fuhrer. His severely cut hair, which also drew comparisons to Hitler, has grown in somewhat, fashioned alongside a graying beard. These days, Mark Thomas's persona calls to mind an itinerant frontier preacher toting a worn Bible in one hand and an axe in the other, ready to quote scripture in exchange for a hot meal, a bath, and a room for the night. Viewed from a different perspective, he might be mistaken for a lax literature professor at a small New England college, a former hippie apt to hold poetry readings beneath a quad's leafing elms at the first gasp of April warmth. By no means reclusive, he no longer hungers for acclaim, preferring a quotidian existence in rural Northampton County, Pennsylvania, alongside the picturesque Delaware Water Gap.

Polite and highly articulate, Thomas has an engaging, deliberate manner of speaking, at once circumspect and inquisitive yet cognizant of the many opportunities he's squandered. Given his intelligence and rhetorical acumen, it is difficult to converse with him without pondering what he might have become if he'd completed his formal education and pursued more traditional endeavors. He is reluctant to relive the parkway murder investigation. "A bad dream from a very distant part of my life," is how he summarized what little he remembered from the late summer afternoon when authorities questioned him at the Roundhouse. As for the "fuzzy answers" he allegedly provided to Philadelphia and New Jersey State Police homicide detectives the night they had him retell his story of hitchhiking home from the shore, Thomas explained, "I had been awake for a long time when this happened....I don't recall the blow by blow of the lie detector test. What I do remember is repeating what I'd heard....the same thing, over and over again," impressions consistent with those drawn by Detective Patterson. He didn't recall traveling to Ocean City that weekend, but can't deny he was there, for he'd hitched rides to the beach on numerous occasions. The name Gerald Stano, he insisted, "doesn't ring a bell." He remains deeply troubled that a number of New Jersey State Police officials continue to view him as a person of interest in the murders of Susan Davis and Elizabeth Perry. "I can assure you, I have no knowledge of what happened." With equal parts angst and frustration, he says of the crime scene off the parkway, "The subject is ghastly... I don't know the details, nor care to know of them." Yet at the same time Thomas remains intrigued by his skeptics, to whom he offered this inference in light of today's scientific advancements in solving cold cases: "I always wondered how [the police] expected me to do such a thing. I was a skinny kid. If I took two lives, don't you think I would have left some of my own blood at the scene?" His own sample, he said, was drawn contemporaneous with his admission to the FCI in Fort Dix, and at some point would have been entered into the National DNA Index System (NDIS), revealing a match if his DNA had been left behind at the Perry-Davis crime scene.

Thomas has shied from controversy since his release from prison, even as his name continues to swirl among lingering Oklahoma City conspiracy theorists. In a broadcast premiering November 1, 2007, he and his ARA foot soldiers were the focus of a darkly themed special on *The History Channel*, titled "Army of Hate." The footage, voiced in a chillingly toned narrative, paints unflattering portraits of each bank robber, suggesting that Thomas's dilapidated Pennsylvania stronghold served as their way station between scores. More recently, the co-authors of a book, *Oklahoma City: What the Investigation Missed, and Why it Still Matters*, suggested once more that McVeigh might've had ties to the masked bandits. They concede, however, that Thomas was the lone defendant from the group able to account for his whereabouts the day the Murrah Building fell.

Mark Thomas's greatest regret in life is the anguish he's caused his family. "I've always been a crusader against injustice," he said, but by his own reckoning admits to "some crazy religious beliefs" he held while maintaining foolhardy alliances with the Christian Identity sect and leading his fatherless minions astray. He considers himself "a reformed Christian" since parting from his extremist views, and his exemplary conduct subsequent to his release from prison aligns with this self-assessment. A father of eight children in all, he is a grandfather to many more, striving to make amends toward those closest to him. "I let my family down," he ruefully admitted. Resuming work as a part-time truck driver, since freed from Fort Dix, "My life has been, What can I do to make it up to them?"

At a time when Mark Thomas was holding rallies as a rising national leader within the Ku Klux Klan, yet still under suspicion by the New Jersey State Police, the Major Crime Unit fielded another seemingly preposterous call from Florida. A final intersecting coincidence loomed yet on the horizon as a condemned voice beckoned from death row, resurrecting faint hope for closure for the Memorial Day murders. Placed by an Oregon psychologist, the communication represented another intervening oddity in the legacy of the doomed investigation, exciting public intrigue once more as newspapers were availed of the latest development. This newest person of interest in the historical murder case, a celebrity in his own right in the wake of his two murder trials, had already been the subject of a made-for-TV movie and a best-selling book since his ten years on death row. What the New Jersey State Police didn't know or might've known all along and kept from the press, was that he'd resided near the heart of their investigation in 1969, just over six miles away from Mark Thomas and Gerald Stano in Montgomery County, Pennsylvania. Though his bloody trail of carnage festered elsewhere, he seemed anxious to share how his murderous impulses took shape during springtime that year in Ocean City, New Jersey.

CHAPTER SIXTEEN

The Six Degrees of Ted Bundy

In the summer of 1970 Raymond and Margaret Perry saw their firstborn daughter Suzanne wed at St. Martin's-by-the-Lake Episcopal Church in Minnesota, in the same quaint chapel where their younger daughter's memorial service was held a year earlier. To the extent he was capable, Raymond appeared stoic as the ceremony unfolded, beaming as he walked Suzanne toward the altar, standing proudly beside the bride and groom as they exchanged vows before a packed congregation.

The Perrys hosted a grand reception for more than two hundred guests at their lakeshore Minnesota cottage, adorning their backyard with pink rose centerpiece bouquets and candlelit tables that glowed beneath a clear moon sky. Despite appearing genuinely contented throughout the evening, Raymond Perry was far from healed as he continued to grapple with the enduring psychological horrors he'd suffered over Elizabeth's death. When he accepted a job transfer from the Bemis Company's corporate headquarters in Minneapolis within the year following her murder, both Perry and his employer fervently hoped a change of scenery and new position might set him on track again and help salvage his failing career.

In October 1970 the Perrys settled into their newly constructed house on Southeast 57th Street in the Parkwood neighborhood of Mercer Island, then a recently developed rural enclave of posh new homes with eastern views of Lake Washington. Life, they surely hoped, might begin anew after all. A rising vice-president at Bemis before his demotion to plant manager at their Seattle factory, in his spare time Perry worked vigilantly to see that other young women not share his daughter's fate. Publicly, he'd always remained silent as to which person he suspected had slain his daughter and her college companion but was certain that whoever was responsible had been given a lift home from the girls just after they left the Somers Point Diner. His concerns were manifested in a vigilant effort to overturn a new state law that legalized hitchhiking throughout the state of Washington, despite its known hazards. In early spring 1972, Perry wrote to Washington Governor Dan Evans, objecting to the controversial bill he signed that legalized the youthful pastime, to become effective May 20, 1972. In an April 29, 1972, editorial in opposition to the new law, journalist Adele Ferguson of the *Ellensburg Daily Record* wrote:

One man who doesn't like it and registered his complaint to Gov. Dan Evans, State Patrol Chief O.C. Furseth and the author of the law, Rep. Jeff Doutwaite, is a prominent Seattle businessman with good reason to hate hitchhiking.

One murdered his daughter and another girl college student near Ocean City, New Jersey in May, 1969.

The other girl was raped and both girls stabbed to death, their killer escaping via the highway and another ride after leaving the girls' car near the scene of the crime.

The Seattle father believes that legalizing hitchhiking in this state removes from the state patrol the useful tool of being able to pick up and check out hitchhikers so they can weed out some of the bad characters.

To appease a vocal minority of citizens like Ray Perry, Evans ordered the law reviewed by the City of Seattle's Crime Prevention Advisory Committee. In December 1972, the committee enacted myriad amendments, limiting where and when a person could hitchhike and at which locations along the highway thumbing a ride would not result in a ticket or arrest. Nevertheless, most provisions of the new bill remained intact, bringing Perry's futile efforts to naught.

Perry's fears came to light a few years after his unsuccessful push to have the controversial measure repealed. It seemed that the cruelest of ironies would continue to shadow his family no matter how many miles he distanced them from their past, for in 1974 several young women of a similar age and physical appearance to his own daughter began disappearing from the communities surrounding his family's new Mercer Island neighborhood.

The first to inexplicably vanish was twenty-one-year-old University of Washington student Lynda Ann Healy, attacked sometime after midnight on February 1, 1974, while asleep in her basement apartment near campus. Woken by a shrill noise permeating the walls of the house at 5517 Twelfth Street, a roommate entered Healy's room later that morning to shut off her alarm clock. Though somewhat surprised by Healy's conspicuous absence, nothing seemed out of the ordinary to her. A tall young woman majoring in psychology, Healy had prepared dinner for a small group friends the previous evening, then headed out for drinks at Dante's, a nearby University District tavern, before returning home some time during the late night or early morning hours. Healy's parents called the Seattle Police department the next afternoon, gravely concerned when they hadn't heard from her, and when her employer said she hadn't reported for her early morning shift at a local radio station where she broadcast the daily ski conditions.

Though initially skeptical that a violent abduction had taken place, Seattle police dispatched a detective to investigate the Healy disappearance. He discovered a slightly bloodied nightgown hanging in Healy's closet, and as he turned back the covers of her neatly made bed, noticed that the sheets and pillow were faintly blotched with what appeared to be bloodstains. No weapons were found near the crime scene during the ensuing investigation, nor did neighbors come forth to recount chilling screams heard echoing within North Seattle's University District that night. In 1974 runaways weren't uncommon, so police didn't initially sweep for prints, surmising that Healy suffered no more than a nosebleed and had gone to seek care.

The Seattle police had answered a similar call nearly three weeks earlier, less than a mile away. Sound asleep in her basement apartment in the early morning of January 4, 1974, eighteen-year-old Joni Lenz was clubbed unconscious with a bed rod and sexually assaulted with a speculum. Though she survived the encounter, due to the severity of her brain injury, the quiet stealth of her assailant and the disorientation of sleep, Lenz blacked out in the midst of the attack. After waking from her coma, she was unable to recall the event or identity of the person who'd fractured her skull. As with the previous crime scene, there were no strewn items, shattered glass, or broken locks to suggest that her assailant had been surprised in the course of a burglary, and her roommates weren't woken during the intrusion.

That the victims were of the same gender, close in age, and lived near one another in basement apartments were the only similarities between the occurrences. Police had no reason to link them to another disappearance a month later, nearly seventy miles away. Donna Gail Manson, a free-spirited nineteen-year-old student at Evergreen State University in Olympia, was last seen leaving her residence hall on the evening of March 12, 1974, to attend a faculty-student music recital across campus. On May 6, coed Roberta Parks disappeared in similar fashion soon after exiting her dorm room and walking along a commonly used path to the student union at Oregon State University.

It wasn't until after eighteen-year-old Susan Rancourt, an Alaskan biology major, went missing from Central

Washington State University, one hundred-twenty-miles from Seattle, that police first took note of a discernible pattern emerging among the disappearances despite the distance separating them. Each was a vulnerably positioned woman in her early twenties. All but one had fashionably long hair parted down the middle. Like Susan Davis and Elizabeth Perry, they were trusting, independent-minded young women, products of loving, upper-middle-class households for the most part, not itinerant nomads who'd fled their sheltered upbringings to take up with a dangerous mountain cult or fringe revolutionary organization. Roberta Parks was the only troubled, lonely soul who might've left town for an overnight stay without telling a friend or packing a bag to take along with her. The likelihood that the same assailant was responsible for the disappearances was a possibility the Seattle authorities now considered more probable than not, even if they refused to publicly acknowledge their suspicions that the cases might be related.

Paul Barclift, a veteran detective with the Thurston County Sheriff's Office in Olympia, Washington, was among the first officials to connect the cases after brainstorming with the campus security chief at Oregon State University, where Roberta Parks had vanished. At the urging of Sheriff Donald Jennings, Barclift transmitted a regional teletype to all police stations in the Pacific Northwest: *All four females...ages 18-21, are considered attractive. They all were attending colleges or universities located on or near an interstate highway...All disappeared, telling no one that they were leaving and took no personal belongings with them...*

In May that year a fifth woman vanished from an alleyway behind the Kappa Alpha Theta sorority house at the University of Washington, last seen in the early nighttime by a friend who'd waved goodbye to her from an upstairs window. In response, nearly one hundred representatives from surrounding jurisdictions gathered for a regional conference at Evergreen State College, wishful that a collective exchange of case files might provide direction, reveal a more distinctive pattern, or uncover leads. Reluctantly, police reached out to newspapers, requesting the public's help in providing tips.

By summertime local headlines warned women of a certain age to stay indoors, or at least not venture outside unaccompanied. Their fears were realized when Janice Ott, a petite twenty-three-year old probation caseworker from Seattle, disappeared from the forested beaches of Lake Sammamish State Park in Issaquah on a balmy afternoon in July when several thousand locals had crowded the sands for a brewery festival. A number of witnesses recalled seeing Ott, wearing a black bikini and reposed on her beach towel, chatting with a young, brown-haired man who spoke with a slight British accent. Dressed in tennis whites, his arm in a sling, he was overheard telling the young woman that his name was Ted and needed help fastening a sailboat to his car. A man fitting a similar description was seen lingering about the park restrooms later that afternoon luring Denise Naslund, a dark-haired nineteen-year-old office worker, toward a light-brown Volkswagen. In the days that followed, nearly one hundred volunteers combed the area while police divers dragged the lake bottom in search of the missing pair.

In the wake of these two well-publicized abductions, a pair of Central Washington University students notified the campus police that they'd been approached one night near the library's main entrance by a suspicious young man wearing an arm sling. He asked for help carrying his schoolbooks to a light-colored Volkswagen Beetle, which he'd parked in a remote unlit area beyond a railroad pass. The two separate incidents occurred at around the same time that Susan Rancourt disappeared, the witnesses recalled.

Provided with only a vague general description and a first name, major crimes detectives from the Seattle Police Department and King County (WA) Sheriff's Office were at a loss to explain the occurrences but deduced that they were attributable to the same perpetrator. In an era before advancements in forensic science more effectively enabled police forces to crack challenging homicide cases, local detectives employed unconventional strategies to hunt the elusive "Ted." Former lead investigator for the Washington State Attorney General's Office, Robert Keppel, Ph.D., who also taught at the University of New Haven's Henry C. Lee College of Criminal Justice and Forensic Sciences, was a newly hired major crimes detective with the King County Sheriff's Office in 1974. He and his colleagues devised an innovative criminal profiling system, feeding scant data compiled from a "tip sheet" into a massive King County payroll computer. The mainframe, occupying nearly an entire room, spat out separate lists of thirty-five hundred young men who lived in the Seattle area, shared the same first name, drove a Volkswagen, and matched the general physical description of the man seen talking to Janice Ott and Denise Naslund.

A police composite, published in local newspapers and broadcast on television reports, drew out a girlfriend, her best friend, and a college professor. They urged police to take a close look at a handsome law school student who'd recently dropped out of classes at the University of Puget Sound two weeks before taking his first-year exams. Detectives ran the name Ted Bundy. Unbeknownst to them at the time, Bundy had accumulated a juvenile record stemming from his involvement in a ski-lift-ticket forgery scheme, and defended accusations of auto theft when he was a teenager. Because he committed the crimes as a minor, his records had been expunged, revealing a deceptively clean background check. Although Bundy indeed resembled the shaggy-haired young man in the sketch, drove a Volkswagen, and lived in Seattle, a few blocks away from where the first three women had vanished, so had dozens of other young men in the "U" District. More names were fed into the computer and cross-indexed for similarities. Possible suspects offered plausible alibis that quickly excluded them. In time the list narrowed to one hundred persons, then down to twenty-five. In each instance the name Ted Bundy couldn't be eliminated.

In September of 1974 a pair of grouse hunters discovered the decomposed bodies of Ott and Naslund strewn near an old railroad trestle in Issaquah, a mile east from the beach where they'd last been seen. Their grisly find confirmed what the public already suspected: the women had perished in a grimly violent encounter. On March 3, 1975, the scattered bones of Susan Rancourt, Lynda Ann Healy, Kathy Parks, and Brenda Ball were uncovered on the slopes of Taylor Mountain in Issaquah. Panic gripped the valleys of the snow-capped Cascades as young women wondered who might fall victim next.

Likely possessed of a gathering sense authorities were closing in on him, Bundy fled for Utah. With the help of a letter of recommendation from Governor Evans, he enrolled at the University of Utah School of Law. Not long after his arrival in the fall of 1974, three young women vanished from the surrounding Salt Lake City area in much the same mysterious circumstances as in Washington. The fresh set of disappearances had crossed state lines, however, with enough time and distance separating them so that authorities from the two states didn't immediately recognize the incidents might be related.

Bundy's arrest transpired as a result of a chance traffic stop on August 19, 1975, when Utah Highway Patrol Sergeant Robert Hayward, answering another dispatcher's call to assist, made a wrong turn and happened by a beige Volkswagen Beetle that had passed him moments earlier as he was seated in his patrol car completing an end-of-shift log. The Volkswagen was parked in front of a house where Sgt. Hayward knew several teenage girls lived. As he flicked on his lights, the driver sped off. After a brief chase, Hayward cornered him in an abandoned gas station parking lot and drew his revolver. Dressed in a fashionable black turtleneck, the young man with shaggy brown hair claimed he was lost and had just returned from seeing *The Towering Inferno,* a film the officer knew wasn't playing locally. A subsequent search of his trunk revealed pantyhose, a ski mask, crowbar, handcuffs, and a length of rope. Recognizing these as a burglar's tools of the trade, Hayward arrested Theodore Robert Bundy for evading arrest.

In the following days the arrest report found its way atop the desk of Detective Jerry Thompson with the Salt Lake City Sheriff's Office. The name Bundy sounded familiar to him, as he'd been investigating the Utah disappearances and fielding tips from outside the state. He searched department files and saw where he'd spoken to one of Bundy's ex-girlfriends, who telephoned him from Seattle in December 1974 to report her suspicions once the authorities in the Northwest had publicly stated that the disappearances might be linked. At long last, wearied investigators from two states had the break they were hoping for.

Though by now he was considered a suspect in the Seattle and Utah murders, no physical evidence tied Bundy to any of the skeletons found in the dense brush on Taylor Mountain. A further background check revealed a former Boy Scout raised by a devoted Christian mother and stepfather in a tree-lined Tacoma neighborhood. He'd graduated with a B average from Woodrow Wilson High School, where he was a semi-popular student, if somewhat withdrawn socially. During the years after Bundy dropped out of the University of Washington in 1968, he'd fielded calls in a Seattle suicide crisis center and worked as a driver for civil rights leader Arthur Allen Fletcher in his unsuccessful campaign for Lt. Governor of Washington State. He'd even chased a purse snatcher down a city street and subdued him till police arrived, a heroic feat lauded in the *Seattle Times.* After graduating from the University of Washington in 1972, Bundy served as an aide to Ross Davis, the Washington

State Republican chairman, and volunteered for Governor Dan Evans' gubernatorial re-election campaign that summer. Though the Perrys were unaware of it at the time, in October that year the same young man whom the Seattle Police were investigating for the random disappearances of the city's young women was appointed by Governor Evans as assistant director of Seattle's Crime Prevention Advisory committee, and was among the members assigned to review the new hitchhiking law vehemently opposed by Ray Perry.

Acquaintances vouched for Bundy's integrity as the Utah State Police maintained surveillance over him. It wasn't until eighteen-year-old Carol DaRonch positively identified Bundy as the man who'd posed as a police officer while attempting to handcuff her inside his car in the darkened parking lot of a Murray, Utah, shopping mall on November 8, 1974, that detectives saw the last of the missing pieces fall into place. While serving a fifteen-year sentence in Utah State Prison for kidnapping DaRonch, Colorado authorities extradited Bundy for charges that he'd murdered nurse Caryn Campbell, who was abducted from the Wildwood Inn ski lodge in Snowmass, Colorado, in January 1975. Her partially nude, bloodied remains were found partly submerged in a nearby snowdrift a month later. Bundy had drawn a small circle on a map of the resort, found when he'd consented to a search of his Salt Lake City apartment. Samples from Campbell's hair matched strands found on the carpet fibers of Bundy's car.

Bewildered by the stunning developments, fellow workers offered unfettered praise, finding the accusations unfathomable to comprehend. Stewart Elway, Bundy's friend dating back to the 1968 Washington State Lieutenant Governor's campaign, was driving when he heard news of the arrest broadcast over his radio. "I almost went into a ditch," he said. "I couldn't believe it."

A young woman who'd worked with Bundy on the 1972 Washington gubernatorial campaign remarked, "It just freaked us out....We thought, how well did we really know him?"

"He was everything you looked for in an assistant," said Ross Davis of the Washington Republican Party. "He had a good analytical mind and worked well with people. He would have had to be a complete Jekyll and Hyde if what they say is true."

Bundy continued to profess his innocence while jailed in Colorado, adamant that he'd been the victim of a systemic cover-up. Justice, he assured his supporters, would eventually clear his name and restore his reputation. He earned notoriety as a wily escape artist in the meantime, leaping out a Pitkin County courthouse window one afternoon after being left unguarded during a break in proceedings prior to the Campbell murder trial in June 1977. For six days he evaded bloodhounds scenting his trail in the nearby Rockies, ducked roadblocks and search parties, and foraged rations from an abandoned hunting cabin where he laid up one night. His feat attained folkloric proportions in the ensuing media hoopla, with Aspen restaurants and resort watering holes naming hamburgers and cocktails after the renegade outlaw. Young men of Bundy's age, playing fearful they might be mistaken for the wanted escapee, sported t-shirts that read *I'm Not Ted.*

After a mandatory facility transfer, Bundy miraculously escaped from another Colorado jail during an evening snowstorm in December 1977, shimmying through a narrow hole left by a ceiling fixture he'd removed from the same nine-by-four-feet Garfield County cell where parkway murder suspect Ronnie Walden tried to hang himself eight years earlier. Stealing a car and hitchhiking a ride to a local airport, Bundy next boarded a flight to Chicago. From there he hopped an Amtrak train to Ann Arbor, Michigan, deciding on a whim that the quiet town and expansive University of Michigan campus would offer the ideal refuge where he might maintain his anonymity. He laid low for a time at a rented room in the YMCA, four miles from the intersection of Glazier Way and Earhart Road, where the body of Joan Schell, one of John Norman Collins's victims, was discovered with a slashed throat and multiple stab wounds in 1968.

Disliking the bitterly cold Midwest, and running short on cash, after a short stay at the YMCA, Bundy stole a car in Ann Arbor and drove to Atlanta before making his way by bus to Florida State University and the leafy quad where Walden had once dreamed of Saturday afternoon glory. He took up residence at a Tallahassee rooming house under the fictitious name Chris Hagen, one of a dozen or so aliases he would assume while dodging federal authorities. For several weeks Bundy managed to elude his pursuers, though by now his mug shot and fingerprints had appeared on the FBI's Most Wanted list. Like a heroin junkie yearning to recapture the unalloyed euphoria of his first opiate rush, it wasn't long before Bundy thirsted for more victims. Clasped in the throes of a spiraling madness, he set loose his wandering demons in the midst of a nightlong drinking binge on January 15, 1978. Donning his burglar's costume and slinking undetected through the unlocked doors of the Chi Omega sorority house, he slaughtered two slumbering coeds with a wooden club and seriously injured two others before making his getaway.

As the search for the killer intensified, Bundy wandered east to Lake City, Florida, where he raped and murdered twelve-year-old Kimberly Leach after luring her from a schoolyard into a white van he'd stolen from Florida State University. He was identified in the same vehicle after attempting to abduct a local police detective's teenage daughter soon thereafter. After a foot chase that ensued following a routine traffic stop of a stolen orange Volkswagen when police caught up to him in Pensacola, Florida, patrolman David Lee arrested Bundy in the same gulf town where Ronnie Walden resided for a time in the early 1970s after trying to pawn a load of scuba equipment at a local dive shop. "I don't even know why I decided to follow him," said Lee. I saw him going out of the town limits. It just goes to show there's no such thing as a routine stop."

In 1979, Bundy was found guilty in the murders of Chi Omega sisters Margaret Bowman and Lisa Levy at Florida State. An Orlando jury reached a similar verdict a year later in his trial for the murder of Kimberly Leach. Both judges sentenced him to die. The two cases sped along separate but parallel tracks toward the electric chair at Florida State Penitentiary in Starke, where Bundy remained housed on death row.

Much of the intrigue initially surrounding Bundy was attributable to his good looks and confident bearing. Relatively tall, with blue eyes, brown wiry shag haircut, an aquiline nose and slender frame, he fit the persona of a companionable local tennis pro, at first glance far more polished and woven of finer character than the other inmates residing alongside him on Q-wing at Florida State Penitentiary. Abused as an infant and beset with a low I.Q., with his disheveled appearance and shifty demeanor, parkway murder suspect Gerald Stano, who for a time occupied the cell beside Bundy, was more illustrative of the archetypal hard-bitten villain marked for execution. Drowsy-eyed, toothless serial killer Ottis Toole, who decapitated Adam Walsh, the six-year-old son of *America's Most Wanted* host John Walsh and lived in the other adjoining cell, fit a similar archetype. Glib and polished, with no history of abhorrent behavior, Bundy didn't give friends and acquaintances pause to glibly remark, *we could tell all along.*

The media seized upon the striking contrast between the ambitious campaign staffer and accused killer, fueling grist for the tabloids. Magazines glowingly cast Bundy as "a rising star within the Republican Party." "Handsome," "brilliant," and "charming" were other flattering portrayals chosen to describe him. Former Seattle newspaper journalist, police detective, and venerable true-crime writer Ann Rule penned his biography in 1980, chronicling the year she worked beside him in a Seattle crisis clinic in 1972, unbeknownst to his double life. The late author's best-selling book, *The Stranger Beside Me,* continues to serve as a primary resource for ensuing works profiling the notorious serial murderer.

By the summer of 1979, while on trial in Miami for the Chi Omega murders, only the governor of Florida had a more recognizable name than Ted Bundy. He relished his sudden celebrity status, turned to smirk devilishly for the cameras as flashbulbs popped outside the courtroom. Groupies young and old clamored for his attention. Newspapers, magazines, television producers, psychiatrists, even moralizing evangelists sought access to him while he held forth in a stark prison visitors room, yearning to understand what evil forces commanded a young man with such a seemingly peaceful temperament to murder over one hundred young women, by some estimates.

As his following waned, Bundy vied for the following he once commanded. To while away the long days of solitary confinement, he offered himself for observation to a select number of writers and psychologists anxious to explore his nuanced madness.

Former *Newsweek* reporters Stephen Michaud and Hugh Aynesworth were among those visitors received by Florida Department of Corrections inmate number 069063. Together they logged countless afternoons interviewing Bundy on death row between 1980 and 1983, meeting him in a sparse visitors room with just a tape recorder between them. Their findings comprised two books, *The Only Living Witness* and *Conversations with a Killer.* The pair had hoped their lengthy, in-depth discussions might offer insight into the multiple unsolved cases thought to involve their subject. Over the course of these numerous exchanges, they set about piercing his carefully constructed façade and deciphering his parlor game tricks.

On some occasions Bundy acted the role of a cooperative participant, conversant and glib. Other days he was distracted and uncommunicative, offering little insight, or arrived stoned from the stash of marijuana his girlfriend had smuggled past guards. The reporters plied their moody subject with vending machine candy and cigarettes in an effort to inspire greater candidness, or at least return him to point when he strayed off topic. From the outset, it became clear to the pair that their assignment would be more challenging than they'd expected, for Bundy was far too clever to provide an outright confession to any single murder. Reasoning with him as though he were a petulant teen boy, Michaud asked Bundy to speculate on the several murders he'd been suspected of committing, allowing him latitude to discuss his crimes without fear of incrimination. Though ultimately successful, this painstaking methodology required wading through a series of deliberately vague responses and dispassionate reflections masking a cunning pretense of self-awareness and narcissistic self-absorption. Referring to himself as "this guy," "that person," this individual," or "the personality," Bundy intimated details of each case hypothetically, but discussed specifics somewhat abstractedly, withholding particulars lest his remarks be misconstrued as an admission of guilt. He referred to murder as "inappropriately acting out" and rape as "satisfying that part of himself." As if aware the reporters recognized such childish transparency, Bundy never slipped into the traps laid by Aynesworth and Michaud as they attempted to exploit the openings offered by his sly ambivalence. Shaping answers into questions of his own, he made a game of alluding to his involvement in several murders but fell short of admitting to any specific one. Conversing in the third person, Bundy surrendered enough information to allow a reasonable inference of his guilt; yet, the more he spoke the less sincere

Bundy seemed, as if he sought to deepen the confusion surrounding him. "He turned the interviews into a game of chutes and ladders with disingenuous pleas of faulty memory," Michaud wrote, "and long silences preventing me from pinning him down."

Though Bundy was unforthcoming with the particulars of each case, he openly grappled to understand the affliction that beset him, articulating as best he could what pathological stimuli prevented him from withholding his raging impulses and attaining the composure necessary to quell their momentum. He consistently maintained that his thirst for pornography and its explicit degradation of women comprised "the entity," "the disordered self," or "the malignant being," terms he used to personify the latent motivation residing within him, a force originating in his childhood fascination with adult magazines and surreptitiously peeking at women through their bedroom windows as they undressed. Unleashed by alcohol, the entity loosened his inhibitions, freeing him to trawl Seattle neighborhoods under the cover of night. "This condition is not immediately seen by the individual or identified as a serious problem. It sort of manifests in an interest concerning sexual behavior, sexual images," he explained to Michaud. "But this interest, for some unknown reason, becomes geared toward matters of a sexual nature that involve violence." The complete possession of a woman, Bundy maintained, was the only act that could satiate the entity's momentum. Murder was a mere afterthought, a necessary means to avoid detection. The first few times he killed someone, Bundy described the aftermath as a "horrifying, guilt-inducing afterthought accompanied by shame and deep remorse." With practice, however, he became desensitized, and the recovery time between crimes grew narrower until "this entity inside was not capable of being controlled any longer, as least not for any considerable period of time."

Bundy's flamboyant antics during the 1980 Kimberly Leach murder trial—where he'd erupted numerous times before Circuit Judge Wallace Jopling, slammed his fist in indignation, attempted to storm out of the courtroom, and insisted upon representing himself against the advice of counsel—served as the basis for an appeal questioning his mental stability and fitness to stand trial. Dr. Emanuel Tanay was one of two psychologists whom Bundy's defense team enlisted to perform a court-ordered psychiatric evaluation in 1987. "Mr. Bundy is driven by a variety of unrealistic motives such as playing games with investigators for no other purpose than the sheer enjoyment of it," Tanay wrote. Bundy, though not "psychotic" in the clinical sense, suffered from antisocial personality disorder. According to Tanay, this condition inhibited Bundy's ability to comprehend the seriousness of the charges against him when he represented himself in Orlando.

U.S. District Court Judge G. Kendall Sharp wasn't persuaded by Tanay's diagnosis. He characterized Bundy as a "diabolical genius," ruling that he fully understood the seriousness of the charges against him and had been competent to stand trial. "Everyone knows that competency is not on trial here," said Sharp. "The death penalty is."

Florida Governor Robert Martinez signed Bundy's third and final death warrant on January 17, 1989. In the frantic last days leading to the execution, his defense team hurriedly prepared a slew of last-minute habeas petitions in federal court after exhausting all remaining appeals at the state level. The enigma surrounding Bundy resurfaced once more as word leaked that he was talking again, returning the media to northern Florida in droves. Fervent with anticipation, news trucks set up camp in a field across from the prison grounds. Florida Department of Corrections officials, unaccustomed to media scope of this magnitude, formed a special press office to receive the avalanche of news inquiries. Hoping to attribute long-dormant cold cases to him, law enforcement officials across the country sought access to Bundy when it became apparent his day was nearing.

Revived by fresh attention, Bundy met with officials from numerous western states against the advice of his attorneys. With the nation's eyes on him again, he resumed a familiar narrative, holding his inquisitors in thrall as they pressed him to elaborate upon his inconclusive responses. Through Diana Weiner, his civil attorney, Bundy presented a deal to Governor Martinez, offering to meet with police detectives from around the country to discuss the thorny specifics of each murder thought to involve him. By telephone hookup, he would guide search parties down the tricky mountain passes in states with rugged terrain, revealing the steep mountainsides where he'd concealed the remains. Remote burial sites only he knew, submerged beneath heavy snowfall and nearly impossible to trek in the dead of winter. The grieving families of countless victims would receive closure at last. As payoff, Bundy would earn a temporary stay. Weiner telephoned Governor Martinez's office in Tallahassee, proposing the terms. "Ted Bundy feels morally compelled as he faces death to do the right thing in terms of resolving any investigations," Weiner told Florida Assistant Attorney General Andrea Smith-Hillyer. "The immediate execution will effectively cripple law enforcement agencies around the country."

Revulsed by the murderer's gall, and wearied by his strategic delays, the governor issued a curt response through the press: "We have sent word back that the rendezvous with the electric chair will be next Tuesday morning at seven." He added, "For him to be negotiating with his life over the bodies of others is despicable."

Desperate, Bundy leveraged what little bargaining power he could muster. Despite advice by one of his lawyers to "shut up, shut the fuck up, and shut the fuck up right now," Bundy reiterated his earlier plan to Washington State investigator Robert Keppel and FBI agent Bill Hagmeier on

January 20: "What I want to do," he scribbled on a legal pad, "to tell the whole truth...nothing more or less...need time and less pressure-filled atmosphere to do it." He assured that he would "give the complete picture of how I came to do what I did....how it was done...plus specific facts of cases."

Three days before his execution, Bundy met once more with Hagmeier and a dispatch of law enforcement representatives from Colorado, Utah, California, Washington, and Idaho to discuss the details of approximately ten cold cases thought to involve him. Presented a map of the region, Bundy feigned an amnesiac absentmindedness each time he came close to pointing where he'd left a victim. Calculatedly imprecise, he was suddenly unable to recall specifics, leaving investigators unable to corroborate his claims. His clarity, he made certain, would uncloud if he were granted a reprieve and given more time. Apprised of Bundy's evasiveness, Florida Deputy Attorney General Jim York told the *Orlando Sentinel*, "Left to his own devices, his history would indicate he'll throw out enough facts to intrigue the listener and then he'll just evade and stall and try to buy time."

Word traveled fast among law enforcement agencies. Ted was ready to talk. Among those authorities wishing to meet with Bundy during his final days were detectives from the New Jersey State Police, anxious to question him about the murders of Susan Davis and Elizabeth Perry.

CHAPTER SEVENTEEN

Origins of Infamy

As the Delaware Valley newspapers had never made reference to Bundy in connection with the parkway murders in the midst of the extensive coverage several decades earlier, several intriguing questions arise as to when the New Jersey State Police first identified him as a person of interest in the Perry and Davis homicides, and why they had a fervent interest in speaking with him prior to his execution. Was he among the thousands of young men the department questioned, though never arrested, during the frantic early weeks of the investigation? Had detectives questioned him in 1969 and released him for lack of evidence along with scores of other young men, keeping the matter from the press in the years that followed for fear of negative publicity?

Constrained by a broad exception to New Jersey's Open Public Record Act, which systemically denies public access to open criminal investigations, no matter how old the case or narrowly construed the request, the New Jersey State Police refuse to confirm or deny whether their detectives had ever questioned Bundy about the parkway case prior to his initial arrest in Utah back in 1975.

Although news of Bundy's connection to the parkway murder investigation wasn't made public until after his death, in 1969 the New Jersey State Police first notified the FBI about the double homicide on the parkway, and for a time the case was monitored, if not actively overseen, by Joseph D. Jamieson, special-agent in charge of the Philadelphia field office. In March 1989 veteran *Seattle Times* journalist Richard Larsen wrote "Bundy and the Jersey Connection," the first article to suggest that as early as 1975 the New Jersey State Police may have been aware that Bundy was living approximately sixty miles away from Somers Point in 1969.

Larsen, a political reporter who'd first interviewed Bundy in 1972 while covering Washington State Governor Evans' re-election campaign, was initially impressed by the young campaigner and envisioned a bright future for him. Similar to Ann Rule, Larsen later chronicled his days covering Bundy's initial arrest and subsequent travails. His book, *The Deliberate Stranger*, was made into a three-part NBC miniseries, with actor Mark Harmon playing the role of the deranged killer. A resident of Mercer Island, Washington, Larsen's interest in the parkway murder investigation was partly attributable to his acquaintanceship with the Perrys, whom he and his wife met after the bereaved family moved to the island a year after the 1969 murders.

According to Larsen's article, "In 1975...investigators learned that during the spring of 1969, Bundy had been living in the Philadelphia area with an aunt and uncle and attending classes at Temple University." But Larsen, who died in 2002, failed to distinguish whether these "investigators" were from the FBI or New Jersey State Police. Nor did he clarify whether state or federal officials possessed any information specifically linking Bundy to the double murders. Former Utah Sheriff's Office detective Jerry Thompson doesn't recall speaking to the New Jersey State Police or learning of their interest in him via teletype communication or otherwise, after first arresting him in 1975. Larsen further wrote, "In recent days [FBI agent Terry Greene] has gathered data on the 1969 murders of Elizabeth Perry and Susan Davis, and those will be reviewed this week," implying that the information would be entered into the FBI's VICAP (Violent Crime Apprehension Program) database, first implemented in 1986. Greene's general remarks did not specify, however, whether the intelligence was culled from agency files dating back to 1969, when they'd monitored the case immediately following the murders, or derived independently of the New Jersey State Police.

Bundy's declassified FBI file provides little insight into his specific whereabouts prior to 1975, revealing minimal information such as fingerprint whorls, possible aliases, a physical description, his birthplace in Vermont, and he was "possibly illegitimate." There is no indication whether he had ever been questioned about the coed slayings near Somers Point. A more thorough examination of this timeframe suggests that the New Jersey State Police didn't show interest in Bundy as a possible suspect in the Davis and Perry murders until June 1977 at the earliest, when the FBI established federal jurisdiction over him after he'd sneaked out the Garfield County Jail in Colorado, and learned from Utah and Seattle authorities that he had traveled quite extensively. His second escape, which generated fervent national publicity, culminated in the issuance of a federal warrant in Denver. Named on the FBI's Most Wanted List in the following weeks, Bundy became a well-known fugitive among state law enforcement agencies nationwide as the bureau disseminated his picture, fingerprints, and biographical sketch via teletype bulletin. As the hunt for him intensified, police departments anywhere between Vermont and California searched for fingerprint matches, crime scene evidence, and investigation notes among their unsolved cases involving the murders of college-aged women to see whether they'd ever questioned Bundy or had him temporarily detained in their own jurisdiction. Consequently, it is reasonable to infer that the Davis and Perry killings were among the multiple cold cases compared with Bundy's profile and *modus operandi*.

Alternately, the FBI may have gathered intelligence on the Davis and Perry investigation prior to 1975 via the New Jersey State Police by way of a psychological profiling course taught by members of the bureau's Behavioral Sciences Unit (today known as the Behavioral Analysis Unit). The BSU formed long before the more sophisticated interagency computer network databases, CODIS and VICAP, formally linked state and federal law enforcement agencies based upon physical evidence and individual offender profiles.

"By about 1960, I had developed a hypothesis that you'd be able to determine the kind of person you were looking for by what you could see at the crime scene," Howard D. Teten, one of the first FBI agents credited with establishing criminal profiling as a science in the Seventies, told *Psychology Today*. Teten taught criminal profiling courses at the National FBI Academy training center in Quantico, Virginia, where he invited top state law enforcement personnel to his classes. Attendees would regularly provide Teten and other criminal profilers with information about regional cases fitting a similar pattern possibly attributable to the same perpetrator. "When I received the information, I would review all the data and prepare a tentative description of the perpetrator. Then I would look at the individual found to have committed the crime and compare the perpetrator to my description."

According to Teten, due to the clandestine nature of profiling during the Seventies, he and other agents purposely maintained scant records of case information shared with them by state police personnel. "In those days profiling wasn't an official program," he explains. "One of our worries was that we'd make a mismatch. We didn't put much on paper as we didn't want to upset our superiors." Detective Robert Maholland and several other New Jersey State Police detectives who'd worked extensively on the parkway murder investigation attended the Academy's police training school at various times during the 1970s. Moreover, field agent Joseph D. Jamison, who kept tabs on the parkway murder case, served as Assistant Director of Training at the Academy between December 1973 and March 1975. Teten doesn't recall receiving any information regarding Bundy as a possible suspect in the 1969 parkway killings while he was an instructor at the academy, or whether Bundy's name had been listed in FBI files prior to his 1975 arrest.

Detective Thomas Kinzer told a *Philadelphia Inquirer* reporter that the New Jersey State Police had attempted to question Bundy about the parkway murders in 1988, the year preceding his execution, but he refused to meet with them. "I have no memory of Ted ever mentioning anything at all about ever being in New Jersey," said Michael Radelet, another of his capital defense attorneys. "My memory-much of it either faded or blocked-was that his first victim was in Washington State circa 1974."

Also unclear is whether New Jersey detectives had flown to Florida to try to meet with Bundy at any point during his final days or limited their scope of inquiry to telephone calls placed through the Florida Department of Corrections. New Jersey Trooper of the Year for 1981, Nicholas Theodos, formerly acting superintendent of the New Jersey State Police and head of the New Jersey State Police Major Crime Unit, was one of the detectives assigned to explore the Bundy connection to the Parkway slayings in the years following his execution. Major Theodos met with Detective Kinzer on at least one occasion to identify any possible nexus between Ted Bundy and the parkway murders. Theodos recalls that Det. Sgt. David Kenna had flown to Florida to meet with Bundy before his execution, along with Det. Ernest Volkmann (Kenna, who served in the New Jersey National Guard following his retirement, didn't return several requests for an interview; Volkmann denies that he was the other detective who'd been sent to Florida.) to question Bundy about the parkway murders. According to John Tanner, a Daytona Beach, Florida, attorney and one of Bundy's spiritual advisers, dozens of law enforcement officials from across the country had travelled to see Bundy, waiting patiently at the prison while he decided whether to provide any final confessions in the hours before his death. Tanner doesn't recall, however, whether New Jersey was among them.

None of the retired New Jersey State Police investigators interviewed for this book recall speaking with Bundy while he was residing in Lafayette Hill in 1969 or during his incarceration in Utah and Colorado. Bundy's aunt, Audrey Tilden, with whom Bundy resided for several months in 1969 while attending school in Philadelphia, doesn't recall the New Jersey State Police ever interviewing her about the parkway murders. She does, however, distinctly remember an FBI agent calling her at home to discuss her nephew's possible involvement in the murders "somewhere along the highways of New Jersey" while specifically referencing the Davis and Perry murders. Although Tilden is unsure of the precise date of this conversation, she remains certain the interview took place after 1969, but long before Ted's execution in 1989. "The [FBI] said they were going to come to my house. I said there was no point in it. It could not possibly have been him." Federal authorities, however, never followed up to interview Tilden in person. Her recollection, if correct, is consistent with the likelihood that the New Jersey State Police first became aware of Bundy's presence in Philadelphia when alerted indirectly by the FBI through the media onslaught after he first appeared on their most wanted list in 1977, or when federal agents recognized similarities among the crime scenes and victims in Egg Harbor Township, Colorado, Utah, and Washington, and subsequently shared their findings with the New Jersey State Police through VICAP after the FBI implemented the database beginning in 1986. At the very least, the FBI's call to Tilden reveals that if federal investigators were in fact aware of Bundy's ties to the parkway murders for a long time prior to his execution, it's doubtful they acquired the case facts independently of the New Jersey State Police.

Whatever answers the New Jersey State Police Major Crime Unit sought on the eve of Ted Bundy's death would have to wait for the time being, as the infamous celebrity inmate, finally heeding the advice of counsel, brought his meetings with law enforcement officials to an abrupt halt, cancelling a 1 p.m. scheduled news conference on January 23, 1989, the day before his scheduled execution. In the meantime, Governor Martinez, refusing to withdraw his last death warrant, insisted that Bundy would be electrocuted early Tuesday, less than twenty-four hours away.

Through Polly Nelson, a court-appointed capital defense attorney with the Washington, D.C. firm of Wilmer, Cutler & Pickering, Bundy sent word that he wished to speak with Dr. Dorothy Otnow Lewis rather than issue a statement to the press. A noted Yale University psychiatrist and author of the book *Guilty by Reason of Insanity*, over the course of her storied career, Dr. Lewis evaluated such infamous madmen as Mark David Chapman (the man who gunned down John Lennon in front of The Dakota apartment building in New York City) and "Beltway Sniper" John Allen Muhammad. In the course of her extensive studies, Lewis uncovered certain traits consistent among society's most violent offenders: brain dysfunction, child abuse, and paranoia. Along with Dr. Tanay, Lewis had provided her professional opinion as to Bundy's mental state at his 1987 evidentiary hearing, testifying that Bundy's alleged exposure to violence at a young age, combined with her diagnosis of bipolar disorder, rendered him incompetent to testify on his own behalf at the trial for Kimberly Leach's murder.

The mood was threaded with somber finality as Lewis and Nelson sat across from Bundy in a glass-walled visiting room on the afternoon of January 23, his last full day alive.

Lewis offered her subject free reign to discuss anything that came to mind, and for four-and-a-half hours she interviewed the man whom a *New York Times* book reviewer once regarded as "the most fascinating killer in modern American history." At turns peaceful and jittery, Bundy's yearning need to explain himself was twisted by the reality of his dire circumstances, as the nearness of death had ferried him into an unsettled mental state marked by a shifty restiveness. Nelson noted that he was "vague, mumbling, acting very furtive, very strange," as though medicated, yet Bundy remained adamant he'd taken no sedatives to calm himself. As his own mother hadn't been to visit with him in nearly three years, perhaps Lewis and Nelson served as reassuring maternal influences as Bundy's imminent demise became an overwhelming reality.

Determined to establish his legacy on his own terms and in his own words, Bundy explained to Dr. Lewis that he'd chosen her for his penultimate interview "because everyone else I've talked with these past days only wants to know what I did. You are the only one who wants to know why I did it."

Authors, former attorneys, and criminal psychologists have posited divergent opinions regarding the origins of Ted's homicidal tendencies. Most agree that dark spirits must have converged upon him at some point during his formative years to incite such unbridled savagery toward young women. "There had to be some history of violence against him...he didn't get that way by reading Playboy," said Bundy's lead counsel, James Coleman.

Robert Ressler, a former FBI criminal profiler who spent a large part of his law enforcement career studying the patterns of violent predators such as Bundy and Chicago serial murderer John Wayne Gacy, was Howard Teten's colleague at the National Academy. In his book *Whoever Fights Monsters,* Ressler wrote, "there were strong indications that

Bundy was physically and sexually abused by members of his family."

Interviewed by a reporter for the *Tacoma News-Tribune* two days before Ted was executed, Louise Bundy said of her son, "He was not a violent person. Yes...he had a temper, but nothing out of the ordinary. In all the years of growing up, we never saw any sign of these violent things. ...we just cannot in any way figure out what would have caused him—if indeed, he did these things, and I still qualify that—what would have caused it....But if he did those things it's a mental illness. A person who would do those things is mentally ill."

Bundy's biographers have offered varying explanations for his pathological deviance. One popular theory suggests that his festering hatred toward women was an affliction rooted in identity deception, as his mother had tricked him into believing that she was actually his sister in an effort to save him the shame and embarrassment attendant to being conceived out of wedlock in an era when being an illegitimate child bore a shameful stigma. Though Bundy never denied he'd been raised to believe that his mother was his sister, and that his maternal grandparents, Eleanore and Samuel Cowell, were his true parents, this revelation didn't have the lasting impact some thought it might when he learned the truth in his early teens, and up until the end of his life Bundy had always expressed unconditional devotion toward Louise.

Author Stephen Michaud wrote of hearing stories that Ted might have been the product of an incestuous tryst between his grandfather and mother. He also suggested that Bundy harbored a class-conscious psychopathy that made him deeply resentful of the women he'd dated, their affluent families a persistent reminder of his own modest beginnings. Though Bundy admitted as much to Michaud during one of their interviews on death row, an alternate version of his formative years, offered by his relatives, veers sharply from the more commonly understood narrative.

Although the Bundys and the Cowells were by no means affluent, they weren't hardscrabble yokels either. Both were respected families in their Seattle and Philadelphia communities, if lacking significant social standing. While Bundy was acutely aware his mother and stepfather had little money and was openly envious of the more prosperous upbringing enjoyed by his cousins in Tacoma, in hindsight these admissions seem more a reflection of his own youthful insecurities rather than a firmly entrenched resentment.

Though generally considered to be class-conscious, Bundy never disclosed, or perhaps never knew, that he was distantly related to a famous confederate general. A comprehensive genealogical history of the Longstreet surname, compiled by Florida historian Rubert James Longstreet through his painstaking mappings of centuries-old New Jersey courthouse records and tombstone inscriptions, provides that Ted Bundy's maternal bloodlines trace back several generations to Dirck Stoffelse Langestraet of Holland. One of Dirck's grandsons, Theophilius Langestraet, was the great-grandfather of Lt. General James Longstreet Jr., appointed by General Robert E. Lee as Commander of the First Corps of the Army of Northern Virginia, who reluctantly led his troops to fight the ill-fated Pickett's Charge at the Battle of Gettysburg.

As further documented in Rubert Longstreet's research of his family's East Coast origins, distant relative James Aaron Longstreet of 5034 Greene Street in Germantown, Pennsylvania, traced his lineage to another of Dirck's grandsons, Dirck "Richard" Langestraet. James possessed official papers from the Monmouth County, New Jersey Orphans Court April 1834 term that corroborated his claims, recording his findings around 1913. Listed in the 1903 Philadelphia City Directory as "sec. & treas Wayne Chemical Company" in Germantown, James Aaron Longstreet was probably Eleanore Miriam Longstreet's father and Ted Bundy's great grandfather.

Rubert Longstreet's account shows to be partly verified by General Longstreet himself in his 1896 autobiography, *From Manassas to Appomattox*. Thus, though several generations removed, Ted Bundy was likely a distant cousin of the trusted adviser whom Robert E. Lee nicknamed "My Old War Horse."

At the 1987 competency hearing Dr. Lewis had also testified that Samuel Cowell, Bundy's maternal grandfather from Philadelphia, was a temperamental alcoholic susceptible to unprovoked outbursts. Ted's homicidal tendencies, she reasoned, were at some level attributable to the horrors he'd witnessed firsthand as a toddler in Roxborough, Pennsylvania, a community several miles outside the city, where he lived with his grandparents until age four.

Never during the several lengthy interviews that he provided over the course of his incarceration, when offering snippets of his early boyhood in the Delaware Valley suburbs, did Bundy hint that his own derangement had originated with Cowell or was any way attributable his unorthodox upbringing. According to Dr. Lewis, her interviews with Cowell's siblings revealed "an extremely violent and frightening" family patriarch in Samuel, a "raging alcoholic" who "swung cats by the tail" and had once flung one of Ted's aunts down the stairs when she arrived home past curfew. Lewis was unsurprised to learn of Bundy's filtered reflection of his childhood. "When a youngster has been horribly traumatized so that he cannot tolerate what he has witnessed…he tends to totally repress," she said.

Dr. Lewis' evaluations have provided an accompanying tragic narrative held steadfast by books, movies, newspaper and magazine articles for the past twenty-five years. (Reached at her New Haven, Connecticut, residence, Dr.

Lewis refused to be interviewed for this book, other than to state that she stands by the version of her courtroom testimony set forth in Michaud's *The Only Living Witness*.) Ted's downfall, Lewis suggested, may have begun farther back than his early childhood, beginning with the unusual circumstances by which his mother conceived him.

Apart from Lewis' interviews, which introduced to America a sordid side of Bundy's childhood that the public had never heard before, most of the general biographical information portraying Bundy's early boyhood first gained attention in the earliest edition of Rule's *The Stranger Beside Me*, published in 1980. Mostly verified, the facts set forth in that edition seem to have been derived from interviews Bundy provided to a Utah prison psychiatrist subsequent to his initial arrest in 1975.

According to Rule, in 1946 Louise Cowell was twenty-three-years old and seven months pregnant when her parents, Eleanore and Samuel, sent her off to the Elizabeth Lund Home on Shelburne Road in Burlington, Vermont. A secluded way station for shamed girls who'd found themselves in a similar predicament, the facility was once known as the "Home for Friendless Women." Though other such facilities were nearer their home in historic Roxborough, Pennsylvania, a middle-class bedroom community located a few miles outside of Philadelphia, Louise likely decided to secret herself in a distant New England state for several months to spare her conservative Christian mother and father the shame of their unmarried daughter bearing an illegitimate child. Louise was said to have been charmed by Jack Worthington, a local man eight years her senior, with whom she worked at a local insurance company. Embellishing his past, he said that he'd attended a local prep school and served valorously in U.S. Air Force. After impregnating Cowell, the noble suitor fled.

"I only talked to him once, when he picked her up one day for a date," said Audrey Tilden, Ted's aunt and Louise's younger sister. "I thought he was a very nice reputable person, but he wouldn't have anything to do with helping pay for Ted when he was born or anything like that. My sister thought it was not right to get rid of the baby."

As further set forth in Rule's account, to further spare her parents the harsh shame of their grandchild's illegitimacy, on October 6, 1950, Louise changed her sons' name to Theodore Robert Nelson. Ted's mother, Rule wrote, selected a commonly pronounced random surname that wouldn't raise questions as to his true parentage. Louise changed Ted's last name once more when he was four-years old after moving with him to Tacoma, where she met and married Johnnie Culpepper Bundy, a Veteran's Administration hospital cook originally from Elizabeth City, North Carolina.

While providing a mostly verifiable blueprint of Bundy's early life, the early edition of *The Stranger Beside Me* never delved far beneath the surface, failing to explore the murky depths of Bundy's origins. Official records surrounding Ted's birth father remain muddled to this day. Who was Jack Worthington? A John F. Worthington Jr. who was born in 1916 and lived in Narberth, Pennsylvania, near Louise during this time period, would seem a likely candidate. According to his 1989 obituary, he performed as a session drummer for local orchestra bands in Philadelphia and had attended Friends Central School, a private Quaker secondary institution. He died in a nursing home weeks before Ted was executed. (Reached by telephone, a close relative of Worthington denied that her father had sired Ted. She further noted that he hadn't served in the Air Force.)

U.S. census records for 1940 verify that at the time of Ted's conception, another John Worthington resided in Philadelphia, born in 1916 as well. Little is known of him, other than he was married to Martha Worthington and lived on Logan Street in the East Germantown section of the city, approximately six miles from 7202 Ridge Avenue. His occupation is listed as "clothing salesman."

A third John Worthington, born in 1915, resided nearby at 5844 Fourth Street in Philadelphia, earning a living as a hat maker.

Louise named Lloyd Marshall as Ted's father when she completed Ted's birth certificate, according to Rule's biography. The author's findings, consistent with Florida Department of State records, also align neatly with a 1940 U.S. Federal Population Census, which reveals that a Lloyd Marshall Jr., born in 1924, the same year as Louise, resided with his parents and younger brother at 226 Osborn Street in Philadelphia, a row home three miles from the Cowells' Ridge Avenue address and within their same 21st voting ward. The census lists Lloyd Marshall Sr.'s occupation as a service manager for Reliable Motors Inc. of 203 N. Broad Street in Philadelphia. His son's present whereabouts, however, are unknown.

On Ted's birth certificate Louise listed 1916 as Marshall's birth year, the same year that two of the three Philadelphia-area Jack Worthingtons were born. And while Bundy's Aunt Audrey confirms that a man named Jack Worthington was Ted's father, what explains why Louise would name Lloyd Marshall, a neighborhood man, as Ted's father instead of Worthington? Was Louise a platonic friend of Lloyd's? Had the two of them enjoyed a fling that caused her to question the true father's identity? As the birthdates of Marshall and Worthington are interchangeable, might she have conveniently switched them on Ted's birth certificate in an attempt to protect their privacy, or had she simply gotten the dates mixed up?

Bundy's "official" Certificate of Birth, issued by the state of Vermont, offers little clarification on the matter. Maintained at the Burlington, Vermont City Clerk's office in Chittenden County, the document was "received" by then City Clerk Frank Wagner on January 24, 1980—thirty-four-years after Ted's birth—and is signed by Johnnie Bundy and Eleanor Louise Bundy. However, the sworn statement on the back of the certificate, attesting to the facts on the reverse side, was notarized in the presence of Vernon M. Johnson in Pierce County, Washington, on July 8, 1953. According to a Burlington County City Clerk's Office representative, the discrepancy in dates may be attributable to Louise and Johnnie submitting this amended birth certificate to the state of Vermont when Johnnie adopted Ted shortly after Louise moved to Tacoma with them after leaving Roxborough, when Ted was four. The representative also confirmed that in instances of adoption, only the newer birth certificate, essentially a certified copy, is reissued to the town clerk in Vermont following the adoption proceeding. To obtain the original certificate from 1946 would require a court order, as the adoption records would likely be sealed and in the possession of the Washington State Department of Health, the state where Johnnie claimed young Ted as a son after he and Louise were married in 1951.

Louise and her newborn son returned to Philadelphia two months after his birth, residing with her two sisters and their parents at the two-story, stuccoed, eighteenth-century white colonial at 7202 Ridge Avenue in Roxborough. This home provided the backdrop for the prevailing theory that Bundy inherited his murderous inclinations from Samuel Cowell, as he'd sheltered newborn Ted and his mother here after their return from Vermont. Although the notion of an abusive upbringing, first introduced through Dr. Lewis' testimony, has held steadfast through the years and was relied upon by Rule in later editions of *The Stranger Beside Me*, a deeper exploration of Ted Bundy's maternal grandfather reveals an entirely different portrait than the more commonly understood version sourced in numerous scholarly publications and myriad biographies.

The oldest of seven children born to Julia F. Cowell, a German immigrant, and William F. Cowell, a Chicago ophthalmologist, Samuel Knecht Cowell was born in Dearborn, Michigan, in 1898, the same hometown of

Caryn Campbell, the nurse that his grandson murdered in Snowmass, Colorado, in 1975. For reasons unclear from the available historical record, at some point during the early part of the twentieth century Dr. Cowell relocated with his family to Woodbury, New Jersey, in Gloucester County, for about ten years. The family then moved to Abington, Pennsylvania, in the 1930s. During this time Samuel courted and wed Eleanore Miriam Longstreet, a young woman from the Germantown neighborhood of Philadelphia where her father, James A. Longstreet, had founded the First Congregational Church on West Seymour Street in 1888.

A devout Presbyterian, Samuel taught Bible school class at his father-in-law's Germantown congregation for several years. Perhaps to raise their three daughters and house the equipment for his thriving landscaping business, in 1945 he and Eleanor moved their family from Shawmont Avenue in Roxborough, after purchasing a spacious three-acre lot at the corner of Ridge Avenue and Domino Street in the same historic northwest Philadelphia community where Revolutionary War soldiers once trooped, lodging at the fieldstone inns set facing the route. City of Philadelphia deed records reflect that in 1945 Cowell purchased the large white-stuccoed colonial at 7202 Ridge Avenue from widower Margaret C. Adams for $5,400. Located a short distance from the old Green Valley Country Club, and extending lengthwise down Domino Lane, with a narrow section fronting Ridge Avenue, the Cowells' home was one of only two residences on the block at the time at the time of its purchase. Fireplaces warmed each bedroom of the rambling two-hundred-year-old colonial, which stood alongside the Miller Funeral Home.

Though his own father had been a physician, Samuel was an outdoorsman and green thumb at heart. Thinly built, yet of wiry musculature much like his grandson, he was handsome with a full head of silver hair and deeply set blue eyes, never too busy to volunteer his time or help a neighbor dig a hole or plant a bush. A member of the Pennsylvania Horticultural Society, Sam prospered as a local landscape architect and gardener, peddling young shrubs and planting small trees with each spring bloom. The community patronized his successful garden mart, *Cowell's Hardy Gardens,* a business he operated from the grounds surrounding his hilltop residence. Each year he sponsored a display booth for his nursery at the Philadelphia Flower Show, an event held annually at the Philadelphia Civic Center.

The Cowells were a frugal, largely self-sufficient family, living within a vastly changing suburban landscape as the rural acreage behind Ridge Avenue was overtaken by suburban expansion after World War II ended. Chickens roosted in a backyard coop, and Sam's daughters canned fruit to store for the winter and grew their own vegetables. Ted's Aunt Audrey, who still resides in Lafayette Hill, the next town over from Roxborough, recalls an idyllic youth spent along Ridge Avenue with her two teenage sisters, Louise and Julia. "It was a good life there," said Tilden. "We had rabbits, we had chickens and ducks. We never locked our doors." Tilden remembers an old barn on the grounds and the detached garage where Sam housed his truck and landscaping equipment, and a small greenhouse that stood near the corner of Ridge Avenue and Domino Lane. This somewhat dilapidated structure, described by one writer as a "fragrant humid hideaway" where a pre-teen Ted Bundy was said to have perused the vast trove of pornographic magazines secreted away by his grandfather, was actually little more than a careworn storage shed.

John Johnstone is the former president of the Roxborough-Manayunk-Wissahickon Historical Society and co-author of the book, *Images of America: Roxborough.* Though Johnstone didn't know Cowell personally, during multiple interviews with local residents he learned that the old man was known about town as an industrious gardener, not a mean-spirited tyrant who served as a malevolent influence on his first grandchild. Young Ted, locals tell Johnstone, used to dote on his grandfather and followed after him around the nursery, often reciting the spelling of words as Sam quizzed him. According to Johnstone, at worst, Ted's grandfather was thought to be a tad eccentric, at times seen muttering to himself as he hoisted shrubs outside his home while tending to his business.

Sylvia Myers, a spry ninety-four-year-old widow and vice-president of the Roxborough-Manayunk-Wissahickon Historical Society, doesn't remember Samuel Cowell, a fellow member of the Roxborough Garden Club, as the universally condemned, sadistically cruel curmudgeon portrayed in the multiple biographies of his grandson. "He was a fine man," Myers said, recalling one occasion as she stood outside Sam's Ridge Avenue home, helping him wrap burlap around a set of young dogwoods he routinely sold at cost to his flower club for $1.19 each, as his toddler grandson stood watching them beside his doting mother. A 1949 *Philadelphia Inquirer* article reveals that Cowell conducted "garden quizzes" and gave talks on "forcing the flowering of shrubs and tree branches" on behalf of the club. In 1964 the *Inquirer* "Garden News" column featured his presentation he gave on "Insects-Friends and Enemies" at the Roxborough-Manayunk Savings and Loan Association." Five years later he was still active with the club, handing out an African violet free to all new members of this club in his capacity as horticulture chairman. As the name Ted Bundy grew more notorious each year the body toll rose, Sylvia Myers and her old friends from the neighborhood remained unable to reconcile the image of a serial killer with the little boy they saw running around his grandfather's yard. "We were surprised to hear these stories of how mean he was," said Myers.

Samuel Cowell sold the Ridge Avenue homestead for $15,000 to Fredavid Construction Company in 1961 upon learning that Philadelphia city officials planned to construct an incinerator at the foot of Domino Lane. He and Audrey moved to smaller quarters on Pulaski Avenue in Germantown after conveying title to the builder, who gave word to Samuel that he'd restore the home at 7202 Ridge Avenue consistent with its original architectural style. Instead, the builder razed the land to maximize its potential as a commercial property with prime footage along an increasingly busy route. Neighbors were kept in the dark as to its sale, as one day the property was suddenly vacant, the abandoned furnishings scavenged by local trash pickers. The family seemed to have vanished, and nobody around town could offer a plausible explanation for their sudden departure. Left untended, a decrepit barn on the homestead purportedly became a favorite gathering spot for neighborhood boys.

Warren Miller, whose father owned the funeral home next to the Cowells, recalls that the property alongside the Millers was in a state of disrepair for several years before it was abandoned and leveled. Today, 7202 Ridge Avenue is the site of a small strip mall, with the entire area eventually succumbing to commercial development. Many of the old fieldstone homes dating back to the revolution were demolished before parts of Ridge Avenue were designated as a historic district. Though intersected by a number of bustling routes, today the avenue reflects much of its original old-world charm.

Collapsing behind the wheel of his truck, Samuel died of a heart attack in 1983, at the age of eighty-five, eleven years after his wife Eleanor, who passed away on April 25, 1971. Sylvia Myers and other members of the Roxborough Flower Club attended his memorial service. He was laid to rest beside his wife Eleanor at George Washington Memorial Park in Plymouth Meeting, Pennsylvania, not far from where his home once stood on Ridge Avenue. Each spring bloom Cowell's selflessness and kind spirit are recalled by Sylvia Myers as she walks past the flowering dogwood Sam planted one season in the backyard of her former row house at the corner of Pechin and Markel Streets in Roxborough, where she lived before moving to a retirement community.

Bundy's cousin Edna Martin, a life insurance professional who resides in Seattle, draws similarly fond memories of Sam, an uncle on her father's side. Martin didn't see Sam very often because she grew up in Tacoma, where her father, Dr. John C. Cowell, Samuel's youngest brother, was a Yale-educated concert pianist and music professor at the University of Puget Sound. Ted was said to have idolized John Cowell and visited him and his children at some point in 1969, during his tenure as music department chair at the University of Arkansas.

"The characterization that [Sam] was a raging alcoholic and animal abuser was a convenient characterization used to make people justify why Ted was the way he was," Martin said. "From my limited exposure to him, nothing could be farther from the truth. His daughters loved him dearly and had nothing but fond memories of him." Martin vehemently disagrees with the notion that Sam "was some kind of monster. It's not true and patently unfair as well as unfounded."

"The best documented evidence of psychotic disturbance was evidence regarding [Ted's] grandmother, Eleanor, Sam's wife," Dr. Lewis testified. "She had been hospitalized on more than one occasion for psychotic depression." Bundy's grandmother never left her house due to agoraphobia, a characterization also derived from Dr. Lewis' testimony, and had been administered electroshock therapy. Bundy's aunt, Audrey Tilden, disagrees with these findings as well. She contends that her mother was an overweight diabetic rendered housebound after suffering a stroke, and never succumbed to psychotic episodes described by Lewis as "being loud and talking too much and being unable to stop."

In a *Miami Herald* editorial published after Bundy's execution, Ann Rule wrote that Bundy had confided the true reason he'd traveled to Philadelphia in 1969: in order to make a side trip to Burlington, Vermont, to find his true father. To Stephen Michaud and Dr. Lewis, however, Bundy disclosed that he'd been traumatized when dumped by his first love, Diane Edwards, a wealthy Seattle girl he met while attending the University of Washington during the 1967 spring semester, and simply needed to get away without any specific destination in mind. This explanation is consistent with the timeline on file with the Florida Department of State, which indicates that Bundy had also sent transcripts to the University of Michigan, Stanford University, and the University of Colorado in early 1967. Though the reasons he offered for traveling to Philadelphia vary according to his multiple accounts, Bundy consistently maintained that he was at a troubled and particularly vulnerable period in his life in the late 1960s, as the breakup with Edwards had psychologically unmoored him. Distracted and lovelorn, he told Dr. Tanay that after returning to the University of Washington in September 1967 and enrolling in several classes, he was still unable to decide on a major: "I dropped out of school in January of 1968, traveled, went skiing in Heavenly Valley (Utah) and Aspen, and then went back east to Philadelphia and then came back....Worked in politics in '68, urban campaigns, and went to Temple University [in] the early part of '69, and then I bounced around a little bit more. But at least I was pulling myself together."

As he recalled this same time period for Dr. Lewis the day before his execution, Bundy revealed that he was at a far more unstable crossroads during his visit to Philadelphia in 1969 than he'd previously disclosed to Dr. Tanay, compelled by the latent psychosis slowly overtaking him. "I decided, well, I'm going to go to Temple," he told Lewis. "It's at that point that I think again that I reached the point of acting out.

In part because it was quickly apparent to me that this place, just a change of place, wasn't going to solve anything."

"Ted just adored his grandfather," Audrey Tilden said, offering yet another explanation why her nephew decided to attend Temple University. Among those interviewed by Dr. Lewis at her New Haven office, Tilden insists that her infamous nephew was never physically or emotionally abused by Sam, nor were she or her two other sisters subjected to cruelty at the hands of their father. Ted couldn't room with his grandparents in 1969, Tilden explains, because the elderly couple had moved into their small Germantown apartment by this time and simply didn't have room for their grandson.

Arriving in Philadelphia with only three-hundred dollars in his pocket, in the winter of 1969 Bundy moved in temporarily with his Aunt Audrey at her two-story brick home on South Warner Avenue in Lafayette Hill. A middle-class, post WWII Philadelphia located the next town over from his grandfather's former home in Roxborough, Lafayette Hill is approximately five miles from Thayer Drive in Center Square, where Mark Thomas spent a large part of his teenage years, and four miles from the split-level where Gerald Stano lived while attending Wissahickon High School. An active member of the Montgomery County Young Republicans and a former delegate to regional political conferences, Audrey Tilden was a single mother whose late husband, George, had been an Aviation Machinist Mate 2nd Class with the United States Naval Reserve stationed at the nearby Willow Grove Airbase, where in 1983 Gerald Stano claimed he'd buried two women "between the road and the fence" of the base. George was one of eleven crewmembers killed when their Lockheed P2V-7 crashed in the Italian Alps on July 19, 1957, when Ted was eleven-years old.

Discontented, and wrought with existential angst as he returned to Philadelphia early in 1969, Bundy enrolled for spring classes at Temple University's College of Liberal Arts after submitting his application on October 30, 1968. His doldrums and residual heartache were likely exacerbated by the leaden skies, frigid climate, and pervasive cynicism afflicting the university that semester. What with the increasingly unpopular Vietnam War, student unrest held at a fever pitch, depleting school spirit during the winter months preceding Ted's arrival. The north Philadelphia campus was rife with war protests and rallies, and student groups regularly hosted speakers stridently mistrustful of the establishment. The radical organization Students for a Democratic Society (SDS) maintained an active presence on campus and angry revolutionaries issued periodic demands to the administration, threatening to hold sit-ins and the like. *Temple News,* the school newspaper, served as the voice of student dissent. The editorials penned by English major Murray Dubin, who became a career beat reporter for the *Philadelphia Inquirer* after graduation, typified the jaded outlook afflicting the urban university. Reporting on the long line of students who stood freezing in the January cold outside Mitten Hall on the same day in 1969 that President Nixon was sworn in for a second term, Dubin wrote in the *News*, "Coming back to Temple University has got to be the biggest bring-down since I borrowed $25 to bet the Baltimore Colts....Maybe, if I was high, I could really get back into the registration rigmarole and that first wild week of classes."

"As we enter into the spring term, Temple University, 1969," he began another column he only thought that offers me any consolation is that I graduate in May." In March of that term, fifteen-hundred students gathered to hear radical Jerry Rubin, founder and leader of the "Yippies" (Youth International Party), and black militant Benjamin Ortiz exhort the throngs assembled in front of Barton Hall at a "Day of Conscience" teach-in. In April, three-hundred students participated in a mock funeral procession, symbolically "burying" the Temple Administration as student leaders acted as pallbearers for the ceremony, toting a makeshift coffin down city streets and placing it at the foot of the university founder's gravesite.

Bundy never partook in the counter-culture activities and mostly kept to himself during his stay in Lafayette Hill. With no car or friends, on school days he rode the commuter bus to campus (likely the SEPTA line), which picked him up and dropped him off at the stop across from the St. Philip Neri Catholic School on Ridge Avenue, a few blocks from his aunt's home. Weekends were mostly spent alongside his younger cousin, an upperclassman at Plymouth Whitemarsh High School, also a short walk from his Aunt Audrey's house on South Warner Road. She held the keys to an old white Dodge she would lend to Ted if she needed him to run an errand or if he wanted to drive to the Plymouth Meeting Mall, the same place Mark Thomas frequently loitered as a teen, and where the New Jersey State Police temporarily set up a room to interview his friends in early June of 1969.

While at Temple, Bundy registered for four classes as student number 207268, according to his official school transcript: *Theater in the Western Culture*, in which he earned an A, as well as *Survey of English Literature*, where he received a B. His grade of "Incomplete" in a political science elective abbreviated *Fld Sess Human Service Adm* suggests he dropped the course at some point during the semester, or neglected to sit for a final exam, if in fact one was a prerequisite to the course's completion. He also earned a B in a psychology course titled *Human Behavior*, completing a total of nine semester hours, a significantly lighter load than during his freshman year at the University of Puget Sound in 1965-66, when he completed twenty-eight. Bundy's less strenuous course selection at Temple was consistent with the directionless path he began while attending the University of Washington between 1966-68, after transferring from Puget Sound. He took just four classes during that two-year span in Seattle, enrolling in disparate courses like *General*

Chemistry and *Intensive Chinese.* This period of emotional tumult was emblematic in his sporadic course selection, another avenue explored by Dr. Lewis in her testimony that Bundy's successful streaks took place while in the midst of a manic high consistent with the symptoms of bipolar disease, yet performed poorly when his concentration failed and his mood turned dark.

"I think what really got me to that point, what pushed me over the edge from thought into action, was often times I would take the commuter train from Philadelphia to New York to Forty-second Street," Bundy explained to Lewis. "I mean, you have the hardest of the hard core."

In 1969 Times Square was a gritty haven occupied by hustlers, prostitutes, and pimps, a year that marked the beginning of what the *New York Times* recently noted as "the golden age of American hard-core filmmaking." Darkly themed films such as *Midnight Cowboy, Shaft,* and *Taxi Driver* were shot on location here, graphically depicting the moral depravity and rampant crime defining Broadway in the late Sixties and early Seventies. As a visitor exited the Port Authority Bus Terminal main entrance on Forty-first Street and Eighth Avenue, he stood less than a block removed from a veritable cornucopia of porn and smut, blinking neon lights, and littered alleyways where transvestites hustled for a fix and bedraggled carnival freaks emerged jangling tin cans before unsuspecting tourists. Many of the historic buildings from the 1930s which have since been restored to their opulent grandeur, such as the Victory and Empire Theatres, ran exploitative "grinder" and "slasher" films that titillated perverse personalities and openly objectified women. Sailors on leave would arrive among these sooty corridors for a cheap blow job or quick lay from one of the many scantily clad underage prostitutes, both male and female, luring them from beneath the entranceways to the XXX peep show theatres, inside where men were known to openly masturbate in the dark shadows thrown beneath the projector glare.

The lurid oasis suited Ted Bundy's persona, his compulsions enticed by the squalid offerings. He admitted to donning a mustache while one of his periodic excursions into the city, assuming another identity with hopes of picking up a random streetwalker, then coaxing her to a seedy hotel room where he could rape her. "It's when we're starting to see this entity begin to reach the point where it's necessary to act out," he explained. "No longer just to read books, or to masturbate, or fantasize, but actually begin to stalk, to look."

While continuing to provide Dr. Lewis with a condensed narrative arc of his life during this time frame, he mentioned that he'd visited Philadelphia in 1968, one year earlier, while in a "highly chaotic" period of his life. He intimated that he'd gone in search of his father this year but refused to say whether this was the primary purpose of his visit. Rather, he felt the need to "get away" from Seattle, to escape what he was becoming of himself there, an aimless drifter struggling far too long with the emotional upheaval of a breakup. Teetering on the precipice of a nervous breakdown, he'd hoped to stabilize himself in Philadelphia but instead succumbed to a deteriorating mental state exacerbated by lack of self-control. His craving for pornography, till now satiated by masturbation, dirty movies along Forty-second Street, or peeping through windows at women as they undressed for bed, no longer satisfied his prurient needs. Instead, his voyeurism served to "decondition feelings of inhibition in engaging in conduct, his ambivalence." As he'd done for Michaud, Bundy referred again to the "entity" urging him to kill. It was at the Jersey Shore, in the spring of 1969, the explained to Dr. Lewis, that he first formulated a specific plan to carry out his *actus reus*.

"In the spring, I went to Ocean City. Ocean City, New Jersey," Bundy told Lewis. "And just hanging out at the beach, and looking at the young women, trailing them around. And my plan again was-I had never done anything like this before-it was, it was very confusing, kind of, and fearful, and yet I felt compelled to continue to, sort of, act out this vision…" He explained that this "vision" was of "some other woman" than his ex-girlfriend Diane Edwards. "Okay, so I was just stalking around the downtown area of this small resort community and I saw a young woman walking along…I didn't actually kill someone this time, but I really, for the first time, approached a victim, spoke to her, tried to abduct her, and she escaped. But that was frightening in its own way. But that was the first—the kind of step that you just—that you don't—that I couldn't ever return from."

Dr. Lewis asked Bundy if he specifically remembered the first time he'd actually killed someone. He hesitated before answering. "It was a couple of years later, but can I just talk about the difference between that one incident at Ocean City and the first time?" He went on to say, "I know that I, in Ocean City, I realized just how inept I was. And so that made me more cautious, and so I didn't do that again for a long time. It scared me. It really scared me."

Lewis allowed him to elaborate, but her interview transcript is devoid of any further reference to the New Jersey killings, for Bundy seemed anxious to switch topics. Before New Jersey State Police detectives were alerted to his remarks in the days following his death, Bundy, seemingly peaceful and resigned to his fate, provided The Rev. James Dobson with a televised one-hour interview where he cast blame upon pornography as the source of society's ills and reiterated his love for his family. Late that night, ABC News and *Nightline* anchor Ted Koppel ran a six-minute piece covering the forthcoming execution, with a detailed expose of Bundy's life and murders reported by veteran correspondent Judd Rose.

Seated outside Bundy's cell, Methodist minister Fred Lawrence shepherded the condemned inmate through his final night while the crowds pressed forward into town. Lawrence described the procedures for execution, replicating as best he could what Bundy could expect after he entered the death chamber thirty feet down the hall within a few hours. He should not fear pain, Lawrence assured, as death would be mercifully swift. "He never said a word," Lawrence recalled. "He held my hands tighter than anyone had ever held my hands....The last four minutes, he raised his head and gazed into my eyes-still not speaking-just gazed intently. I didn't see fear, or uncertainty. He just seemed to want to hang on a little longer before he disappeared. It was like holding on to a dead man."

Florida State Penitentiary Superintendent Thomas L. Barton met with Bundy at 6:15 a.m., hoping that Bundy, with dwindling prospects of reprieve, might blurt a last-minute confession. For the last time, the New Jersey State Police again tried to gather information about the parkway slayings through an intermediary. "Ted, I have some inquiries from Illinois and New Jersey," Barton said, while last minute preparations for the execution proceeded unabated down the hall.

Bundy replied, "I can say without question, that there is, nothing for instance that I was involved in in New Jersey or Illinois."

A cadre of guards gathered Bundy from his cell forty-five minutes later. They escorted him thirty feet down the hall toward the chamber itself, where a small number of the press and victim family members had been invited to witness the execution from behind a partitioned viewing area. Robert McMaster, a press officer with the Florida Department of Law Enforcement, watched the prisoner come undone as he was led toward the chamber door. So shaken was Bundy, McMaster remembers, that his legs went out from under him as a bevy of guards dragged him through the door and seated him in the electric chair. Shaking his head and trembling throughout, Bundy managed to remain calm while his wrists and ankles were strapped to the chair's arms and legs, electrodes connected. His eyes darted beyond the glass, gazing at the assembly of onlookers seated before him.

"Give my love to my family and friends," Bundy quietly uttered, when asked if he'd any last words he wished to share before a dark veil was lowered across his face. A wall phone, through which the governor issued last-second reprieves, rang once. An official answered and shook his head before quickly replacing the receiver. Nods were shared among prison officials, somber glances signifying what was to transpire next. Swiftly, a hooded executioner threw down a wall switch, and in the glimpse of an instant a current bearing two thousand volts surged through Bundy's innards. Smoke rose from the metal cap and dampened sponge fastened atop his shaved scalp. His convulsing limbs tightened for a few seconds within the electricity's unrelenting grip, then released as the power was cut off. Manacled in a crumpled spasm of scorched flesh, Theodore Robert Bundy was pronounced dead at 7:16 a.m.

Outside the chamber, as the sun rose behind the prison grounds, the anticipation of the early morning electrocution grew rampant for the two hundred or so onlookers and news reporters impatiently teeming on the pasture across the road from the Florida State Penitentiary. Mike Mello, one of Bundy's death row attorneys, commented that the field across Route 16, clogged with traffic, "had all the trappings of a late night county carnival,' with gleeful bystanders providing doughnuts and coffee while crafty vendors sold tiny, pin-sized replicas of the electric chair.

Word of Bundy's death was signaled by way of a yellow legal pad, waved high from the outstretched hands of a wire service reporter who'd stepped outside the death chamber to deliver the message. Free to exult, the expectant throngs let out a gleeful roar while a scattering of revelers chanted in unison to the 1969 hit "Na Na Hey Hey Kiss Him Goodbye." Fireworks were lit off. A chorus of off-duty cops broke into chorus, altering the timeworn lyrics of the camp ballad, "On Top of Old Sparky" to "He bludgeoned the pooooor girls, all over the heaaaad, now we're all ec-staaatic, Ted Bundy is deaaad." A short time after the crowds dispersed, a white hearse ferrying Bundy's corpse drove slowly past a herd of gleeful onlookers seeking a glimpse. "You would've thought it was the Super Bowl," remarked evangelist James Dobson.

A random photographer snapped a picture of Ted's blanketed corpse peacefully reposed on a morgue slab before he was carted to the funeral home. Electrical burns had shredded a seven-inch strip of his bare scalp. The tabloid *Weekly World News* published a front-page close-up of Bundy's freshly sutured head wound, his waxen eyelids fixed closed in a tranquil calm. One Florida lawmaker, sickened after reviewing the gruesome autopsy findings of the Alachua (Fla.) County Medical Examiner's Office, publicly sought a co-sponsor for a bill that would offer condemned inmates the choice between electrocution and lethal injection.

In 2011 an untainted vial of Bundy's blood was discovered in an evidence room refrigerator at the Columbia County (Fla.) Sheriff's Office. Though a flurry of public attention arose in the wake of the startling find, to date no state law enforcement agencies have publicly announced a match to evidence found in their cold cases after Bundy's DNA profile was uploaded into the CODIS database.

Bundy's presence in Ocean City and Philadelphia comprises one segment of an uncanny geographical proximity he shared with numerous key suspects and myriad participants in the 1969 coed murder probe. His death set off a number of troubling questions that remain unanswered today, due in part to the secretive nature of the ongoing investigation. Was Bundy seen by anyone in either Ocean City or Somers Point near the time Perry and Davis were murdered? Were his revelations about the two coeds, uttered reflectively as he neared his execution in 1989, sincere or just another desperate ploy to prolong his life? Within hours of his execution, a number of plausible answers slowly emerged as the name Ted Bundy was reintroduced into the Garden State Parkway murder investigation.

CHAPTER EIGHTEEN

Ocean City

Arthur Norman, a Portland, Oregon clinical forensic psychologist and erstwhile member of Bundy's capital defense team, was the first person to publicly disclose Bundy's connection to the parkway murders. He first encountered the serial murderer in 1986, when assigned to interview him by a Florida state agency representing inmates in their death penalty appeals. Norman, who'd spent more than eighty hours speaking to Bundy while he was on death row, contacted the Atlantic County Prosecutor's Office in New Jersey within several hours of Bundy's execution.

"He said he had dealt with Bundy a couple of years ago and spent some time with him and had certain information about the deaths of two girls in the area in 1969," according to prosecutor Jeffrey S. Blitz, who led the prosecutor's office for twenty-two years. "[Norman] was calling collect from California and did not have his notes," Blitz told a Philadelphia newspaper, "so we set up a more formal telephone conference for [this] morning which will involve me, the investigators and him." Blitz further stated that what information Norman had provided him at this time was of insufficient detail to decide Bundy's guilt.

Norman had known of what crucial knowledge he wished to share with Blitz ever since he interviewed Bundy on October 31, 1986. However, he didn't immediately notify the Atlantic County Prosecutor's Office of the incriminating information because he was bound by an oath of confidentiality. Norman informed a Portland newspaper that Bundy "told me in no uncertain terms" that his first murders were of two young women in the Philadelphia region.

As he would explain to Dr. Lewis some three years later, in 1986 Bundy told Norman that while he was living in Philadelphia in early 1969, he found himself journeying to New York City via train, where he routinely viewed violent pornography in Times Square. "Talk about being pushed to the edge," Bundy said. He reverted to form during the interview, speaking in the third person. "So, after being more or less detached from people for a long period...didn't have any friends, didn't go anywhere, just more or less had school and then sort of entertained himself with his pornographic hobby and drove to the shore and watched the beach and just saw young women lined up along the beach." With little prodding from Norman, Bundy wistfully recalled the balmy spring afternoons he'd spent along the Ocean City boardwalk promenade. "You know, it's like an overwhelming kind of vision, eventually found himself tearing around that place for a couple of days. And eventually, without really planning anything, he picked up a couple of young girls. And ended up with the first time he had ever done it. So when he left for the coast, it was not just getting away, it was more like an escape."

Norman was certain that Bundy was cryptically referencing the parkway murders. When asked by the psychologist whether he'd experienced any remorse or shame in murdering the two young women, Bundy replied, "Yeah, yeah, I had this kind of extraordinary, catastrophic kind of despair. This horror. This fear of getting caught. It's just an extraordinary trauma, you know. And one that is shocking in many respects. You tend to break all the conventions. And a lot of social taboos. And then there's, of

plays on the jukebox. In reality, Chino came away with a far different impression of her first meeting with Bundy at the Sandpiper Bar in Seattle in September 1969. "The song 'Lodi' by Creedence Clearwater Revival was playing on the jukebox," she said. "As we walked in, Ted was sitting across the bar, nursing a beer. I saw a look on his face I'll never forget. I was frightened, I can't describe it but never saw anything in my life like it. It was a faraway look, as if he had done something to me in his mind."

Unlike Kloepfer, Chino had always sensed something amiss about Bundy and was never lulled by his charisma. Where her close friend was beguiled by the charming young man with humble origins, Chino saw an opportunistic thief and seasoned con artist, a sneak who would lie to suit whatever purpose or occasion. She was among the first persons to contact Salt Lake City Sheriff's detective Jerry Thompson once she felt certain that her friend's steady boyfriend fit the description of the man police were looking for there and in Washington. "I am lucky to be alive today," she says. "Let me repeat. I am lucky to be alive today."

A smiling, confident twenty-two-year old Ted Bundy strolling the Bay Avenue sidewalks on a warm May evening in Somers Point, effortlessly mixing with the college weekenders guzzling foamy tap beer at Tony Mart's circle bar. Weaving his way anonymously through the transient crowd spilling into the parking lot outside Bayshores nightclub across the street. Beautiful college girls dressed in bellbottoms and halter-tops leaning against cars, smoking with friends, laughing. From there, trawling inconspicuously among the pleasantly drunken and stoned patrons riding out the dwindling night at the Dunes on Longport Boulevard. Saddling up to the bar while waiting patiently for the perfect moment to approach a susceptible young woman, light her cigarette, leaning into her ear to deliver a well-rehearsed line. Given his good looks charismatic charm, Bundy might've easily ingratiated himself with two pretty coeds like Susan and Elizabeth at any number of nightclubs or at the Somers Point Diner before persuading them for a ride back to his aunt's home in Philadelphia, then murdered them for sport in the Jersey Shore woodlands for the sense of accomplishment and control it provided him.

During the years of his confinement, Bundy enjoyed keeping his captors at bay as they conjectured how to accurately define him. He selectively chose which parts of his life to divulge and made a game of leaving his inquisitors to fill in the blank spaces, challenging psychologists and detectives to devise their own conclusions. Consistent with his selective memory and circumspect disclosures, Bundy held secret a far greater connection to Ocean City than he ever mentioned to Dr. Lewis or Dr. Norman, part of a family life he seldom elaborated upon unless free-associating or when asked to summon fond remembrances.

Not only did Bundy fail to tell his biographers that he'd descended from a famous civil war general, and didn't confide that he'd lost an uncle in a mountainside plane crash—two tragically colorful associations for a young man thought to be somewhat dismissive of his quotidian Tacoma upbringing—he also withheld that he had visited Ocean City several times during his youth. According to his Aunt Audrey, on multiple occasions over the years Bundy stayed with relatives at the Twenty-sixth Street home of his great grandfather, James A. Longstreet Jr. Faded family photographs show Ted as a toddler, playing in the sand alongside his doting grandfather Sam and posing in his mother's arms near Fourteenth Street and the boardwalk, with the Ocean City Fishing Pier visible in the background. When he broached the topic of Ocean City with Dr. Lewis and Art Norman, Bundy also withheld that his great-grandfather may have previously served as vice-president of the Ocean City Beachfront Owners Association in 1926, and owned at least one oceanfront property lot along the boardwalk between Eleventh and Twelfth Streets. A 1912

Ocean City newspaper article described its construction progress as a "cinderblock building between the new theatre and the Golden Galleon, costing $40,000. …The Longstreet building will occupy a frontage of 84 feet by a depth of 64 feet."

Verified Bundy sightings during his visits to Philadelphia, or firsthand encounters while he was at the Jersey Shore near the time of the 1969 parkway murders, have thus far eclipsed accounts of his numerous visits to the beach community. According to former New Jersey State Police Detective Thomas Kinzer, who in the wake of Bundy's death investigated his day-to-day forays while he was enrolled at Temple and living in Lafayette Hill, "We didn't get calls from anybody who knew him….I don't think we got one call." The detective's recollection, however, varies significantly from several witnesses who claim they personally met or saw Bundy in the Philadelphia region in the late 1960s and at or near the Ocean City beaches around the time when Davis and Perry were slain.

Somers Point security guard Albert Hickey remembers sitting at his Egg Harbor, New Jersey, home one night, watching a nightly television report covering one of Bundy's trials in Florida during the late 1980s. Upon noticing the serial murderer's smug grin, Hickey turned to his wife. "Damn if he don't look just like him!" Hickey exclaimed, referring to the young man he saw wearing a yellow turtleneck and jumping into the back of a convertible shortly after it entered the Somers Point traffic circle. "Seeing him on TV, the guy looked just like Bundy," said Hickey. "There was a certain turn Bundy had when he looked to face the camera that was the same as the guy had when he got into the car." Hickey claims that he notified the New Jersey State Police as soon as he learned that Bundy was a possible suspect in the parkway slayings. "At some point I called the state police when Bundy was in jail confessing to these murders. I asked them if he was in Somers Point that night carrying a flight bag. They ignored me. I never heard a thing back from them."

"I read an article on Bundy and the parkway murders, and I absolutely believe that Ted Bundy killed those girls," said Pat LaWall from Philadelphia. "I stayed in Ocean City with my best friend and her family, who owned a summer home there. We spent a couple weeks each summer beginning in 1968. One summer we spent our time at the Ninth Street beach by the jetty because that was the most popular spot. There was a guy who hung out at the beach each day who constantly tried to get us to go with him. The three of us were scared of him because he looked strange with his bushy hair and beard and never wore a bathing suit or shorts, and he looked very out of place. He had his arm in a sling. We would occasionally see him getting into his car, which he parked on Ninth Street. It appeared as though he was living in his car. He seemed to have a ton of things in there. He drove a Volkswagen Bug. He told us he was from California and his name was Ted Bluchell and that he used to be in the band The Association.

"We found him extremely creepy," LaWall said. "His eyes were shifty. He did seem to favor talking to me, and I found many excuses to get away from him. At that time, I had long brown hair parted in the middle, which was the style. It wasn't until twenty-plus years later, when I was watching a show on Ted Bundy, and they showed a picture of him with bushy hair and a beard, that I knew it was him. You don't forget someone who really scared you. In this same show, they mentioned the New Jersey coed murders. They said Bundy may have been involved, and I was convinced at that moment that he was."

"It finally made sense, the way he was at the beach in jeans, so out of place and so determined to get someone to go with him," LaWall said. "Everyone else was just hanging out enjoying the sun with friends. He was all alone. It also explains why he would tell us that his name was Ted

Bluechel and that he was in The Association. I think he was making that up to impress us to go with him."

Cathy Kalb, a teacher from the East Falls section of Philadelphia, remembers a man of similar appearance approaching her when she was a teenager at the Jersey Shore the summer after she'd graduated from Gwynedd Mercy College in 1969. That season Kalb shared a rental home in Sea Isle City, a compactly spaced resort community divided from Ocean City by a narrow isthmus. As she and a friend were lazily sunning themselves on the beach one afternoon, they were approached by a clean-shaven young man whom Kalb recalls was "very ordinary looking and very polite." He had a cast on either his arm or his leg, as Kalb remembers, and asked her for a ride to the Crab Trap, a popular Somers Point restaurant and cocktail lounge adjacent to the diner where Elizabeth and Susan were last seen. As operating a car's manual transmission requires a certain degree of dexterity, with the left foot releasing the clutch while the right hand maneuvers the gear shift into place, "Ted" struck Kalb as suspicious when he told her that he couldn't shift the gears on his Volkswagen due to his injury, yet had been able to drive and parallel park on a nearby street. As this was the same year Perry and Davis were murdered, when she read of Bundy's stratagem in luring women several years later, and that he'd admitted to spending time in Ocean City that spring, Kalb thought the coincidences too numerous to overlook.

On a rainy day in 1966, sixteen-year-old Barbara Masson from the Philadelphia suburb of Levittown, Pennsylvania, drove to the local Pomeroy's department store at the Shop-a-Rama Mall, near where she lived with her parents. While shopping, she realized that a young man wearing a long trench coat was following her from aisle to aisle, periodically ducking from sight, then reappearing and looking her way. As she prepared to leave the store, she noticed the same man lingering by the inside glass doors of the front entranceway, staring directly at her. His unsettling behavior instinctively caused Masson to pause before walking past him and into the darkened parking lot alone. She asked a security guard to escort her out the building and to her car, a shrewd decision she realizes that may have saved her life. Her memory of the harrowing incident remained repressed until she saw a picture of Ted Bundy in the newspapers following his execution. Masson "literally dropped the paper" upon seeing the photo of the same young man she is unequivocally certain had stalked her that rainy evening several years earlier. "Something about the way he looked at me. I distinctly remember his face...he was staring at me... I'll always remember the way he looked at me." The event traumatized Masson to the extent that she never picked up any books about the Bundy murders after reading of him in the local newspaper. To this day she harbors no doubt that Ted Bundy was the man who had been following her.

In his early seventies today, Stephen Golden is a semi-retired account manager for the International Paper Company in Orlando, Florida. One busy weekend afternoon in the late spring of 1969, a few months before receiving orders to report to DaNang in Vietman, where he would serve a tour of duty with the Air Force until 1970, Golden was stationed at Fort McGuire Air Force Base in central New Jersey. This was a turbulent period for military stations around the country, for anti-war activists frequently targeted bases with bomb threats and random acts of terrorism. As a nineteen-year-old security policeman assigned to monitor the civilian traffic entering the front gates, Golden was to board each bus, examine each passenger's identification, and inquire why they wished to enter the base. Large commercial buses would often stop there, for it was on the same route as a number of other bus depots. Normally two guards manned the front entrance, but on this afternoon Golden's unit were short-staffed and traffic was unusually busy.

After boarding one of the buses, Golden noticed two disheveled young men occupying a pair of seats. Neither of the men was toting a suitcase, travel bag, or other belongings. Both lacked identification of any sort, refused to provide Golden a plausible reason why they wished to enter the base, and wouldn't disclose their destination. As was standard procedure, Golden escorted them off the bus and ordered them to wait inside the gates while he phoned the base police desk sergeant for assistance.

The taller of the two men, who appeared to be in his twenties, began approaching Golden. Ordered to stop and stand against a wall, he stated that he was traveling to Philadelphia. At first he seemed friendly, but drew Golden's suspicion when he inquired about the .38 service revolver holstered to the soldier's waist. His companion, who stood about six inches shorter, was approximately eighteen years old, with curly black hair. He whispered in the ear of his taller companion, who asked Golden, "Do you know about the two girls murdered in Ocean City?"

Golden didn't immediately respond and is fairly certain this was before Davis and Perry had been reported missing.

"We killed those girls!" the taller man exclaimed.

"He had an evil stare on his face," Golden said of the man's brash utterance. "I will never forget it." Seconds later, after briefly leaving the men unattended so he could check the passengers on another incoming bus, they vanished, having swiftly boarded an outbound bus. The New Jersey State Police were notified of the incident and stopped the bus. From what Golden learned, the two young men had already disembarked at a subsequent stop and were never questioned.

"Several years ago, I saw an FBI picture of a young Ted Bundy," said Golden. He was immediately reminded of the taller of the two young men, who'd sinisterly claimed responsibility for the parkway murders. "I believe the man I pulled off the bus was Ted Bundy. I would bet on it."

In the spring and summer of 1969 commercial artist Wesley Meier from Pennsburg, Pennsylvania, was a twenty-year-old temporary employee at the Shore Memorial Hospital emergency room in Somers Point. His duties included processing intake information for doctors assigned the graveyard shift between 11 a.m. and 7 a.m. In the early morning hours of May 30, 1969, a short time before Davis and Perry were killed, a young man wearing a red plaid shirt and khaki pants arrived at the emergency room, calmly asking Meier to remove his arm cast. As this was the middle of the night, the request seemed unusual to Meier, for most of the patrons who stumbled through the emergency room entrance were either drunken teens immersed in a bad hallucinogenic trip, or incoherent drunks looking for a bed where they could sleep off a night of partying at the Bay Avenue bars a few blocks away. The young man was in his early twenties, with brown, neatly combed hair that was "neither long nor short," as Meier remembers. "He was extremely engaging….Half of the kids who came in were high. He seemed like a clean-cut non-hippie."

The young man explained to Meier that he'd recently hitchhiked to the shore from Pennsylvania, yet refused to fill out a chart with his personal information as required by hospital regulations. Meier then asked for a phone number, so he could contact the parents, hospital policy if there were any question that the person seeking treatment might be underage. "What bothered me was as soon as I started to ask questions, he wanted to get out of there," Meier explained. Though the young man grew unnerved when asked to present identification, he remained exceedingly polite and ingratiating. As was protocol, Meier asked to see a driver's license, which revealed an address in King of Prussia, a Montgomery County, Pennsylvania suburb. There was no answer, however, at the number given to Meier as he left the lobby to place the call.

When Meier returned, he saw where the stranger in the cast had struck up a friendly conversation with Detective Andrew Gifford of the Somers Point Police Department, whose officers would periodically stop in at the hospital as part of their patrol duties. (Gifford died of a heart attack in 1994.) Meier overheard the young man tell Gifford that he was hungry and asked for the name of a place where he could eat. The detective suggested that he try the Somers Point Diner, a short walk away, and offered him a lift. As the pair walked out the front doors, this was the last time Meier saw or heard from the young man.

A few days later, while Meier was working his first shift following the news bulletin that the bodies of Perry and Davis had been discovered in the parkway woods, detectives and plainclothes officers from the New Jersey State Police arrived at the emergency room in droves, asking employees if they had seen a young man wearing a white t-shirt arrive at the hospital in the hours after the women were killed. From what the state police told Meier, a man fitting this vague description was seen leaving a bar with Davis and Perry, consistent with the composite released in the newspapers two months after the murders. Meier told New Jersey State Police investigators about the young man with the cast, but felt that the police "tuned me out" out once they heard him recall that the somewhat suspicious young man he met hadn't been wearing a white t-shirt. As with over two thousand other young males who'd been investigated, the questioning grew heated toward Meier as investigators tried to ferret out the true murderer.

"For forty-five years I've been haunted by the information I know," Meier said. He was working in his office outside of Quakertown, Pennsylvania, in 1989, faxing a document to Taiwan, when he glanced at a Philadelphia news program showing a photo of recently executed serial killer Ted Bundy. "As an artist, I remember faces," he said. Following the telecast, Meier telephoned the Atlantic County Prosecutor's

Office and asked for Prosecutor Jeffrey Blitz, who was unavailable to speak with him at the time. Instead, Meier was referred to an investigator. "I told him I was certain that Ted Bundy came into the emergency room that night." Much to Meier's surprise, the investigator seemed underwhelmed by the new information. He told Meier to "just forget about it" when he offered to drive to the prosecutor's office and provide his statement in person.

Approximately five years ago, Meier again called the Atlantic County Prosecutor's Office and met with Captain Bruce K. DeShields, providing the investigator with a statement. DeShields confirms that he did meet with Meier on this occasion, heard his account of that night, and pulled the Davis and Perry case file after speaking with him. However, he wasn't able to draw any definitive conclusions about the information Meier supplied him and refuses to make any comments about the Perry-Davis case, as it remains an open investigation.

Bundy was familiar with Ocean City, periodically traveling to the resort community with his family several times prior to the spring of 1969. If he had schemed to murder two young women there, he was provided ample opportunity during these visits to familiarize himself with the beach area, scope out the boardwalk, and identify potential victims.

According to a representative from the Temple University Special Collections Department, final exams for the 1969 spring semester were administered between April 28 and May 2 that year. Finals for evening courses and basic studies classes were held from May 5 through May 10. So, at the latest, Bundy would have completed his semester twenty days before the parkway murders. This timeframe is factually consistent with his earlier admission that he "he didn't have much to do...." as late spring approached.

Though such abundant free time would've offered Bundy ample occasion for traveling to the beach and releasing the "entity" that had consumed him during his visit to Philadelphia and numerous excursions to Times Square, Bundy's Aunt Audrey insists that her nephew was present at her Lafayette Hill home during the entire 1969 Memorial Day weekend. She knows for certain, she says, because she distinctly remembers her family's activities during special occasions such as holidays. As she recalls, while Ted and her teenaged son were playing basketball that weekend on the small hoop in her backyard, Ted fell on an ankle, "either severely twisting it or breaking it." (Hearkening back to his athletic prowess, Bundy once boasted to Stephen Michaud that his deft hoops skills drew the admiration of black inmates on death row during their exercise period in the prison courtyard.) Audrey immediately drove her nephew to the emergency room at nearby Chestnut Hill Hospital following the accident, the same facility where Gerald Stano toiled in the computer department before he was fired for stealing money from his female co-workers' purses in 1973. Audrey insists that a hospital doctor placed Bundy's ankle in a cast for several weeks, thereby incapacitating him at the time the murders took place sixty miles away. According to a Chestnut Hill hospital employee, patient records dating as far back as the 1960s would have been destroyed by now or viewable on microfiche only. Absent a court order entered upon the formal application of a living relative or authorized representative of the deceased's estate, any such request would be denied under the Pennsylvania Health Insurance Portability and Accountability Act.

Consistent with Audrey's recollections, a chronological summary of Bundy's activities during 1969, archived at the Florida Department of State, reads, "Fractured right ankle in Philadelphia." However, the injury is noted under Bundy's activities for September that year, four months after Davis and Perry were slain. "He couldn't have done anything like that at the shore," Tilden is adamant. "For weeks he was in a cast. It could have been someone else who did what they thought he did, but it certainly wasn't him. Ted was here with us."

Former New Jersey State Police Lt. Major George Joo, a South Jersey baseball umpire and office manager with the Burlington (N.J.) County Medical Examiner's Office, retired from the state police in 2000, at a time when detectives and troopers from the Major Crime Unit were periodically assigned to review cold cases in hopes that a fresh look at their investigative files would uncover new information. The Perry-Davis case was among those he studied. "As I recall, we were leaning toward Bundy, hoping that he'd spill his guts," said Joo.

"We've looked at Bundy, but there was no evidential value that Bundy did it," Detective Kinzer told an *Atlantic City Press* reporter in 1994. "Looking at his M.O., and what he has done in the past, we can't exclude him, but we don't have anything to link him."

Ted Housel, the Atlantic County prosecutor from 2007 until 2012, offered a somewhat contradictory assessment. In 2009 he announced that his office had begun a fresh review of the Perry-Davis case file, saying, "There wasn't enough evidence to rule out Ted Bundy."

Due to their cryptic nature, Bundy's remarks about Ocean City are intriguing yet lead to further confusion. In speaking with Dr. Norman in the days before his execution, Bundy unequivocally distinguished his first attempts at abduction from his first planned murder, specifically referencing "when you kill someone" in the context of the Perry and Davis slayings. Moreover, he never qualified his remarks about Ocean City to Norman, as he did for Dr. Lewis.

Nevertheless, what Bundy confided to Norman should be interpreted with a fair degree of skepticism, as a number of logical arguments may refute the revelations uncovered during Bundy's interview with Dr. Lewis, when he admitted "stalking around the downtown area of this small resort community," and spotting "a young woman walking along... spoke to her, tried to abduct her, and she escaped." Foremost, if he had truly attempted such a feat near the center of town, an area encompassing the boardwalk area and tourist motels, it stands to reason that this person would have reported the incident to the Ocean City Police Department. As Bundy's admission that he'd spent time in Ocean City broke publicly amid the national publicity attendant to his execution, wouldn't this person have come forward to the New Jersey State Police, or contacted the newspapers to say she was nearly a Ted Bundy victim, especially in light of the indelible impression he'd made on the women he encountered? Although it was characteristic of Bundy to weave the truth throughout his lies in an effort to bargain for more time, a pair of troubling conclusions may be inferred by his remarks: the young woman he'd try to abduct was either Davis or Perry, or the "couple of girls" he told Art Norman he'd seen "lined up along the beach" and "picked up" were in fact both Davis and Perry.

A 1993 *Philadelphia Inquirer* story about the parkway murders, written by columnist Larry Lewis, was published to coincide with the twenty-fourth anniversary of the unsolved slayings. In the article, Lewis interviewed *Seattle Times* reporter, *Deliberate Stranger* author, and Perry family friend Richard Larsen. The renowned journalist, who passed away in 2001, told Lewis that he unequivocally believed the parkway killings were Bundy's first "adult, planned crimes," part of "a complete circle from the East Coast to the West Coast, back to the Rocky Mountains and then down to sunny Florida." Having listened to Art Norman's recorded interviews with Bundy, Larsen theorized that as Susan Davis and Elizabeth Perry drove down Ninth Street in Ocean City and crossed the bridge into Somers Point on their way home, they were "heading into a trap" laid by Bundy, whom Larsen surmised had stalked them on the beach and familiarized himself with the parkway woods in preparation for their murders.

Bundy's chilling reminiscences of the Ocean City boardwalk are hauntingly similar to a story he'd shared with writers Michaud and Aynesworth while retelling of an attempted abduction of a young woman on a city street at night, an incident that took place in the days leading to what he told them was his first murder. While omitting the name of the city where the crime occurred (the authors surmised the location was Seattle), Bundy described for Michaud what he felt after he'd struck a woman on the head with a piece of wood, and she escaped after falling to the ground. "What he'd done terrified him," Bundy said. "Purely terrified him. And he was full of remorse....Fear of discovery, sure. Fear of a number of things. He was horrified by the realization that he had the capacity to do such a thing, or even attempt—that's a better word—this kind of thing. He was terribly fearful that for one reason or another he might be apprehended." Bundy added, "It was clear to him, I think, that the course of conduct he had engaged in on that first, monstrous, occasion, as it were, was totally inappropriate. Fraught with danger, badly thought out." As Bundy clearly identified two separate incidents many years apart, one presumably in Seattle, the other in Ocean City, as the watershed epiphany that prompted him to confront the escalation of his violent behavior, which recounting is true?

In March 1989 numerous state investigators and FBI agents who'd partaken in Bundy's final interviews attended the Bundy Multi-Agency Investigative Team conference at the FBI Academy in Quantico, Virginia, to share case information. For the next three years following the conference, specialists from the agency's Visual Investigative Analysis Unit consulted with investigators around the country to ascertain the regions Bundy had traversed over the course of his lifetime, hoping to solve dormant cases thought to be attributable to him. Despite the fact that an FBI agent called Audrey Tilden at her Lafayette Hill, Pennsylvania, home to ascertain Bundy's whereabouts on May 30, 1969, New Jersey State Police spokesman Barry Roberson said, "The FBI is aware of our Perry-Davis double homicide, however, we were not invited or notified about the Bundy conference, and do not have anyone there."

The FBI's 1992 FBI Ted Bundy Multiagency Investigative Team Report, a compilation of their findings, officially concluded that Bundy was responsible for twenty killings nationwide, all in the western United States. Offering a general timeline of Bundy's peregrinations, the report is comprehensive yet inconsistent, making no reference to any coordinated effort between FBI agents and New Jersey State Police into the parkway murders, or of when agents had called his Aunt Audrey, at a time, she recalls, that was "long before" he was executed. For example, the report reads that in January 1969 Bundy was "enrolled for one semester [at] Temple University, Philadelphia, Pennsylvania," with no mention of his periodic jaunts to New York City while living with his aunt. The report also asserts that Bundy left for the West Coast in May of that year, when he "travelled to San Francisco, California, and stayed with friends for two or three weeks." If accurate, this would place Bundy outside the Jersey Shore area at the time Davis and Perry were killed, for they were last seen alive on May 30, 1969. The following entry for the same month, however, indicates that he "moved to and worked in saw mill, Tacoma Washington," without specifying what day of that month he allegedly moved from California to Washington, or vice versa, and failing to account for what he'd told Dr. Lewis: "In the spring, I went to Ocean City. Ocean City, New Jersey."

The consistent manner by which Bundy approached and assaulted his victims, revealed by him at length to Michaud and Aynesworth while he was imprisoned in Florida, and later described for Dr. Lewis, was explained in the multiagency report. "Bundy differentiated between 'dry runs' and 'abductions.' He defined a dry run as picking up a woman and releasing her unharmed to test his skills. An abduction was an incident in which an intended victim managed to escape." In further summarizing Bundy's M.O., the report read, "Generally, Bundy's crimes followed a particular pattern. He would feign an injury and indicate he needed assistance or he would portray an authority figure such as a police officer. ...Bundy typically looked for victims at places where young people gathered, such as colleges, beaches, ski resorts, and discos."

Bundy's behavioral pattern is entirely consistent with the theory that in May 1969 his mental state had deteriorated to the point where he was no longer able to contain his raging impulses. Having already familiarized himself with the Ocean City area by admittedly "hanging out at the beach, and looking at the young women, trailing them around," as he told Dr. Lewis, he decided upon the resort area as a strategically convenient location to employ his sympathy ruse to pick up Davis and Perry before murdering them in a previously scouted location along the parkway.

While Bundy's *modus operandi* seemed to match how Perry and Davis may have been abducted, their manner of death bore none of his latter signatures. Bundy, for example, never killed in pairs, preferring instead to target vulnerable, isolated young women under the guise of seeking help. He typically bludgeoned his victims over the head, rarely, if ever, stabbing them to death. Often transporting his victims to carefully selected disposal sites in remote locations, he later desecrated their corpses, behavior inconsistent with the crime scene alongside milepost 31.9.

Primarily owing to fear of detection, serial killers change behavioral patterns over time, which might explain why Bundy's M.O. evolved over the years. According to Sessions, "A serial killer...improves significantly as he progresses, choosing his victims, murder and body disposal sites and methodology more carefully. He becomes more sophisticated."

Bundy biographer Richard Larsen offered *Inquirer* columnist Larry Lewis a similar analysis to justify his conclusion that the Davis and Perry murders were Bundy's first, explaining that in 1969 Bundy was a sloppily prepared, inexperienced killer who hadn't yet honed his craft or mastered the skills necessary to avoid capture.

Why then, when presented the opportunity, didn't Bundy admit to the Davis and Perry murders when questioned by Dr. Lewis the day before he died? After all, what did he have to lose? Likely for the same reasons he was reluctant to discuss a number of other unsolved murder cases in which he was a suspect-he was withholding crucial information in desperate hope of bargaining for a last-minute reprieve.

"I think Bundy was manipulative and would have said or done anything to change his fate," says former Florida Department of Law Enforcement spokesman Robert McMaster, who fielded calls from law enforcement officials in several states during the serial killer's final days and witnessed his execution. "I wouldn't trust anything he said during those last twenty-four hours."

Atlantic County Prosecutor Jeffrey Blitz's similarly dismissive remarks, wherein he concluded that psychologist Art Norman's remarks "lacked specificity," fail to account for Bundy's purposeful vagueness. Though Bundy never declaratively admitted to any single murder and consistently spoke in the third person when describing his victims, Blitz failed to consider the distinctive pattern of Bundy's masterful riffing-that is, making cryptic reference to his crimes, surrounding himself with inculpatory circumstantial evidence, and placing himself at the scene of murders later confirmed to have involved him.

"Ted liked to play with people, he wanted you to know he wasn't lying," says Bill Hagmeier, the former FBI agent who was present alongside Bundy in the days leading to his execution, unsuccessfully urging him to name all his victims. Bundy told Hagmeier that he'd killed thirty women in total, comprised of eleven victims in Washington, eight in Utah, three in Colorado and Florida, two in Idaho and Oregon, and one in California. The former agent doesn't recall fielding any calls from the New Jersey State Police requesting to speak with Bundy during this time.

Under the auspices of the FBI's National Center for the Analysis of Violent Crime, in the two decades since Bundy's death, the bureau has launched numerous studies detailing the behavioral patterns of serial killers such as Bundy in an effort to assist state police departments nationwide in identifying similar predators residing within their own jurisdictions.

The bureau officially defines the term "serial killer" as "the unlawful killing of two or more victims by the same offender(s) in separate events." Whereas a mass murderer slays a number of persons during a single episode (as in the Columbine massacre), the handiwork of a serial killer like Bundy is identified by a "cooling off" period of days, months, or sometimes years between murders. Either purposefully or unintentionally, serial murderers often follow a general behavioral pattern that links their cases based upon a multitude of factors, including a consistent method of operation, similar age range and gender of victims, use of a similar weapon, and geographical proximity of crime scenes. As if challenging investigators, they frequently leave behind a unique set of indicators at each murder site, often manifested in the form of ego-driven ritualistic behavior and signature acts that identify each murder as their own.

The early science of serial murder profiling, developed by agents from the agency's Behavioral Science Unit, was limited for the most part to an inclusive and somewhat limited examination of the serial murderer's personality type, gleaned primarily from the offender's perspective during interviews. (Although the bureau continues to actively profile serial murderers, they've replaced the term "profiling" with the more generic "Criminal Investigative Analysis.") One of the bureau's first published studies on the subject of profiling, developed in the 1980s, established a serial offender classification system divided into two broad categories. Generally speaking, an *organized* offender was defined as an individual who plans his murder in great detail, displays a certain degree of control at the crime scene, and uses restraints upon his victims. Among other characteristics, a more spontaneous *disorganized* offender lives alone and in the general proximity of the crime scene, kills in a fit of rage, leaves behind his weapon, poses the corpse, and doesn't use a vehicle at any point during the commission of the crime. There is also evidence of *overkill,* or gratuitous acts of violence unnecessary to subdue his victims.

What remnants lay scattered in the underbrush off milepost 31.9 combined aspects of both offender categories. Davis' clothes were piled neatly beside her nude body, suggesting that her killer was calm and collected when perhaps ordering her to undress at knifepoint, not consumed in a manic frenzy. Repeated stabbing was listed as the cause of death for both victims; yet, the autopsies also revealed that each had sustained blunt force trauma about the body and facial area as well, indicating that their killer had acted beyond sheer necessity. According to investigative historian Peter Vronsky, Ph.D., author of *Serial Killers: The Method and Madness of Monsters* and contributing writer toward numerous anthologies on this subject, "Once the disorganized serial killer approaches his victim, he usually carries out a powerful 'blitz' attack that is very quick, vicious, and highly violent….multiple stab wounds, a high number of blows to the head and body…..excessively more wounds than necessary to cause death."

Perry was fully dressed, yet two newspapers reported that her underwear were missing, indicating that the perpetrator may have taken them as a "souvenir," or memento of his killing. In their book *Profiling Murders: An Investigative Tool*, criminal justice professors Ronald M. Holmes and Steven T. Holmes undertook to classify serial killers based primarily upon their motives. "The immediate reason for a serial killer to take a souvenir from a crime scene is so that he has a reminder of what has transpired," according to the authors. "It reminds the killer not only of the event, but of what has taken place during the event. The souvenir is also part of the psychological gain realized by the murderer during the kill."

The disposal site at parkway milepost 31.9 illustrates the difficulty of bifurcating the actions of serial killers and their crime scenes into two succinctly defined categories, for characteristics of the disorganized offender were revealed here as well. For example, a watch, presumably belonging to the killer and likely torn from his wrist during a struggle, was found near the bodies. A week after the murders a group of Girl Scouts discovered the keys to Davis' convertible while picking flowers along the side of the parkway two miles north of the crime scene, suggesting they were flung from an assailant's fleeing vehicle, or hastily ditched there if the murderer had fled by foot. Though their bodies were concealed beneath a light scatter of leaves and sticks, Davis and Perry did not appear to have been murdered elsewhere, then transported down the parkway embankment and dumped at the location in the woods where maintenance worker Elwood Faunce discovered them three days later. Conversely, judging from the blood spatter on the trees nearby, a lack of drag marks leading into the woods and the positioning of the bodies, New Jersey State Police detectives have consistently stated that the victims were left behind at the same location where they were killed. The lack of forethought in leaving Davis and Perry so close to the parkway, and allowing their convertible to remain abandoned in plain sight, suggests that their murderer may have been ill-prepared and acted spontaneously, neglecting to consider disposing them in a more remote location deeper in the woods to better avoid their discovery.

Acknowledging the inherent limitations and apparent inconsistencies in their classification system, the bureau formally recognized a crossover of characteristics among organized and disorganized serial murderers in their 1992 *Crime Classification Manual.* In 2014 the bureau's National Center for the Analysis of Violent Crime (NCAVC) published a more comprehensive five-year study of serial murderers, comprising a broader sampling of 480 victims involving 92 offenders, with their crimes spanning a forty-two-year period between 1960 and 2006. The results provide an updated and more precise methodology for identifying serial killings than the bureau's earlier studies.

The 2014 study concluded that in 72.3% of the 480 cases, the offenders committed the murders in the state where they resided. Of the remaining 27.7%, the murders took place either immediately adjacent to state borders, geographically nearby, or close to where the perpetrator had an occupation, such as a truck driver, requiring interstate travel. In rarer instances the offenders were transitory drifters who traveled cross-country, like Bundy. Most of the murderers claimed two to four victims and had no previous acquaintance with them. Strangulation was the primary cause of death, followed by blunt force trauma and stab wounds. In more than half of the cases, the offenders removed more than one item from the crime scene. The majority of the items taken were clothing or shoes. Females comprised 85% of the victims in the study, with the largest percentage between fourteen and twenty-nine years of age. Most victims were Caucasian, also the primary racial composition of the offenders themselves.

The study also concluded that 329 of the 480 murders were sexually motivated, as displayed by perverse inclinations varying from the more conventional expressions of sexual assault such as vaginal, anal, and oral penetration. These motivations are often revealed at the crime scene in peculiarly ritualistic manifestations unnecessary for the perpetration of the murder itself, such as posing a victim, binding him or her, or evidence of necrophilia. Such distinct and uniquely bizarre "signatures" reflect a sexual disorder commonly known as paraphilia, a deviant conduct motivated by a murderer's sexual fantasy, which serves as a substitute for more traditional forms of arousal.

As opposed to the other serial murderers studied, at the time of their first kill most serial sexual murderers had a prior criminal record, with 70.4% of them claiming three or more victims, and 77.8% using a ruse or con as the method of approach. The murders took place mostly in outdoor public areas, and in 75.1% of these cases the victims were found nude or partially nude. Bindings were used in approximately one-third of the cases, and an article of clothing was the most commonly taken item from the victim.

According to Ronald M. Holmes and Stephen T. Holmes, these types of serial murderers, known as "lust" and "power/control" killers, "realize sexual gratification through the homicide, making it an eroticized experience." They also "connect sexual gratification with personal violence, have a need to see the distress of their struggling victims, and bondage serves this purpose."

Louis B. Schlesinger, Ph.D., a Professor of Psychology at the John Jay School of Criminal Justice, has authored papers, testified in numerous trials, and published ten books on the subjects of homicide, sexual homicide, and criminal psychopathology. According to Schlesinger, "ritual and signature are fantasy-driven, repetitive, crime-scene behaviors that have been found to occur in serial sexual homicide." In the course of his work he found that "offenders have been reported to engage in various crime-scene behaviors that are unnecessary in the commission of the homicide. These unnecessary activities served a psychological purpose. The offender needed to engage in such actions to feel sexually gratified." Such sadistic crime scene behaviors "have been found to be an outgrowth of the perpetrator's deviant sexual fantasies, wherein the murder and the repetitive acts are parts of the offender's sexual arousal pattern."

A few dollar bills and coins were found in Elizabeth Perry's purse nearby her body, and she was wearing a three-carat diamond ring and gold charm bracelet, likely eliminating robbery as the assailant's primary motive. Whether utilizing the more limited criteria of earlier FBI criminal profile analysis, the motivational model offered by Holmes and Holmes, or the bureau's more recent and comprehensive serial murder and serial sexual murder behavioral profiling data and methodologies, the crime site near milepost 31.9 clearly revealed the markings of a sex crime, though the rape of either or both victims was never confirmed due to the degree of decomposition that had set in during the three day delay between the time of the murders and when the bodies were discovered. Davis was discovered facedown and completely nude, her clothes piled neatly beside her. Though neither victim was strangled, evidence of deviant sexual deviation was readily apparent, for one victim either had her neck bound to a tree with her own bra, or it had been tied into her hair. It would seem unlikely that the killer used the victim's bra as the primary method of restraint, if in fact the bra had been used to bind her neck to a tree, for her arms would be free to defend herself against his attack. Instead, tying her wrists together would seem a more effective way to render her helpless. The way Susan's body was found indicates that her assailant may have used the undergarment to begin choking her in the course of murdering her, perhaps deriving gratification while stabbing and beating her, or in order to pose her corpse in the moments after she died.

Apprised of the crime scene indicators left behind in the woods off milepost 31.9, though without reviewing the investigative file held by the New Jersey State Police, Dr. Schlesinger characterizes the Perry and Davis killings as sexual murders. In such instances, said Schlesinger, "violence takes the place of the murder. Violence is sexually gratifying."

Vernon Geberth, a retired commander of the New York City Police Department, draws a similar conclusion about the Perry-Davis double slayings. The author of *Practical Homicide Investigation: Tactics, Procedures, and Forensic Techniques*, a manual recognized in law enforcement as "the Bible of Homicide Investigation," Geberth has more than forty years of experience investigating, supervising, and consulting on over eight thousand criminal investigations. "My perspective is that the mere fact that she's tied with her own bra is a sexual act," he said of the murder scene alongside the parkway. Tying with her own undergarments is the classic indicator of a sex offender."

According to Criminology Professor Stephen T. Holmes of Central Florida University, however, "Sexual deviants don't tie people up to trees with their bras....that's someone who's combining elements of sexual hedonism....you're looking at a mission-oriented serial killer there," he says regarding the Davis-Perry crime scene. The selection of a murder site along a wooded path, too, is another distinguishing characteristic of serial killers, according to Holmes.

The FBI's statistical profiling data and evidence from various crime scenes support the strong probability that Susan Davis and Elizabeth Perry were abducted and murdered by a sexual serial killer who was roaming New Jersey in 1969. While allowing for standard deviations, were today's FBI crime scene analysts to apply the bureau's most recent empirical data to the 1969 Garden State Parkway murders, their methodology could reasonably point to Davis and Perry's killer as an unmarried white male with a criminal record, in his twenties or thirties at the time of the murders, who was living in New Jersey or in a bordering state like Pennsylvania, New York, or Delaware. Psychopathic, rather than psychotic, he probably would've had murdered at least three young women prior to Memorial Day in 1969, with physical dominance over the victims his primary sexual fulfillment.

To be certain, there are several unsolved "lust" killings from the state dating back to the late 1960s and early 1970s with enough similar crime scene indicators to infer that one or more serial killers were afoot in the region during that time period, exhibiting a preference for sadistically murdering young Caucasian females in their teens and twenties, all outdoors.

On April 8, 1969, the body of eighteen-year-old Irene Blasé from Bogota, New Jersey, was found partly submerged in a creek off Highway 80 in Saddle Brook. Fully dressed, she'd been beaten and strangled with a piece of electrical wire, though hadn't been sexually assaulted.

Three months later, thirteen-year-old Jacalyn Harp from Midland Park, just north of Saddle Brook, was found beaten about the face and strangled with a cord from a high school banner she was carrying. Her corpse, police surmised, had been tossed in a ditch in a wooded area along Goffle Creek. She hadn't been sexually molested either.

Denise Falasca, fifteen, from Closter, New Jersey, was the third Bergen County teen strangled that year. Her body was discovered on July 15, 1969, on an isolated road outside a Saddle Brook, New Jersey, cemetery, just one mile from where Irene Blasé was found murdered. Choked to death with her own crucifix, Falasca "had been punched around before she was strangled," according to a Bergen County spokesperson, and "had a black eye and several bruises on her chin and face." Her pink bra was found "loose around her neck," according to a newspaper report. As with the other two victims, she hadn't been raped.

In 1969 Assistant Bergen County Prosecutor Michael Gross told the *New York Daily News*, "There are definite similarities on the murders. They could be the work of one man."

In 2000, however, former Bergen County prosecutor Larry McLure told the *Bergen (NJ) Record* that authorities were never certain that a serial killer was active in North Jersey. "I don't think we ever had a sense that there was a connecting factor," McClure said. "We had a series of unsolved homicides, a number of which involved young ladies. Trust me: They've been referenced and cross-referenced."

On June 8, 1970, just a few days before Sterr and Dunbar were pilloried by Captain Paterra for failing to report the discovery of Davis' convertible, two beach patrolmen from the Wildwood, New Jersey Police Department made a gruesome discovery within the damp night shadows underneath Hunt's Amusement Pier. The body of Carol Hill, a petite twenty-year-old from the gritty Kensington neighborhood of Philadelphia, had been found strangled, her head buried under an oblong mound of tightly packed sand stuffed down her throat. She'd been severely beaten about her arms and thighs, with bite marks visible on her neck. Nearby, police discovered a piece of insulated electrical wire likely used to strangle her. Her green skirt was pulled above her waist, and her panties had been torn off. As with the Perry and Davis murders, the murderer had left behind a peculiar signature that investigators withheld from the press: a silk or satin bow had been neatly tied around her private area. Had the same murderer struck twice at the shore, just one year apart? Though Wildwood authorities clearly had jurisdiction, there were enough similarities between the parkway killings and the Hill murder to justify the intervention of the New Jersey State Police, who "practically took over" the investigation, according to a retired Wildwood Police Department detective. Strangely, within months of Hill's slaying, the Wildwood Police Department sent Detective Ralph Sheets to Michigan to interview parkway murder suspect John Norman Collins, though Collins was already incarcerated at the time of Hill's murder.

On November 27, 1970, the nude battered corpse of Allentown, Pennsylvania, resident Sharon Ann Branweiner, a nineteen-year-old second year student at Lehigh Community College, was found on an oil-slickened road, sometimes used as lovers' lane, leading to a coal plant northwest of Allentown. According to Lehigh County (PA) District Attorney George Joseph, her bra and stockings were knotted together and wrapped twice around her neck. After the knot was tied, the two stocking ends were again wrapped twice around her neck. Her clothes were strewn beside her, and she'd been run over by a car.

The year 1974, termed "The Year of Fear" by *Washington Examiner* writer Diane Diamond, saw a precipitous uptick in serial killings nationwide. "At the time, the [Behavioral Sciences Unit] had no idea how devastating a year 1974 would turn out to be," retired FBI special agent Jim Clemente told Diamond. "Some of the most brilliant and prolific serial killers would launch their destructive careers at that time."

In January that year, the body of fourteen-year-old high school freshman Suzanne Garden was found in the woods of Toms River, New Jersey, a coastal town situated approximately sixty miles from Egg Harbor Township and three miles from the Garden State Parkway. Garden, found partly clothed, had been stabbed and severely beaten, though the cause of death was listed as strangulation. A penknife, believed to be the murder weapon used to kill her, was located near the crime scene, but police weren't able to trace it back to its owner. Her money and jewelry had been left untouched.

Five weeks later eighteen-year-old high school senior Cindy Leslie was found strangled with her own belt in the woods between Messenger and Water streets in the same town, approximately four-hundred feet from the northbound lanes of the Garden State Parkway, and nearly six miles from where Garden had been found. Like Garden, she'd been stabbed and beaten as well, but not sexually assaulted. Due to the "striking similarities" of the cases, at the time both an FBI profiler and local authorities believed that the same perpetrator committed both murders.

Did the same person who killed them slay these several women from New Jersey and Pennsylvania between 1969 and 1974? Though for a time he refocused attention on the Perry-Davis cold case, due to his public notoriety Ted Bundy overshadowed numerous other violent sexual predators who resided in the Mid-Atlantic states during this time period, with signature characteristics similar to the crime scene beside milepost 31.9 of the Garden State Parkway.

CHAPTER NINETEEN

More Serial Killers and Scenarios

Opportunities to murder innocent young women were abundant for the rogue's gallery of violent sexual predators who were prowling the northeastern and Mid-Atlantic states around the time when Susan Davis and Elizabeth Perry were murdered. Some of these dangerous sociopaths attained notoriety for their horrific crimes elsewhere in the country and were apprehended before they claimed more lives. Others, more chameleonic and adept at anonymously immersing themselves within the permissive youth culture of the hippie free-love era, skillfully eluded detection for decades. The predations later attributed to them bore a similar *modus operandi* and signature as to how Perry and Davis were murdered. Young women in their teens and twenties, the victims claimed by these men were found nude or partly nude, alone or in pairs. Each had been severely beaten about the face and upper body area. They were strangled or slain with a knife or other hand-held weapon, providing their killer a tactile thrill in satisfying a particular fetish. Their remains were often concealed within brush and buried in shallow graves, or dumped alongside rural roads, creeks, and dense woods near roads and highways. The whereabouts of each murderer on May 30, 1969, remains uncertain, yet none were known to be incarcerated on this date.

New Jersey State Police Lt. Jeffrey Kronenfeld, who retired from the Major Crime Unit in 2015, wouldn't confirm whether he or other detectives had questioned any of these offenders to ascertain their whereabouts on May 30, 1969. A brief biography of these predators, along with a summary of their criminal history, is as follows:

ROBERT ZARINSKY

He once identified himself as "Lieutenant Schaefer, leader of the Neo Nazi American Republican Army." Stoutly built, with loose, curly brown hair and long mutton-chop sideburns, in the 1950s and 1960s Robert Zarinsky, a diagnosed paranoid schizophrenic, garnered a reputation in his hometown of Linden, New Jersey, as a thick-wristed roughneck bully with a temperamental disposition. He'd accumulated a lengthy criminal record in his teens and twenties while working as a deliveryman for his father's produce business, making deliveries among the Raritan Bay in the northeast section of the state. As he grew older his crimes assumed an increasingly menacing turn, with petty thievery, armed robbery, and vandalism serving as cover for his darker homicidal impulses, allowing him to avoid detection for lengthy periods of time.

Perpetually clad in a white muscle t-shirt, the former amateur weightlifter often pulled up alongside underage girls walking in pairs along town streets and in nearby beach towns, enticing them with the promise of alcohol and a ride in his white Ford Galaxy convertible. Like Ted Bundy, Zarinsky removed the inside passenger side door handle in order to trap his victims, rendering them helpless against escape.

Zarinsky was extremely active during the summer of 1969, roaming the North Jersey coast and its nearby back roads in search of young women. One of his first known victims was Sharon Kennedy. One afternoon, under the guise of offering her a ride home, Zarinsky drove the fourteen-year-old Linden resident to a remote rock quarry near the Monmouth County beach town of Atlantic Highlands. He proceeded to beat her with his fists and bound her hands over her head with her bra as she sat stunned in the front seat, too disoriented to fend off his blows. He subdued her after she broke free and escaped toward a nearby stream, dragging her roughly back to his car. Seemingly oblivious, Zarinsky calmly drove Kennedy home after the harrowing encounter, behaving as if nothing unusual had just transpired between them. Traumatized for a number of years, Kennedy didn't report the incident to local authorities until eight years later, a time that coincided with a series of shocking murders and disappearances that rocked the blue-collar community.

On August 25, 1969, Zarinsky allegedly abducted seventeen-year-old Rosemary Calandriello of Atlantic Highlands, New Jersey. She had been sent by her parents on an errand to buy milk just two blocks from their home when she vanished. Once news of her disappearance was published by the local newspapers, two local boys notified local police they'd seen Calandriello in the front passenger seat of a car on the day she was reported missing, seated alongside a young man fitting Zarinsky's description. A neighborhood mother had also contacted the Linden Police Department, providing a detective with the license plate number of a similar vehicle, driven by a man of similar description, seen luring the woman's twelve-year-old daughter into his car two days before Calandriello's disappearance. Police also learned that several weeks earlier Zarinsky had tried to coax teen friends Darlene Curren and Donna Johnson toward his car outside at the same bowling alley in Middletown Township near where Calandriello was last seen.

Though four girls had clearly identified him as the same perpetrator suspected of abducting Calandriello, Zarinsky managed to avoid sentencing. The similarities between cases led police to name Zarinsky as the prime suspect in the March

28, 1969, slaying of seventeen-year-old Linda Balabanow from Union, New Jersey, though he was never charged. Bound with electrical wire, her beaten corpse was found nude from the waist down, bobbing in the Raritan River a short time after she'd been reported missing. Zarinsky was also a prime suspect in the 1974 murders of Doreen Carlucci and Joanne Delardo from nearby Woodbridge, who were found strangled with electrical wire near a dead-end road, ten feet from one another, concealed with dead leaves. Like Elizabeth Perry, one of the women was nude except for her shoes, the other partly clad in a work shirt.

In 1975 a jury convicted Zarinsky of Calandriello's murder, though her body was never recovered. While serving a life sentence, a DNA match led to Zarinsky's indictment for the November 4, 1968, murder of thirteen-year-old Jane Durrua from Keansburg, New Jersey, whom he had sexually assaulted and bludgeoned to death on her way home from school, discarding her partly-clad remains beside an abandoned railroad track in the grassy fields near Keansburg High School.

Zarinsky testified at his last court appearance in 2008 while dying of pulmonary fibrosis. Deputies rolled him into the hearing room on a gurney, a tube feeding oxygen through his nose. He maintained his plea of innocence until his death at Bayside State Prison in Bridgeton, New Jersey, later that year, where he'd been serving a life sentence for the murder of Calandriello.

In February 2016, the New Jersey State Police and Monmouth County (N.J.) Prosecutor's Office announced that the results of a recent DNA test had linked Zarinsky to the 1965 murder of eighteen-year-old Mary Agnes Klinsky. The gruesome crime scene revealed haunting similarities to the 1969 parkway murders, as Klinsky's crumpled, nude remains were found beneath the guardrail off exit 118 of the Garden State Parkway, near the entrance to Telegraph Hill Park. The Raritan Township (N.J.) High School senior had died of blunt force trauma to the head and had been sexually assaulted. As with Elizabeth Perry, Klinsky's jewelry, including her Hazlet High School class ring, was found on her body, eliminating robbery as Zarinsky's primary motive. In addition to exhibiting a consistent manner of killing in targeting young, vulnerable women in the Jersey Shore vicinity near Raritan Bay, Zarinsky grouped his victims in Monmouth and adjacent Ocean Counties, consistent with a serial killer's need for a comfort zone and satisfying a predilection to be near his home and familiar with his dumping grounds. Perry and Davis fell slightly outside this range in Atlantic County, and were killed one county away, in Ocean County to the south. This grouping of similar victims suggests that his murders transpired within his targeted area, consistent with FBI conclusions about serial killers.

EUGENE PAUL CLAWSON

In April 1970, the bodies of two nineteen-year-old West Virginia University coeds, Karen Ferrell of Quinwood, West Virginia, and her friend Mared Malarik, of Kinnelon, New Jersey, were found buried in a shallow grave near a highway in the woods south of Morgantown, West Virginia. They'd disappeared after hitchhiking near campus on April 19, 1970.

The West Virginia coed murders were referenced by garrulous New Jersey State Police Detective Jack Kreps in a 1970 *Philadelphia Bulletin* article published on the one-year anniversary of the Garden State Parkway murders. Because of the unique similarities between the cases, Kreps informed the reporter that his detectives would travel to West Virginia to investigate a connection if their state police arrested anybody there.

The *Bulletin* never followed up with a story, and the West Virginia coed murders remained an unsolved case of mostly regional interest until 1976, when Eugene Paul Clawson of Port Marion, Pennsylvania, who was incarcerated at the time in the Camden County (N.J.) Jail for two unrelated sex crimes, admitted to his cellmate that he'd been having nightmares about the West Virginia coed murders, sharing with him the grisly details.

When West Virginia State Police detectives visited Clawson in New Jersey, he confessed to decapitating the West Virginia coeds with a machete after holding them by gun point, raping one as the other remained tied in the front seat, then disposing of their skulls down an abandoned mine shaft near his hometown of Port Marion, near the West Virginia border. He was sentenced to life in prison in West Virginia after a lengthy and well-publicized trial. During the proceedings, Clawson's attorney argued that his client had fabricating the story after reading a similar tale in a pulp detective magazine.

Also while incarcerated, and after confessing to the murders of Malarik and Farrell, Clawson, diagnosed by psychiatrists as a "compulsive and repetitive sex offender," pleaded guilty to nine charges of abducting and raping his thirteen-year-old neighbor at knifepoint after forcing her into his car and driving her to a nearby wooded location hear his home, where he ordered her to disrobe before raping her. The assault, which took place on February 22, 1974, occurred at a time when Clawson was residing at Broadlane Road in Winslow Township, New Jersey, approximately 2,000 feet from the Atlantic City Expressway and about thirty miles from Somers Point. He also pleaded guilty to raping a fifteen-year old Gloucester County boy in his car in a separate incident in January 1973 and received a thirty-year sentence for both crimes.

A defense witness at the Farrell and Malarik murder trial testified that Clawson had been working at the Weyerhaeuser Paper Company in Philadelphia, Pennsylvania, on the night of the murders in West Virginia. As such, Clawson was likely in the area as early as 1970, providing him ample opportunity to venture to the Jersey Shore.

Though ultimately convicted of the West Virginia murders, a number of West Virginia police investigators remain convinced of Clawson's innocence, attributing his jail cell confessions to the bizarrely incoherent ramblings of slow-witted, sexually confused man who yearned for a sex-change operation and often cross-dressed while living in the Philadelphia area in the 1970s. Today he remains incarcerated in West Virginia, where he serving a life sentence for the murders of Malarik and Ferrell.

RODNEY ALCALA

The winning contestant on a 1978 episode of *The Dating Game*, Rodney Alcala was a West Coast serial killer whose string of murders during the 1970s went unnoticed until he abducted and murdered twelve-year-old Robin Samsoe from Huntington Beach, California, on July 2, 1979, discarding her remains in the foothills of the Sierra Madre Mountains in southern California. Today he remains imprisoned in California for Samsoe's murders, but investigators have also linked him to numerous unsolved slayings of young women across the country.

Alcala effortlessly immersed himself within the L.A. and Greenwich Village club scenes of the late Sixties and early Seventies. He often lured his victims to remote locations under the pretense of being a professional photographer. Years after his arrest for Samsoe's murder, authorities discovered a trove of approximately eight-hundred photographs, mostly of young women, stashed in a Seattle storage locker belonging to Alcala. The Huntington Beach, California Police Department posted several hundred of the pictures online, eliciting responses from a number of women across the country who recalled being approached by Alcala and being asked to pose for him in various states of undress.

To this day, many of the women in the pictures remain unidentified, leading authorities to conclude Alcala might've murdered them shortly after the pictures were taken. DNA samples connected one of the young women, a pregnant brunette astride a parked motorcycle, joyfully leaning back on the seat, was later identified as twenty-eight-year-old Christine Ruth Thornton, whose body was unearthed in a remote patch of land near Granger, Wyoming, in 2015.

It was thought for a time that Alcala's victims were limited to the West Coast. Between 1969 and 1971, however, he was residing on the East Coast, enrolled in an NYU film class taught by famed director Roman Polanski, wanted by California authorities for the 1968 abduction, beating, and rape of a twelve-year-old schoolgirl in Hollywood, California. During these years as a fugitive, he also worked as a counselor at a New Hampshire arts summer camp, assuming the alias John Berger, before a camper identified him from an FBI Most Wanted List.

In 1971 Alcala murdered a New York City airline stewardess in her Manhattan apartment, strangling her, as well as Ellen Hover, the daughter of a Manhattan nightclub owner.

Another of the photographs gathered from Alcala's trove shows an unidentified young woman seated beside a motel pool, laughing while holding a Kodak Instamatic camera manufactured in the late 1960s. She appears to be smoking a cigarette as she poses, presumably for Alcala, in another photo taken at the same poolside, her head turned to the right. The plastic palm trees in the foreground reflect the unique kitsch architecture of Wildwood, New Jersey. The second-floor balcony railing, as well as the yellow and white-striped awning and umbrellas adorning the pool terrace, appear identical style to what was formerly the Golden Nugget Motel on Ocean Avenue in Wildwood Crest, presently known as the Beach Colony Motel. (The present owners refuse to confirm a match with the railing in the picture.) Though the photo is inconclusive, if the motels are indeed one in the same, this would place Alcala at the Jersey Shore, not far from where Davis and Perry were killed when he was on the East Coast in the late 1960s.

CHARLES D. HALEY, JR.

On June 6, 1974, twenty-year-old glass factory worker Charles D. Haley Jr. from Seabrook, a small farming town in southern New Jersey, abducted two young women at knifepoint from separate locations in the nearby town of Bridgeton, binding them by the wrists and forcing them into the trunk of his car. Unbeknownst to Haley, a tenth-grade dropout and Army veteran who'd served time in Leavenworth Federal Penitentiary on robbery charges, he was discreetly followed in his car by two witnesses who tracked him some forty miles, starting at Bridgeton and proceeding down the Black Horse Pike into Atlantic County. Haley was pulled over near the intersection of Fire Road and the Black Horse Pike after local police were notified by CB radio of Haley's erratic driving, as he was reportedly "forcing cars off the road." This location, adjacent to the Shore Mall in Northfield near the Garden State Parkway, is situated approximately 4.5 miles from where Davis and Perry were murdered. When Egg Harbor Township police officer Edward Jones approached the vehicle, a black, 1961 Chevrolet Impala with racing stripes and a Swastika sticker in the rear window, he heard muffled cries coming from the trunk. He freed the two victims before arresting Haley, who attempted to grab the officer's gun while he was being frisked. One of the kidnap victims told a reporter that Haley said he had murdered eleven other girls and that she had lived longer than any of the others he'd abducted.

After his arrest on reckless driving charges and resisting arrest, and while incarcerated in the Atlantic County Jail, Haley told investigators he'd killed two young women and buried their bodies in Cumberland County, New Jersey, not far from Bridgeton. He subsequently led police on a one-mile trek into the woods near Pittsgrove Township. There, submerged in a shallow stream, lay the bodies of Barbara Woods, nineteen, and Cheryl Murphy, sixteen. Each had been reported missing several months earlier.

Haley confessed that he'd abducted Murphy at knifepoint from the Bridgeton High School bathroom three months earlier, forced her in the trunk of car, then led her into the woods where he raped her, beat her, and stabbed her "three or four times."

A month later he lured Woods into his car from a near a local bus stop. He then took her to his apartment, bound and raped her, before taking her to the woods where "he strangled her and stabbed her" near where he'd killed Murphy. While in a Salem County, New Jersey, jail, Haley was questioned by state, county, and local authorities concerning any possible connection between these slayings and the unsolved murders of Cindy Leslie and Suzanne Garden in Toms River.

According to a June 11, 1974, *Courier NJ) Post* article, "Sources said police were investigating Haley's connection with the killings of two coeds whose bodies were found off the Garden State Parkway near the Somers Point interchange June 2, 1969." Atlantic County Prosecutor Richard Williams told the newspaper, however, "I have no information at this point to believe that there is a connection between Haley and the killing of the two coeds."

Haley kidnapped a guard while in prison and attempted suicide on at least one occasion. He died on June 2, 1991.

Whether they were the unwitting victims of a randomly violent abduction or targeted by a serial sexual predator, on the morning they were killed, Davis and Perry likely encountered somebody who was quite familiar with the woods surrounding milepost 31.9 and knew in advance of the precise location where he would murder them.

Owing in large part to substantial outgrowth from the Atlantic City casino boom of the late 1970s, Egg Harbor Township has undergone a considerable degree of commercial and residential development since 1969. Today professional office buildings and strip malls clutter Fire Road, while cornfields have yielded to golf courses and self-storage facilities. Flourishing big-box stores and busy chain restaurants have displaced the plywood fruit stands that once stood along Route 9 and Tilton Road in nearby Linwood, forever altering the landscape of what was once a primary access route to Ocean City and other South Jersey coastal towns.

Although the township population has more than quadrupled since the summer when Davis and Perry were slain, the surface roads and sleepy neighborhoods closer toward milepost 31.9 remain largely rural, with quaint Victorian houses set alongside bait shops, small marinas, and garden markets. With the exception of the New Jersey Turnpike Authority's removal of several hundred old trees between mileposts 30 and 64.5 in 1991 and in 2011, the implementation of metal guardrails, and the addition of an upscale housing development built parallel to and behind the stretch of woods where Davis and Perry were found murdered, "Nothing much has changed in that area of the parkway near Patcong Creek," says Gary Giberson, the four-term mayor of Port Republic, New Jersey, who helped forge the box culverts along the parkway in 1954, the year of its completion. Nearer the spot where the girls were killed, the privately owned land between mileposts 31.5 and 40 remains preserved within the same pine groves and intersected by the same timeworn paths that were here in 1969. Because the surrounding topography of Egg Harbor Township remains substantially unchanged, with a reasonable degree of accuracy one can deduce the most probable route of escape Susan Davis and Elizabeth Perry's murderer chose when fleeing the crime scene.

Much of this conjecture depends on whether the girls' murderer was a hitchhiker or had driven a car that he used to lure the girls to pull over to the side of the parkway. In either case, spackled with drying blood and likely bearing defense wounds inflicted by two able-bodied young women fighting for their lives, Susan and Elizabeth's assailant was faced with a perilously winnowing amount of time in which to contemplate his getaway. Had he been driving and pulled over to the parkway shoulder before subduing his victims, a passing motorist might've noticed his car and Susan's convertible parked behind one another and stopped to offer help or walked down to have a peek between the trees. A patrolling state police trooper could stop to inspect the vehicles and run their tags, perhaps search further into the woods. If he'd arrived by foot instead, did the killer deliberately pause for a moment to contemplate his surroundings in deciding which way to travel, or quickly scatter in a random direction while in the throes of panicked desperation? Had he driven past the area on an earlier occasion, predetermined where he'd kill Davis and Perry, and coolly rehearsed his escape beforehand?

Most of the initial news reports supported the conclusion that Davis and Perry were slain by a hitchhiker. One unnamed New Jersey State Police investigator surmised as much, sharing his thoughts with *Philadelphia Daily News* reporter Joe O' Dowd several days after the murders. His belief, similar to what Raymond Perry surmised, was that the killer, whom he termed "sex-crazed," and "somebody looking for action," had been hiding in the backseat of Susan's convertible at the diner. He theorized that their killer held a knife to her throat within minutes after she left the Somers Point Circle and "began jabbing at her neck" to force her to pull over. Soon thereafter he ordered both girls into the woods, where he first killed Elizabeth, "just to show

[Susan} that he meant business," then raped and murdered Susan.

If he had been a hitchhiker with no immediate means of transportation at his disposal, the options presented to Davis and Perry's murderer would've been severely limited, for the brackish tributaries and acres of salt marshes along this section of the parkway would've provided him scarce opportunities for a clean getaway. He might've first considered backtracking to Ocean City to hitch a ride from someone heading out of town, instinctively sensing that the area would soon be swarming with detectives once the bodies were found, despite his efforts to conceal them with sticks and leaves. In the summer of 1969 buses to Philadelphia departed almost hourly from the Ninth Street and Atlantic Avenue stop in Ocean City, beginning at 6:20 a.m. Buses followed a similar schedule to points north, hauling vacationers and weekend partiers to the Port Authority terminal in New York City in regular intervals throughout the weekend, with the first ride leaving the downtown beach area at 7:15 a.m. The Pennsylvania Reading Seashore Line trains, no longer in service, departed to Philadelphia from the Tenth Street station on a regular schedule during the summer as well.

To reach Ocean City by foot, Susan and Elizabeth's killer would've needed to proceed southeast from the crime scene. He couldn't have traveled far in this direction unless he had decided to swim, for tramping a hundred or so yards along the twisting path that bisects the woods at this point would dump him onto Ocean Heights Avenue. Continuing beyond the opposite side of this road, the path empties onto a small beach on the banks of Patcong Creek. The water is approximately sixty yards wide at this turn with a swift current flowing under a culvert crossed by both directions of the parkway, in plain view of local crabbers reeling in traps and boaters leaving Clayton's Marina toward Great Egg Harbor Bay. Assuming he had forged the tides and made it to the opposite banks of the creek without being swept into an adjoining channel, he would've emerged drenched in saltwater and dripping with mud as he attempted to inconspicuously navigate his way past the homes on the opposite side of the creek.

The shortest distance between milepost 31.9 on the northbound lanes of the parkway and its intersection with Steelmanville Road, the nearest surface road north from where Perry and Davis were slain, is approximately three-hundred yards north as the crow flies. Considering the vicinity of where patrolman Lou Sterr first saw Susan's convertible three days after the murders-parked on the shoulder near milepost 31.9, some one-hundred yards north from the murder scene, according to several newspaper reports, we can eliminate any likelihood that the murderer, if at all clearheaded, was foolish enough to thumb a ride from another motorist driving on the parkway from any point remotely near Davis' parked car. He would also risk exposure if he'd turned around and began walking east, for he'd have to cross through an open field then owned by the Aspenberg family of Somers Point before sneaking between the homes facing Blackman Road.

The murderer might've first settled upon a westerly direction of travel instead, following the narrow path directly in front of him leading away from the murder site and onto the grass between the edge of the woods and parkway shoulder. From this point he could've dashed across the parkway and hid behind the trees on the median dividing the north and southbound lanes, about a hundred feet away, timing his escape across the road to breaks in the flow of traffic. In 1969 only a smattering of tall pines and oaks shadowed this section of the road. The median, which is approximately one hundred feet wide at this point, would've confined the murderer to just two narrow points of egress, north and south. The evergreens and bushes gather here in meager clumps, providing inadequate cover, thereby rendering the sparsely wooded interior plainly visible to a driver casually glancing sideways from either direction of traffic. Due north from this point the thin canopy gradually tapers into an open gulch. This opening, which remains today as it was in 1969, is flanked to the east by a sloping grass hill that ascends to the parkway shoulder at the point where the highway crosses Steelmanville Road. As pedestrians seldom frequent the hill, within this narrow clearing the murderer would be plainly visible to passing motorists.

If Susan and Elizabeth's assailant headed due north and managed to thread his way through the median clearing without being spotted, slinking undetected through the quiet neighborhoods of Cardiff and Bargaintown would prove difficult, and the more populated bordering towns of Linwood and Northfield would prove a more formidable challenge as the sun grew higher, and he risked exposure in the gathering daylight. His presence would become less noticeable at this early hour only if he'd reached the next exit along the parkway, within the vicinity of the Searstown Mall on the Black Horse Pike in Hamilton Township, off exit 36. From here he could've easily hitched a ride or boarded a bus to Philadelphia, New York, or Atlantic City. The mall, however, was located several miles away.

In a more likely scenario, the murderer didn't walk out of the woods to cross the parkway after recalibrating his bearings, nor did he immediately backtrack to Ocean City. If he had been a hitchhiker, his most instinctive means of escape would have been to remain hidden for a time behind the tree cover beside the parkway shoulder. Obscured by the trees, he might've headed in a northern direction on the well-beaten dirt path parallel to the parkway and leading back toward Steelmanville Road, flanked to the west by the foliage beneath the grassy embankment and advantageous sightline beside the northbound parkway lanes. Yet even if he'd crept silently past the Flanagan's home without being seen or heard by its occupants, and failed to rouse the backyard dogs and farm animals, this direction would've led him a distance of only three hundred yards before emptying onto the road, where again, he risked detection by Bargaintown locals who regularly used these back roads. From here he might've turned west and briefly sought cover for a time under the shadowy parkway overpass, or dashed into the woods at the avenue's intersection with Mt. Airy Avenue, near where junk dealer Robert D'Amore allegedly witnessed Mark Thomas run as the eccentric junk dealer slowed his truck.

Whatever direction the assailant chose, at each turn the roads and waterways in this area would've boxed him in, severely hindering his chances of escaping the crime scene without being seen. Consequently, it seems unlikely that Susan and Elizabeth's murderer initially thumbed a ride from them at the Somers Point traffic circle as they left the diner. The location of Susan's keys, discovered by Girl Scouts within a patch of grass between the parkway and Fire Road (Route 561), two miles north from the murder scene and approximately thirty feet from the right northbound lane of the parkway, suggests a far greater probability that they were hastily tossed from a moving vehicle. Even if their murderer were a hitchhiker, and decided to grab the keys from the ground to steal Davis' car, it is doubtful that a man who'd just brutally slain two women would carry with him such an incriminating piece of evidence, possibly containing his fingerprints, before spontaneously tossing them in a location so near the road where they could be easily found, especially when he could've promptly disposed of them in Patcong Creek.

Nobody is as familiar with these woods and the concealed paths threaded within them as intricately as Egg Harbor Township native Patrick Flanagan. Fifty-one years old, with the grizzled features and seamed forehead creases of a Jersey pines woodsman, Patrick resides a few hundred feet from Garden State Parkway in the same Steelmanville Road home that once belonged to his parents, the late James and Viola Flanagan. He continues to operate James Flanagan & Sons Hog Farm, a prosperous hog-raising business his father founded on this land in 1967, raising piglets before shipping them off to a supplier in Pennsylvania for butchering. As Patrick also maintains a flourishing scrap metal business, discarded appliances, car chassis, and hog pens are arranged neatly beside either side of the path leading from his backyard and slightly uphill into the parkway woods behind his house.

One day in the early 1970s, when Patrick was a young boy, his father took him for a stroll beyond the dirt driveway beside their home and up the sloping path that leads into their woods. After walking with his son several hundred feet along the path, which has been widened into a firebreak in recent years, James Flanagan pointed to the split oak alongside which Susan Davis and Elizabeth Perry had been found. Snapped in two by a recent windstorm, today the rotted log rests at a forty-five-degree angle atop a carpet of dead leaves and pine shoots, perpendicular to a second path leading out of the woods and onto the grass aside the parkway shoulder.

Owned by the Flanagans since 1964, this land held a strangely timeless fascination and morbid sense of adventure for Patrick when he was young, the lingering puzzle of the coed murders like an intriguing Hardy Boys case, with the trees and bushes and trails containing the clues needed to solve the mystery. Patrick and his neighborhood friends would often explore their wooded surroundings, imagining themselves as a band of young sleuths challenged to find the knife used in the grisly slayings. Today Patrick treats his land with the care and respect he learned from his father, leaning to grab scraps of plastic shopping bags and other scraps of windblown litter impaled in the parkway shrubbery as he walks along the same path taken when his dad first showed him the precise location where the bodies were found.

Because the murders occurred on the late Mr. Flanagan's property and so near his home, in 1969 the state police interviewed him and his brother John as part of their investigation into the coed murders. Did they recall seeing any odd strangers trespassing across their land or know of any locals with the cunning to carry off such an atrocity? As Patrick recalls, the sudden appearance of random miscreants was common fare living this near the parkway, with his wistful boyhood reminiscences tainted somewhat by the emergence of a few ominous intruders over the years, each of whom his father viewed askance in the decades following the murders.

One weekend night in the early 1970s, as Patrick and his brothers and sisters were ensconced in the family's den watching a television movie, two random men came knocking on the door to his family's home on Steelmanville Road. Purporting to have car trouble, the pair asked Mr. Flanagan if they could borrow his phone. Generally hospitable, though suspicious of strangers ever since the coed killings, he wisely denied their entry, saying he didn't have a phone and suggesting they might check up the street. Soon thereafter Patrick learned on the news that the men had recently escaped from a nearby mental asylum.

On another occasion a dirty shirtless wanderer, barefoot and wearing ragged cutoff jeans, ambled aimlessly toward their homestead, clutching a staff in one hand. "He kept saying 'The answer is in the stick...the answer is in the stick,'" Patrick recalls, muttering to the young boy and his father as if possessed or under a spell. The man's menacing appearance unsettled his father enough to shoo Patrick into the house, preparing for a confrontation.

Patrick emphasizes that his backyard woods, though part of his family's property, were sometimes used as illegal dumping grounds. Locals would surreptitiously back their trucks into accessible openings off Steelmanville Road and Ocean Heights Avenue, prompting his father to erect a chain fence to cordon off the area. Patrick once saw a large pentagram drawn into the sand near the murder site. Another local recalls finding abandoned car parts and an old jewelry box among the scattered debris. Could the murderer have been a local, familiar with the area? "That's what I think," says Flanagan.

Ocean City native Cheryl Collins, who lived on Central Avenue in Egg Harbor Township between 1956 and 1986, remembers the parkway murders as well. "In 1969 I was thirty-four years old. We all knew about the incident. I had a four-year-old child. A lot of us felt trepidation because we didn't know if we had a serial killer." She says, "I would think that two healthy college-aged students would put up a good fight against a single person. These were two strong ladies. I don't think it was one person."

While newspapers initially reported that the autopsies revealed superficial wounds on the necks of Perry and Davis, theorizing that each victim was held at knifepoint at some point during their abduction, nearly all detectives and persons with knowledge of the investigation believe that the killer acted alone.

Other than the three Delaware County, Pennsylvania, youths who'd fallen asleep in the tan mustang they parked behind Susan's convertible at the time when the girls were murdered, the only other vehicle seen near the crime scene was a dark sedan the state police surmised was a 1958 Pontiac, parked slightly ahead of Susan's light-blue Chevrolet. State Police referred to this car in the court-martial proceedings in 1971 against patrolman Lew Sterr as "probably belonging to the killer." Consistent with the discovery of the keys, a witness' recollection of this car reintroduces the lingering possibility that the killer was behind the wheel, driving off after murdering both women.

The three young men who'd been sleeping in the Mustang each passed lie detector tests, clearing them of any involvement in the murders. On his own volition, one of them returned to the Absecon barracks with his father, voluntarily submitting to a second round of questioning. Why weren't they woken by bloodcurdling screams or desperate cries for help when two people were being savagely beaten two hundred feet from them? If the murderer had premeditated the killings in such a manner, how did he manage to silently pull over in plain view of another vehicle and not wake its three dozing passengers? Did Susan and Elizabeth willingly follow him down the grassy embankment?

It is difficult to imagine two young women not crying for help or being unable to subdue one man threatening their lives. Unless, of course, their captor had frozen them into submission. According to *Whoever Fights Monsters* author Peter Vronsky, "a disturbingly significant number of serial killers pose as police officers. This gives them a convenient pretext to approach and gain control over their victims without the necessity of putting them at ease." The FBI, too, cites law enforcement disguise as a useful coercive tool for serial killers, providing them with a convenient ruse to hold their victims at bay.

Perhaps the murderer had been an off-duty policeman with a siren mounted on his dashboard, stopping Susan and Elizabeth for a traffic violation, quietly marching them toward the woods before killing them. Florida serial killer and former police officer Gerard Schaefer, for example, often used his police badge to coerce victims, pulling them over with the threat of arrest before escorting them into the woods, handcuffing them to trees and nooses before stabbing them to death.

There were no skid marks near Susan's car, signs of askew parking, erratic footprint patterns or other irregularities visible along the path to the crime scene to infer that Susan and Elizabeth were held against their will or had been dragged kicking and screaming down the grassy embankment alongside the parkway shoulder. The theory that a law enforcement officer, or a man posing as one, had slain Perry and Davis intrigues at least one retired New Jersey State trooper.

Lt. Karl Ulbrich, the co-owner of a boutique detective agency in southern New Jersey, spent twenty-five years on the force, where he served for a time in the Major Crime Unit and as a supervisory member of the New Jersey Attorney General's Shooting Response Team. Ulbrich didn't focus on any particular suspect after reviewing the Davis and Perry case file several decades after the murders. Nevertheless, he believes that the women were somehow induced into willingly following their captor after Susan parked her convertible. "It appeared to me that they stopped for a reason," Ulbrich is certain. "They were compliant," As such, the lauded investigator believes that the murderer was a man of convincing persuasion, probably a security guard or someone posing as a police officer.

The Somers Point Police Department deployed a large contingent of "special officers" to harness the overflowing crowds during the busy summer seasons of the late 1960s. Their beat included crowded nightspots such as Bay Shores Cafe, Tony Mart's, the Anchorage Tavern, and the perpetually crowded Point Diner. These part-time employees, tasked with managing unruly drunken revelers and breaking up the occasional bar fight spilling onto the Bay Avenue sidewalks, also worked weekend night patrol near the Somers Point traffic circle. They weren't issued white Dodge squad cars or standard uniforms like full-time officers or provided with official badges.

"They really weren't professional, like the full-timers," says retired Somers Point Police Chief Orville Mathis, who headed the department's detective bureau in the 1970s and retired from command in 1987. "A lot of these guys were wannabe cops. They would walk the avenues and act as a deterrent, and only worked during the summer. Good background checks weren't really done on them in those days. If they were deemed qualified, however, some were issued revolvers." Mathis doesn't recall hiring any officers who appeared suspicious in retrospect, or who were questioned in the coed murders.

The general location of where Davis's car was found on the morning of the murders-approximately one hundred yards north of the murder scene-reflects that the killer didn't spontaneously coerce the girls into the woods immediately adjacent and perpendicular to where Susan had stopped her car on the parkway shoulder. More likely, he knew beforehand of both well-camouflaged openings that faced the parkway and had the girls accompany him in a southeast direction back toward the nearest path, affording him the shortest and most direct way to the stand of trees where he killed them. According to Patrick Flanagan, there was only one other trail with an entrance facing the parkway in 1969, and it was located approximately fifty feet north of milepost 31.8. As these two path entrances, located between mileposts 31.8 and 31.9, were indistinguishable from one another and not readily visible from the parkway, the man who abducted Susan and Elizabeth mostly likely knew precisely where either path began.

The girls were last seen between 5:45 and 6:45 a.m. This time frame coincided with last call at several nearby all-night bars, including the Dunes on Longport Boulevard, the Jug Bar on the same road, and Brownie's Lodge in Bargaintown, roadhouses located just a few miles from the murder scene and frequented by some rough locals and bikers. The man who would soon kill them might've just left one of these establishments, highly intoxicated and delirious with fatigue at having been up all night drinking, with sleeplessness exacerbating his psychosis and copious amounts of alcohol significantly lowering his inhibitions. He had probably practiced his routine beforehand, on different occasions perusing scores of other pretty and seemingly innocent coeds while near the Somers Point Circle. But the right set of circumstances and ideal pair of victims hadn't line up in his favor as they did now.

The sleep-deprived murderer, infused with a potent mix of alcohol, loneliness, rage, and sexual frustration, may have first targeted the girls when they were eating at the diner, studying their mannerisms, recognizing in them two well-dressed, attractive young women who were suitable prey. He likely waited for them in the diner parking lot until they walked outside, fixating upon them in their brief absence, increasingly aroused in knowing he would soon control them. He was probably driving right behind them as they got into Susan's convertible and drove out from the diner parking lot. But the girls, giddy with anticipation at the exciting weekend that lay ahead, and bombarded from all angles with the sights and sounds of a busy traffic circle replete with hitchhikers holding signs, were too distracted to recognize that they were being closely followed on MacArthur Boulevard and through the Somers Point tollbooth.

As they neared Patcong Creek, the killer began signaling for Susan to pull over. He was probably so intoxicated, delusional with anger, or single-mindedly obsessed by the time Susan hit her turn signal that he simply didn't see the tan Mustang parked along the shoulder. Or his fear of detection was overwhelmed by his urge to kill both her and Elizabeth. In discussing the victim selection process of serial murderers in their book *Profiling Violent Crimes*, Criminology Professors Ronald Holmes and Stephen T. Holmes described such an obsessive mental state: "The nature of a serial murderer's compulsion is such that it precludes any prolonged or self-imposed delay in acting out his brutal urges..."

Trooper Sterr found Davis' purse untouched on the front seat of her empty convertible within hours of her death. Elizabeth's purse, however, was discovered strewn in the woods near her body three days later, its contents mostly intact. This evidence again supports the likelihood that Susan willingly accompanied her abductor into the woods under some sort of pretense after she pulled over and felt safe enough to leave her purse behind with her friend. It seems highly unlikely that Susan would've insisted on taking her purse along with her if accosted at gunpoint, or if forced out of the car with a revolver pointed at her or a knife held to her throat. When Susan didn't return to the car, Elizabeth went into the woods to check on her friend, bringing her own purse along with her rather than leaving it unattended on the side of the road.

The murderer likely hurried Susan toward one of the entranceways between mile markers 31.8 and 31.9, walked her down the path approximately two-hundred feet, and once sufficiently out of sight, put a knife to her throat, stood her against a tree and forced her to disrobe. He threatened to cut her throat if she screamed, and Susan was rendered silent, submissive with shock and terror. Elizabeth, now having second thoughts about leaving her friend and concerned by her prolonged absence, took her own purse and followed the same path into the woods. Shocked by the horrific scene unfolding before her once she reached her friend and captor, the killer likely threatened to cut Susan's throat if Elizabeth screamed. Seconds thereafter, and sensing safety in numbers, Susan tried to escape from his grasp, and was stabbed in her neck and stomach as she fought back, her eyeglasses falling off in the process. Elizabeth, reeling and in shock by what she was seeing, was rendered frozen in her tracks as the killer lunged toward her, by now consumed by a maniacal frenzy. His watch was pulled free from its cuff during the ensuing altercation, which was probably over within a few minutes. He then lashed Susan to a nearby tree with her own bra as she lay dying. The coroner concluded that stab wounds were the cause of death for each victim. It seems improbable, again, that the killer would have used a bra to restrain Susan while repeatedly stabbing her. Instead, he probably used the undergarment to either pose the corpse as a serial killer might, or perhaps began the process of choking her, depending on how tightly he'd tied the bra, after she was incapacitated by her knife wounds. He then took along Elizabeth's underwear as a memento of his conquest. Immediately afterward, when his anger and sexual arousal subsided and the reality of what he'd done set in, he quickly concealed the bodies under a cover of leaves and twigs and plotted his escape.

Familiar with the contours and intricacies of the Egg Harbor Township woods, Susan and Elizabeth's murderer probably rehearsed the abduction beforehand. Just as a serial killer might perform a "dry run," he cruised the southern stretches of the Garden State Parkway, scouting for potential victims among the countless pretty young women who regularly drove this route to Ocean City and Somers Point, or targeted them outside the diner. Today, one woman shares a harrowing account of a similar fate that might've awaited her if she didn't act quickly.

The fear of being murdered by Susan and Elizabeth's killer hadn't subsided yet for twenty-three-year old south Jersey native Barbara Solem on Memorial Day weekend in 1970. That she might also end up as one of his victims, savagely beaten, repeatedly stabbed, and left to die in the woods on the side of the road, still haunted her a year after the gruesome slayings when she was spending her summer at the Jersey Shore.

One early evening that weekend, after settling into a summer rental home she shared in Margate, New Jersey, with four teachers, Solem decided to meet for drinks with her boyfriend and some of his friends that night at the Emerald Room nightclub on Cedar Avenue in Wildwood.

On her way to Wildwood, Solem decided to stop at the Somers Point Diner to get herself a burger and a Coke. While rounding the traffic circle, she noticed a New Jersey State Police trailer parked upon side of the circle. A large foldout sign had been propped on the grass beside it, requesting information about the coed murders and providing a public hotline for witnesses to call. She remembered that the same trailer had been placed in the same location one year before, for authorities had hoped they might gather leads from out of-towners in the area for the perennially busy Memorial Day weekend and the returning young college crowds frequenting the numerous bars along Bay Avenue.

As she got up to leave the diner, Solem recognized the portraits of Susan and Elizabeth gazing at her from behind the cage of a newspaper vending machine near the entranceway, as the first anniversary of the murders had rekindled interest in the case. With their long, straight hair and pretty faces, the images of Davis and Perry lingered with Solem as she walked to her car, for she noted the resemblance to herself and her girlfriends. Two young women near her age, the unwitting victims of a horrific crime nearby, whose murderer continued to elude police one year later. A young woman venturing out alone suddenly acquired an uneasy meaning fraught with worry and concern.

Later that night in Wildwood, after partying into the early morning hours at the Emerald Room, at about 2:30 a.m. Solem left the bar with plans to return to her apartment. She stopped at a gas station in North Wildwood before embarking on the half-hour drive home to Margate via the parkway. Just after purchasing a soda at a convenience store adjacent to the fueling island, she noticed a short, dark haired, young clean-cut man staring at her from beside the gasoline pumps. She looked away from him, as something about his hovering presence and unwavering gaze unsettled her. She quickly hopped into her old jalopy, a biege, 1959 Chevrolet sedan (though not 100% sure, Solem is fairly certain her car was an

Impala, the same model as Susan's convertible) and headed for home, thinking nothing more of the leering stranger, yet vaguely troubled by him nevertheless.

She drove nervously along the deserted parkway, her head beams sweeping across the darkened marshes. Solem's Chevy had been breaking down quite frequently as of late, and here she was out here alone on a highway in the pitch darkness of early morning. Cool tidal winds drafted through the broken passenger side window. Her desolate surroundings resurrected a prickly sense of isolation and vulnerability. She was reminded once more of Susan Davis and Elizabeth Perry, found murdered along this same road just one year earlier.

After cruising a few more miles, Solem glimpsed a pair of headlights brighten suddenly in her rearview mirror. She glanced out her side window as a black car pulled alongside her, stunned to recognize the same dark-haired young man who'd been watching her at the gas station moments earlier now frantically waving his hands, motioning for her to pull over. Terrified by his erratic swerving, for a moment Solem thought he was trying to veer her off the road or desperately trying to alert her that someone was lying in wait for her in her own back seat. She quickly glanced over her shoulder and saw nobody there. Flushed with adrenaline, she floored the gas pedal and shot away, praying her engine would hold the acceleration.

No sooner did the stranger's headlights recede in the darkness behind Solem than they appeared once more, his car's front end forcefully knocking into her back fender. She knew because of her broken window that she was vulnerable and risked danger if she was forced to stop or pull over to the side of the road. Shaking, she tried keeping her wits about her as the stranger again pulled alongside, as if making a game of forcing her off the highway. She smashed her foot on the accelerator, desperately hoping to attract the attention of a police cruiser, praying the man would give up pursuit.

Yet within seconds he was next to her once more, this time drifting into her lane, blocking her as she tried to shoot past him. Then in an instant the man in the dark car inexplicably sped off into the distance, his taillights trailing off into the dank mist. A fleeting sense of relief overwhelmed Solem, as the horrific episode had finally come to an end.

But just as soon as the lights disappeared within the black horizon, once more they reemerged ahead of her, forming a picture in the distance. Through the haze of her headlights she saw that the man had parked lengthwise in the middle of the parkway, perpendicular to her car. There he stood beside his car, wildly waving his arms in the air as if beckoning Solem to stop for a grave emergency. She swung sharply to the right without slowing, narrowly avoiding him, and sped as fast as she could to the Somers Point toll booth, where she hysterically told the attendant her story, providing a description of the car and driver. The attendant didn't seem to take her seriously, however, and so Barbara left for her home, glancing in her rear view mirror every few minutes as she drove down the quiet streets of Margate, rattled by what had just happened.

As nearly fifty years has passed, Solem can only recall that the driver of the black vehicle that had nearly run her off the parkway had dark short hair, was tall and reasonably good looking. She doesn't remember any other specific features. Might she have been his next victim?

"I was raised in foster homes," says Solem. Though trusting, she was keenly aware of her surroundings, sensing a situation where her friends might have thought otherwise. "Very quickly, I realized I was in a very vulnerable and dangerous situation. Obviously this person meant me harm….to this day my presence of mind blows me away. I was relatively sober at three in the morning…that was the worst and most insane summer of my life. The diet pills were why I was alert."

The following day Solem drove to Somers Point and reported the incident to the state police trooper manning the trailer at the circle. Perhaps the trooper was approaching the end of his shift or was immune by now to the large number of fruitless tips he and his fellow troopers had pursued from the cramped quarters of the trailer. Maybe he wasn't familiar enough with the investigation to recall that witnesses had seen a black car of a similar model and year parked in front of Susan Davis's convertible near the time of the murders, one that New Jersey State Police Captain Paterra thought had belonged to the killer. Perhaps he didn't find this young woman's tip worthy enough to dispatch a radio bulletin and follow up on the lead. Though not blatantly disputing her account and concurring that the stranger from Wildwood had undoubtedly meant her harm, the trooper merely shrugged. "Because I hadn't seen the other driver's license plate number," Solem recalls, "the officer said there would be little the police could do."

AFTERWORD

In 2009 construction began on several new bridges connecting Somers Point and Ocean City. Though the traffic circle was razed in the process, replaced by a large traffic stop, and the Route 52 causeway was widened with more traffic lanes, the diner where Susan and Elizabeth ate their last meal remains a favorite eatery with tourists and locals alike. The former New Jersey State Police Troop A barracks at 244 White Horse Pike in Absecon, once the temporary hub of the Davis and Perry murder investigation, stands vacant today. A dense jungle of verdant weeds, resembling the ancient ruins of a lost city, have reclaimed the driveway where Wesley Davis once identified his daughter's Chevrolet after it was towed from Blazer's Garage. The troop headquarters in Hammonton, where the investigation was centered thereafter, closed as well. A massive new state of the art facility opened in Buena Township, New Jersey, in 1996. The Ninth Street boardinghouse where Susan and Elizabeth spent their last night alive is now a private residence.

Wesley and Marjorie Davis lived into their nineties, dying within two weeks of one another at a Florida assisted living facility in 2016. I spoke briefly with Mr. Davis in 2009, a few weeks before *The Origins of Infamy* was published. An extraordinarily polite and gracious gentleman, he wished me great success with my book but declined to comment further, saying that in recent years he and his family had chosen to refrain from speaking publicly about his daughter's murder investigation.

Margaret Perry died in Seattle, Washington, in 2005, on her eighty-third birthday. Raymond Perry returned home to St. Louis, Missouri, after his wife passed away. By 2010 he'd remarried, and that year I attempted to reach him at the assisted living facility where he resided. I had fervently hoped to share with him what my research at that point had uncovered, for I learned that he was ailing and had little time left. Through his daughter Suzanne he relayed a message that he didn't wish to talk about the case. He died soon thereafter.

While writing this book, I had hoped that with recent advancements in forensic science technology I would open my computer one day to read where the New Jersey State Police had recovered some previously overlooked crime scene evidence from beside the parkway. Perhaps detectives or laboratory personnel had uncovered a lost set of fingerprints from Susan's convertible, failed to notice a previous blood specimen, or inadvertently misplaced a swatch of clothing on another evidence shelf. My last conversation with the state police regarding this matter took place in 2011. A detective within the Major Crime Unit offered that several years earlier his department had received some federal funding for DNA analysis of dormant cold cases. The Perry and Davis case, he said, was among those where evidence was submitted for analysis. "We have nothing," he said, when I asked him to provide a general assessment of the case. Although he wouldn't elaborate, I gleaned from his succinct remarks that either no useful specimen had been gathered from the crime scene, or what *had* been preserved likely failed to produce a "hit," or profile match, within the federal and state databases of criminal offenders. Either that, or the perpetrator of these horrific crimes died before passage of the Justice for All Act of 2004, the federal law requiring defendants convicted of a federal crime to submit a DNA sample upon their conviction.

In 2016, then Governor Chris Christie signed into law a bill adding indictable disorderly offenses to the list of crimes requiring submission of a DNA sample to New Jersey authorities upon a defendant's conviction, thus augmenting a state profile database previously limited to violent offenses. In addition to this encouraging news, with recent advancements in technology, most notably "touch" DNA analysis, today forensic pathologists are able to gather a usable genetic profile from as few as fifteen to twenty cells a perpetrator might have left behind at the crime scene in instances where there aren't any usable traces of blood or semen. The cells are often revealed on a part of the victim's clothing that the perpetrator would've handled, or applied significant pressure to during the commission of a sex crime, such as underwear, bra, ligature, etc.

Given the secrecy surrounding the Perry-Davis homicide investigation, I don't know if the New Jersey State Police ever re-submitted the scant crime scene evidence to their Office of Forensic Sciences crime lab in Hamilton, New Jersey, at any time since 2011. I previously filed two written requests to review the investigative file under New Jersey's Open Public Records Act and was rejected on each occasion. My requests were deemed to fall within the "active criminal investigation" exemption to the Act. According to the law, any "open" criminal investigation, defined as a case that hasn't been solved, no matter how old, is considered active, thus invoking the broadly construed exemption. Seeing how the New Jersey State Police Records Unit denied my efforts to solicit even the scantest documentation on two separate occasions, and recognizing the nearly insurmountable appeals process, I saw no purpose in submitting a third request.

I'm also uncertain whether New Jersey State Police detectives expanded the scope of their investigation to include questioning the scores of aging men presently listed within the Cape May and Atlantic County Sex Offender registries. As serial sex offenders tend to seek victims near where they live, and are statistically apt to repeat similar crimes, perhaps the culpable party continues to reside locally.

In their defense, the state police are responsible for enforcing laws, not drafting them. And as the Perry and Davis case is among thousands of unsolved homicides vying for their investigative resources, with budget restraints and a constant influx of murder cases the Major Crime Unit understandably directs more state resources and manpower to solving newer cases with fresher witness recollections and better preserved evidence.

I broached this topic with a Baltimore, Maryland, cold case detective one afternoon in 2016. While he was similarly dumbfounded as to why the Major Crimes Unit wouldn't discuss the Perry-Davis investigation with me in any but the most vaguely general terms, he agreed with me that given the nearly fifty years that have passed, the chances are slim to none that a case this old will ever be solved unless a usable DNA sample is found or a confession is offered. Homicide cases simply must be prioritized.

In April 2018 New Jersey Attorney General Gurbir Grewal announced that a panel, led by former state Supreme Court Justice Virginia Long, would meet later in the year to discuss the possibility of allotting funding for a statewide cold case unit comprised of former police detectives. Hopefully they will heed the advice of renowned Seattle police detective and FBI profiler Robert Keppler, who was among the first detectives to label Ted Bundy as a person of interest in the Seattle murders of 1974. Keppler remarked about serial murder investigations in general, "when a detective reviews a difficult long-term case it's worthwhile to go back and look at what was done in the first few months. More than likely, the killer's name or a key clue to his identity will appear in those early files." According to Keppel, the killer "is apt to be among the first suspects known to the police."

If Keppel's theory is correct, the New Jersey State Police have already interviewed the young man who killed Susan Davis and Elizabeth Perry. Is he walking among us today, secretly harboring his horrific secret?

From 1990-1991 I worked in an insurance claims office in Haddon Township, New Jersey, my first full-time job out of college. As my desk was located near the coffee maker in the file room, each morning an amiable middle-aged man with longish curly hair and a protruding beer gut would say hello to me as he stopped to fill his mug. On one occasion Paul Serio sat down in the chair next to my desk, extolling the virtues of working for our company, offering tips how to better organize my caseload. Paul was a casualty adjuster who specialized in processing the overflow of catastrophic claim in regions where natural disasters had struck. His work took him to offices like ours all over America for brief stays. The several clunky pewter rings that adorned his fingers, along with his prolonged absences from the office, inspired water cooler talk; Paul had been married eight times, it was said, and on weekends he jousted at medieval renaissance fairs, thus explaining the rings.

One day, less than three years after I last saw Paul and had left the company, I received a call from a former co-worker in New Jersey. He informed me that Paul had recently appeared on the America's Most Wanted television program. In 1983, a wealthy Aspen, Colorado, real estate developer named Paul Hamwi hired Serio and his accomplice, Robert Beckett Sr., to murder Hamwi's ex-wife in Florida. Paul held by her neck while his accomplice stabbed her in the heart and strangled her with a telephone cord. The two men then stripped her from the waist down to make the hit job appear as a botched robbery, not a murder-for-hire plot.

At a pre-trial competency hearing, Paul testified that he had multiple personalities. At times he would lapse into the part of a woman, a ten-year-old boy, or a medieval character named Duke Angus. One day on the stand he scratched his hand until it was bloody and asked the judge, in a child's voice, "Are you going to shave my hair and put me in the bad chair today?"

A Fort Lauderdale jury found Paul Serio guilty of murder. I remembered how unfailingly polite he was toward me, and seemingly good-natured. He was always cheerful and in a good mood, walked with his chin raised, and said hello when we passed one another in the hallway. He was gracious without seeming unctuous or wanting something from me. There was nothing he said or did that betrayed his carefully cultivated persona. As we never ventured beyond the cordialities of our initial greeting, socialized during lunch, or went out for beers together after work, I never saw his lurking dark side, nor was I privy to glimpses from his carefully hidden past. Other than a peripatetic lifestyle, which allowed him to move from town to town across the country, nothing about Paul's demeanor seemed strange in retrospect. Yet by the time I'd met him he'd been a hired killer. He'd fooled me. Our instincts can be deceiving, I thought. How many of us have worked in the same office alongside a cold-blooded killer and not sensed danger? In the midst of the parkway murder investigation, I wondered, had the state police inadvertently overlooked a clever suspect like Paul?

In the early stages of my research I spent several winter afternoons in Ocean City and Somers Point. I would often stand beneath the old Magnolia tree on the Somers Mansion grounds and look out over the Somers Point traffic circle below me, to the diner across the way and the causeway to my west, hoping that scenes from that Memorial Day might unfurl before me from this heightened elevation, or offer alternate perspectives. Replicating Susan and Elizabeth's travels, one day I parked in the diner parking lot and drove between there and mile marker 31.9, just as the girls had done. Factoring breaks at stoplights and pausing to slow through the Somers Point tollbooth, I calculated that it took roughly four and a half minutes for Susan and Elizabeth to travel this distance. That's how quickly it all happened.

I once laid down in the woods near where they were murdered, where I heard and saw a small gathering of crows perched high in the limbs overhead, cawing. I read in several places where crows possess magical powers, are sacred spirit animals that guide souls into the afterlife. That they visit the dying and return to the place of death shortly thereafter. Their presence can be interpreted as an omen or a blessing. Understanding their call can open portals that offer answers to life's most vexing questions. As I sit at my desk in Milford, Connecticut, typing these final words, somewhere in the trees outside my window I hear a crow. I wonder if he is channeling a message from Susan and Elizabeth, and what they are trying to say.

PICTURES

Elizabeth Perry, 1968 yearbook photo,
Minnetonka (MN) High School
courtesy of Elizabeth Holl

Susan Margarite Davis

"Sue"

2805 Laurel Lane
Camp Hill, Pennsylvania 17011

Independent Study
Secretary of Senior Class
Varsity Basketball
Varsity Hockey
Varsity Softball
Vice-President of G.V.C.
Modern Dance
Portfolio
Academian
Buck Hill Falls
Prayer Breakfast
Art Creative
Music Creative
Science Creative
Dramatics
Swimming
Girls Chorus

Silence is golden, but she prefers silver.

Hey, guess what...Rabbits...1:30...Blow-up... First period sport report...Wink is too better than Fizzies!...By the way, Penn Harris tomorrow...Who pays the tip?...Grandma's house...Hood...See you next year Pam!

*Susan Davis 1967 yearbook photo,
Harrisburg (PA) Academy
courtesy of Harrisburg Academy*

Walter Syben's 9th Street boardinghouse
in Ocean City, New Jersey
Google Images

Ocean City boardwalk, summer 1969
courtesy of Ocean City (NJ) Historical Museum

Somers Point Diner (with traffic circle
in foreground), summer 1969
Temple University Libraries, SCRC, Philadelphia, PA

*Booth along windows inside Somers Point Diner, where
Susan and Elizabeth ate shortly before they were murdered.
photo by author*

*Milepost 31.9, northbound lanes, Garden State
Parkway, Egg Harbor Township, New Jersey
photo by Lindsay Wilson*

*Perry-Davis crime scene location, woods alongside Garden
State Parkway, Egg Harbor Township, New Jersey
photo by author*

*Dive watch found near Perry-Davis crime scene
courtesy New Jersey State Police*

*Suspect Mark Thomas (seen upper right corner), who
was also a member of the Aryan Republican Army
FBI photo*

*Philadelphia Police Department headquarters
Google Images*

Detective Harry Patterson, New Jersey State Police
courtesy of Deneen Patterson Gove

New Jersey State Police barracks on
Route 73, Berlin, New Jersey
photo by author

The young man in the foreground is Thomas Ronald Walden, 22, of Cario, Ga. who led law enforcement officers from several states on a chase last week which ended Sunday when he was taken to Denver by a U. S. Marshall. Also in the picture from left to right, are Chief Robert Husted, Sheriff Ralph Baker and Undersheriff Les Eccher.

*Perry-Davis murder suspect Ronnie Walden outside
jail in Glenwood Springs, Colorado, summer 1969.
courtesy of Glenwood Springs Historical Society*

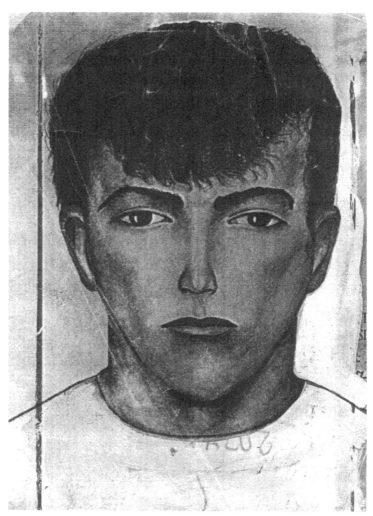

*Composite sketch of Perry-Davis murder
suspect, as described by witnesses
courtesy of New Jersey State Police*

WANTED BY THE FBI
INTERSTATE FLIGHT - MURDER

THEODORE ROBERT BUNDY
DESCRIPTION
Born November 24, 1946, Burlington, Vermont (not supported by birth records); Height, 5'11'' to 6'; Weight, 145 to 175 pounds; Build, slender, athletic; Hair, dark brown, collar length; Eyes, blue; Complexion, pale / sallow; Race, white; Nationality, American; Occupations, bellboy, busboy, cook's helper, dishwasher, janitor, law school student, office worker, political campaign worker, psychiatric social worker, salesman, security guard; Scars and Marks, mole on neck, scar on scalp; Social Security Number used, 533-44-4655; Remarks, occasionally stammers when upset; has worn glasses, false mustache and beard as disguise in past; left-handed; can imitate British accent; reportedly physical fitness and health enthusiast.

CRIMINAL RECORD
Bundy has been convicted of aggravated kidnaping.

CAUTION
BUNDY, A COLLEGE-EDUCATED PHYSICAL FITNESS ENTHUSIAST WITH A PRIOR HISTORY OF ESCAPE, IS BEING SOUGHT AS A PRISON ESCAPEE AFTER BEING CONVICTED OF KIDNAPING AND WHILE AWAITING TRIAL INVOLVING A BRUTAL SEX SLAYING OF A WOMAN AT A SKI RESORT. HE SHOULD BE CONSIDERED ARMED, DANGEROUS AND AN ESCAPE RISK.

FBI/DOJ

Ted Bundy Most Wanted poster
FBI photo

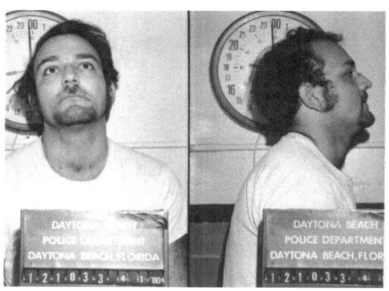

Serial killer and Perry-Davis murder suspect Gerald Stano
photo Daytona Beach Police Department

Elizabeth Perry Memorial, located at Animal
Humane Society, Golden Valley, Minnesota
photo by Elizabeth Holl

For More News About Christian Barth,
Signup For Our Newsletter:

http://wbp.bz/newsletter

Word-of-mouth is critical to an author's long-term success. If you appreciated this book please leave a review on the Amazon sales page:

http://wbp.bz/tgspma

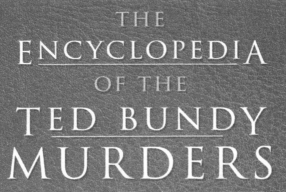

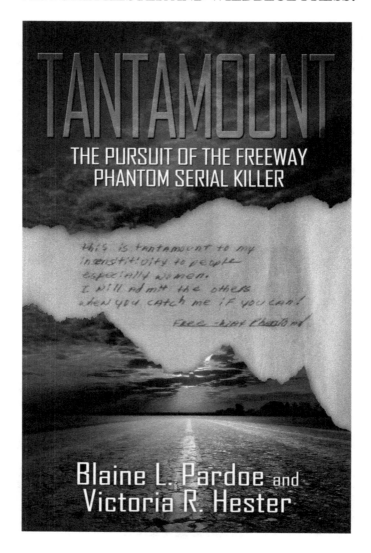

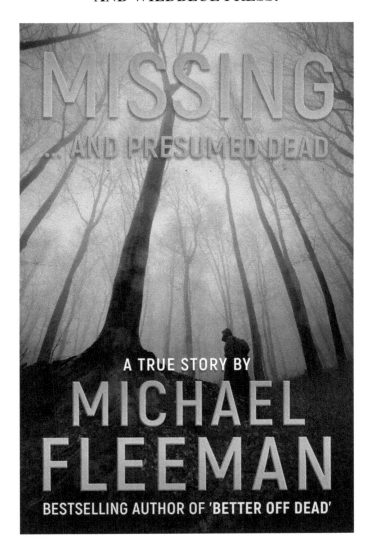

See even more at:
http://wbp.bz/tc

More True Crime You'll Love From WildBlue Press

BOGEYMAN: He Was Every Parent's Nightmare by Steve Jackson *"A master class in true crime reporting. He writes with both muscle and heart."* (Gregg Olsen, New York Time bestselling author). A national true crime bestseller about the efforts of tenacious Texas lawmen to solve the cold case murders of three little girls and hold their killer accountable for his horrific crimes by New York Times bestselling author Steve Jackson. *"Absorbing and haunting!"* (Ron Franscell, national bestselling author and journalist)

wbp.bz/bogeyman

REPEAT OFFENDER by Bradley Nickell *"Best True Crime Book of 2015"* (Suspense Magazine) A "Sin City" cop recounts his efforts to catch one of the most prolific criminals to ever walk the neon-lit streets of Las Vegas. *"If you like mayhem, madness, and suspense, Repeat Offender is the book to read."* (Aphrodite Jones, New York Times bestselling author)

wbp.bz/ro

DADDY'S LITTLE SECRET by Denise Wallace *"An engrossing true story."* (John Ferak, bestselling author of Failure Of Justice, Body Of Proof, and Dixie's Last Stand) Daddy's Little Secret is the poignant true crime story about a daughter who, upon her father's murder, learns of his secret double-life. She had looked the other way about other hidden facets of his life - deadly secrets that could help his killer escape the death penalty, should she come forward.

wbp.bz/dls

BODY OF PROOF by John Ferak *"A superbly crafted tale of murder and mystery."* – (Jim Hollock, author of award-winning BORN TO LOSE) When Jessica O'Grady, a tall, starry-eyed Omaha co-ed, disappeared in May 2006, leaving behind only a blood-stained mattress, her "Mr. Right," Christopher Edwards, became the suspect. Forensic evidence gathered by CSI stalwart Dave Kofoed, a man driven to solve high-profile murders, was used to convict Edwards. But was the evidence tainted? A true crime thriller written by bestselling author and award-winning journalist John Ferak.

wbp.bz/bop

CPSIA information can be obtained
at www.ICGtesting.com
Printed in the USA
LVHW021926130720
660549LV00012B/1837